An Introduction to
Partnership Law

An Introduction to
Partnership Law

Geoffrey Morse LLB, Barrister

Reader in Law, University of Liverpool

Financial Training

First published in Great Britain 1986 by Financial Training Publications Limited, Avenue House, 131 Holland Park Avenue, London W11 4UT

© Geoffrey Morse, 1986

ISBN: 1 85185 025 2

Typeset by Kerrypress Ltd, Luton, Beds
Printed by Livesey Ltd, Shrewsbury

All rights reserved. No part of this book may be reproduced or transmitted in any form or by any means, electronic or mechanical, including photocopying, recording, or any information storage or retrieval system without prior permission from the publisher.

Contents

Preface vii

Table of Cases ix

Table of Statutes xiii

1 Partnerships and Partnership Law 1

What is a partnership? — Partnership law — Essentials of a partnership — Partnerships then and now — Partnerships: variations on a theme

2 Establishing a Partnership 25

Questions and answers — Formal partnerships — Partnerships by association — Investing in a partnership — Partners and employees

3 Legal Controls on Partnerships 58

Public and private controls — Restrictions on the freedom to contract — Restrictions on freedom of association — Restrictions on choice of business name — Partnerships and the public domain

4 Partners and Outsiders 70

Potential problem areas — Liability of partners for contracts — Liability for other wrongs — Nature of the liability — Duration of the liability

Contents

5 Partners and Each Other   102

Contract and equity — Fiduciary duties — Contract: implied terms — Expulsion clauses — Assignment of the partnership share

6 Partnership Property   134

Problems and possibilities — What is partnership property? — Business premises: leases and licences — Goodwill: a note

7 Dissolution and Winding Up   146

Dissolution — Winding up — Partial dissolution — Distribution of assets: insolvency

Index   173

Preface

There is a tendency to regard the subject of partnership in the same light as Ebenezer Scrooge regarded his famous partner Jacob Marley, i.e., as an unnecessary reminder of times past. It is true that partnerships grew, flourished and then declined in number before the First World War, and that the private company has since inherited the earth so far as small businesses are concerned. But circumstances change and the growth in prestige and financial status of the professions in recent times has created a renaissance of the partnership form. Lawyers, accountants, surveyors, doctors, etc. are now linked together in partnerships, often in forms undreamt of in 1890. It is to the everlasting credit of the Victorian judges that they created a business form which has proved to be both strong and flexible enough to adapt itself to EEC-wide firms of accountants when it was designed for the small parochial business in Victorian England. The form has also been exported to many Commonwealth countries and applies throughout the UK. Companies, once partnerships' great rivals, are now frequently encountered as partners themselves.

Partnerships in the late twentieth century therefore play an important role in the economic life of the country, and the laws applicable to them deserve study on that ground alone. But if that is thought to be a sterile reason for academic study, partnership law provides a perfect cross-section of the strands which together form the basis of the lawyer's art. Based on the common law concepts of contract and agency, subjected to equitable considerations in the form of fiduciary duties and governed by a part-codification in the Partnership Act 1890 (the simplicity of which can but reflect on the style of modern legislation), partnership law has had to adapt to modern state regulation, taxation, insolvency laws and business property law. A student can thus encounter the common law, equity, statutory interpretation and public law in one microcosm. Partnership law is not an historical relic but a dynamic and complex interrelationship between the various members of the legal cast.

Preface

This book is an introduction; that does not mean that it avoids all the difficulties or tries to explain every point in a sentence. It is an attempt to present the partnership canvas in a modern context with light and shade — some of the more complex areas are dealt with in sufficient detail to provide the reader with, if nothing else, a clear grasp of what the problem is. I have used Scottish and Commonwealth cases where these provide better, more recent, or sometimes the only examples of the points they are making. But it remains an introduction (there are no footnotes) — it does not, for example, contain precedents for partnership deeds, nor does it provide a compendium of every point which a practising lawyer might need. It is a book for the student or anyone who wishes to understand what partnerships and partnership law are all about. Taxation, one of the modern interfaces which partnership law has had to come to grips with, is dealt with only from the point of view of its impact on partnership law. The reverse impact of partnership law on taxation is a complex area which requires a detailed knowledge of taxation generally.

My thanks must go to seventeen years' undergraduate partnership classes who have always shown a keen interest in this subject, to my colleagues Anne Morris and Christopher Ryan, who helped and advised me and to my admirable secretary Edith Jones, who typed the manuscript and bore all my second (and third) thoughts with fortitude. The publishers have been efficient and courteous — no author can ask for more. Finally to my family, who as always supported me and kept me to a very tight schedule, I give my thanks and the promise to be available for Monopoly etc. more often in the near future.

The final responsibility for all errors and omissions is, of course, mine. The law is stated as known to me on 1 March 1986.

Geoffrey Morse
Liverpool
March 1986

Table of Cases

Aas v Benham [1891] 2 Ch 244 (CA) 108, 109, 110, 112
Abbott v Abbott [1936] 3 All ER 823   31
Agriculturist Cattle Insurance Co, re (Baird's case) (1870) LR 5 Ch App 725 (LJJ)   71
Arbuckle v Taylor (1815) 3 Dow 160   88
Ashbury Railway Carriage & Iron Co Ltd v Riche (1875) LR 7 HL 653 (HL)   23
Australia & New Zealand Banking Group Ltd v Richardson [1980] Qd&R 321   21
Badeley v Consolidated Bank (1888) 38 Ch D 238 (CA)   33, 35
Badham v Williams (1902) 86 LT 191   162
Bagel v Miller [1903] 2 KB 212   97
Baker v Lintott [1982] 4 WWR 766   63
Barclays Bank Trust Co Ltd v Bluff [1982] 1 Ch 172   165
Barnard, re (Martins Bank & Trustee) [1932] 1 Ch 269   49
Barnes v Youngs [1898] 1 Ch 414   126
Belfield v Bourne [1894] 1 Ch 521   151
Bell's Indenture Trusts, re [1980] 3 All ER 425   92, 94
Bennett v Richardson [1980] RTR 358 (DC)   54
Bentley v Craven (1853) 18 Beav 75   107
Bevan v Webb [1901] 2 Ch 59 (CA)   117, 118
Bevan v Webb [1905] 1 Ch 620   110
Biss, re [1903] 2 Ch 40   110
Blisset v Daniel (1853) 10 Hare 493   127
Blyth v Fladgate [1891] 1 Ch 337   93
Boardman v Phipps [1967] 2 AC 46 (HL)   108, 109, 110, 113
Boehm v Goodall [1911] 1 Ch 155   156
Bonnin v Neame [1910] 1 Ch 732   130
Boston Deep Sea Fishing & Ice Co v Ansell (1888) 39 Ch D 339   107, 130
Bourne, re [1906] 2 Ch 427   154
Brenner v Rose [1973] 1 WLR 443   110, 111, 112
Brewer v Yorke (1882) 46 LT 289   157
Briggs & Co, re [1906] 2 KB 209   75
British Homes Assurance Corporation Ltd v Patterson [1902] 2 Ch 404   89
Brooks v Brooks (1901) 85 LT 453   32
Brown, Janson & Co v Hutchinson (No 2) [1895] 2 QB 126 (CA)   132
Bunny (D & H) Pty Ltd v Atkins [1961] VLR 31   43
Byrne v Reid [1902] 2 Ch 735 (CA)   123, 124
Campbell v McCreath 1975 SLT 5   81
Canadian Pacific Ltd v Telesat Canada (1982) 133 DLR (3d) 321   11
Canny Gabriel Castle Jackson Advertising Pty Ltd v Volume Sales (Finance) Pty Ltd (1974) 131 CLR 321   136
Carmichael v Evans [1904] 1 Ch 486   125, 148
Carter Bros v Renouf (1962) 36 ALJR 67   140
Cheeseman v Price (1865) 35 Beav 142   150
Churton v Douglas (1859) John 174   144
Clark v Watson 1982 SLT 450   161
Clifford v Timms [1908] AC 112   148
Clode v Barnes [1974] 1 All ER 1176   88
Const v Harris (1824) Turn & R 496   102
Cook v Rowe [1954] VLR 309   141
Coope v Eyre (1788) 1 H Bl 37   8
Court v Berlin [1897] 2 QB 396   97
Cox v Coulson [1916] 2 KB 177 (CA)   14
Cox v Hickman (1860) 8 HL Cas 268 (HL)   12, 33, 34, 35, 38, 51
Craig v Finance Consultants Pty Ltd [1964] NSWR 1012   121
Croft v Day (1843) 7 Beav 84   68
Cruikshank v Sutherland (1922) 92 LJ Ch 136 (HL)   103, 161
Cruttwell v Lye (1810) 7 Ves Jr 335   144
Curl Bros Ltd v Webster [1904] 1 Ch 685   144
Customs & Excise Commissioners v Evans [1982] STC 342   2
Davies v Braithwaite [1931] 2 KB 628   6
Davis v Davis [1894] 1 Ch 393   34, 36, 139, 140
Davy v Scarth [1906] 1 Ch 55   156

Table of Cases

Daw v Herring [1892] 1 Ch 284	32
Deacons v Bridge [1984] 2 All ER 19 (PC)	63, 64, 69, 145
Deucher v Imperial Gas Light & Coke Co Ltd [1925] AC 691 (HL)	24
Dickenson v Gross (1927) 11 TC 614	29
Dixon v Dixon [1904] 1 Ch 161	155
Dodson v Downey [1901] 2 Ch 620	131
Drughorn (Fred.) Ltd v Rederiaktiebolaget Transatlantic [1919] AC 203 (HL)	82
Dungate v Lee [1967] 1 All ER 241	27, 62
Dyke v Brewer (1849) 2 Car & Kir 828	98
Eardley v Broad (1970) 120 NLJ 432	138
Ebrahimi v Westbourne Galleries Ltd [1973] AC 360 (HL)	18, 50, 114, 151
Edwards v Bairstow [1956] AC 14 (HL)	26
Edwards v Worboys (1983) 127 SJ 287 (CA)	64
Ewing v Buttercup Margarine Co Ltd [1917] 2 Ch 1	67
Fall v Hitchen [1973] 1 WLR 286	6, 7
Federal Commissioner of Taxation v Everett (1980) 54 ALJR 196	136
Floydd v Cheney [1970] Ch 602	104, 155
Fort, re (ex parte Schofield) [1897] 2 QB 495	41
Franklin and Swaythling's Arbitration, re [1929] 1 Ch 238	124
Furniss v Dawson [1984] AC 474 (HL)	14
Garner v Murray [1904] 1 Ch 57	168, 169, 171
Garwood's Trusts, re [1903] 1 Ch 236	128, 129, 132
Gieve, re (ex parte Shaw) [1899] WN 41 (CA)	41
Goode v Harrison (1821) 5 B & Ald 147	61
Green v Hertzog [1954] 1 WLR 1309 (CA)	168
Green v Howell [1910] 1 Ch 495 (CA)	126, 127
Hamlyn v Houston & Co [1903] 1 KB 81 (CA)	87
Handyside v Campbell (1901) 17 TLR 623	150
Harrison-Broadley v Smith [1964] 1 WLR 456	142, 143
Harvey v Harvey [1970] ALR 931	137, 138, 142
Head, re [1894] 1 QB 638	170
Hensman v Traill, *The Times*, 21 October 1980	63
Hexyl Pty Ltd v Construction Engineering (Aust.) Pty Ltd [1983] 2 NSWLR 624	83
Higgins v Beauchamp [1914] 3 KB 1192, (1914) 111 LT 1103, (DC)	77
Highley v Walker (1910) 26 TLR 685	116
Hill, re [1934] Ch 623	55
Hitchman v Crouch Butler Savage Associates (1983) 127 SJ 441	126
Hogar Estates Ltd v Shebron Holdings Ltd (1980) 101 DLR (3d) 509	105
Howes, re [1934] Ch 49	170
Hudgell Yeates & Co v Watson [1978] 2 All ER 363 (CA)	45, 149
Humble v Hunter (1848) 12 QBD 310	82
Industrial Development Consultants Ltd v Cooley [1972] 1 WLR 443	109
Inland Revenue Commissioners v Graham's Trustees 1971 SC (HL) 1	148
Inland Revenue Commissioners v Williamson (1928) 14 TC 335	26, 28
Jackson v White [1967] 2 Lloyd's Rep 68	26
Jones v Jones (1870) 4 SALR 12	138
Keech v Sandford (1726) Ca *t* King 61	110
Keith Spicer Ltd v Mansell [1970] 1 All ER 462	8
Kelly v Tucker (1907) 5 C&R 1	119
Kendal v Wood (1871) LR 6 Ex 243	76
Kendall v Hamilton (1879) 4 App Cas 504 (HL)	95, 96
Kennedy v Malcolm Bros (1909) 28 NZLR 457	76
Kirkintilloch Equitable Co-operative Society Ltd v Livingstone 1972 SLT 154	87
Latcham v Martin (1984) 134 NLJ 745 (PC)	159
Law v Law [1905] 1 Ch 140	105
Lee v Lee's Air Farming Ltd [1961] AC 12 (PC)	52
Lonergon, re (ex parte Sheil) (1877) 4 ChD 789 (CA)	42
Lovell and Christmas v Beauchamp [1894] AC 607 (HL)	61
Lynch v Stiff (1944) 68 CLR 428	44
Lyne-Pirkis v Jones [1969] 1 WLR 1293 (CA)	64
McLeod v Dowling (1927) 43 TLR 655	32
Manley v Sartori [1927] 1 Ch 157	164
Mann v D'Arcy [1968] 1 WLR 893	11, 79
Mara v Browne [1896] 1 Ch 199	93
Marsh v Stacey (1963) 107 SJ 512 (CA)	55
Martin v Thompson 1962 SC (HL) 28	123
Matthews v Ruggles-Brise [1911] 1 Ch 194	122
Meagher v Meagher [1961] IR 96	166
Meekins v Henson [1964] 1 QB 472	88
Megavand, re (ex parte Delhasse) (1878) 7 ChD 511	39
Mercantile Credit Co Ltd v Garrod [1962] 3 All ER 1103	78

Miles v Clarke [1953] 1 All ER 779
        137, 138, 143
Ministry of Health v Simpson [1951] 000
 AC 251 (HL)   95
Moss v Elphick [1910] 1 KB 846 30, 31, 32
Neilson v Mossend Iron Co (1886)
 11 App Cas 298 (HL)   32
Newstead v Frost [1980] 1 All ER 363
 (HL)   13, 23, 24
Noonan, re [1949] St R Qd 62   115
North Cheshire & Manchester Brewery
 Co Ltd v Manchester Brewery Co Ltd
 [1899] AC 83 (HL)   68
Northern Sales (1963) Ltd (Ministry of
 National Revenue (1973) 37 DLR (3d)
 612   35
Olver v Hillier [1959] 1 WLR 551 151
O'Sullivan v Management Agency &
 Music Ltd [1985] 3 All ER 351 (CA) 61
Oswald Hickson Collier & Co v
 Carter-Buck [1984] 2 All ER 15, (1982)
 126 SJ 120, (CA)   64
Page v Cox (1852) 10 Hare 163 123, 124
Palumbo v Stylianou (1966) 1 ITR 407 53
Pathirana v Pathirana [1967]
 1 AC 233 (PC)   107, 164
Peake v Carter [1916] 1 KB 652 (CA) 132
Peso Silver Mines Ltd (NPL) v Cropper
 (1966) 58 DLR (2d) 1   110
Peyton v Mindham [1972] 1 WLR 8
        64, 127, 148, 150
Pocock v Carter [1912] 1 Ch 663 143
Polkinghorne v Holland (1934) 51 CLR
 143   74
Pooley v Driver (1877) 5 ChD 458 (CA)
          39, 40, 42
Protheroe v Protheroe [1968]
 1 WLR 519   110, 111, 112
Public Trustee v Mortimer (1985)
 16 DLR (4th) 404   87, 90, 94
Queensland Mines Ltd v Hudson (1978)
 18 ALR 1 (PC)   110
R v Knupfer [1915] 2 KB 321   149
Ramsay (W.T.) Ltd v IRC [1982] AC 300
 (HL)   14
Rayner & Co v Rhodes (1926) 24 Lloyd
 LR 25   50
Reed v Young [1984] STC 38 49, 52
Regal (Hastings) Ltd v Gulliver [1942]
 1 All ER 378 (HL)   109
Rennison (E) & Son v Minister of Social
 Security (1970) 10 KIR 65   7, 53
Rhodes v Moules [1895] 1 Ch 236 90

Rolfe v Flower Salting & Co (1866)
 LR 1 PC 27   98
Rolled Steel Products (Holdings) Ltd v
 British Steel Corporation [1984] BCLC
 466 (CA)   24
Royal British Bank v Turquand (1856)
 6 E & B 327   73
Rudd & Sons Ltd, re [1984] 3 All ER 225 24
Rye v Rye [1962] AC 496 (HL) 142
Salomon v A. Salomon & Co Ltd [1897]
 AC 22 (HL)   1, 16
Saywell v Pope [1979] STC 824
       10, 11, 13, 26, 29, 53
Senanayake v Cheng [1966] AC 63 (PC) 152
Sims v Brutton (1850) 5 Exch 802 91
Singh v Nahar [1965] 1 WLR 412 138
Skipp v Harwood (1747) 2 Swanst 586 158
Smith v Baker [1977] 1 NZLR 511 31
Smith v Gale [1974] 1 WLR 9   163
Sobell v Boston [1975] 1 WLR 1587
         155, 164, 165
Solicitor's arbitration, re a [1962]
 1 All ER 772   125
Steinberg v Scala (Leeds) Ltd [1923]
 2 Ch 452   61
Stekel v Ellice [1973] 1 WLR 191 54, 55, 56
Strathearn Gordon Associates Ltd v
 Commissioners of Customs & Excise
 (1985) VATTR 79   9, 12
Taylor v Good [1974] 1 WLR 556 (CA) 8
Tendring Hundred Waterworks Co v
 Jones [1903] 2 Ch 615   91
Thompson's trustee v Heaton [1974]
 1 WLR 605   111
Thom's Executors v Russel & Aitken 1983
 SLT 335   162
Tower Cabinet Co Ltd v Ingram [1949]
 2 KB 397   43, 100
Trego v Hunt [1896] AC 7 (HL) 144
Trimble v Goldberg [1906] AC 494 (PC) 113
United Dominions Corporation Ltd v
 Brian Pty Ltd (1985) 60 ALR 741 12, 104
Varley v Coppard (1872) LR 7 CP 505 141
Waddington v O'Callaghan (1931) 16 TC
 187   29
Walker v Hirsch (1884) 27 ChD 460 36
Walker West Development Ltd v F.J.
 Emmett Ltd (1979) 252 EG 1171 (CA)
           36, 53
Waterer v Waterer (1873) LR 15 Eq 402 140
Watson v Haggitt [1928] AC 127 (PC) 163
Watteau v Fenwick [1893] 1 QB 346 83
Watts v Driscoll [1901] 1 Ch 294 (CA) 130

Table of Cases

Waugh v Carver (1793) 2 H Bl 235   12, 33
Welsh v Knarston 1972 SLT 96   154
Wheatley v Smithers [1906] 2 KB 321   77
Whitehill v Bradford [1952] 1 All ER 115   64
Whiteman Smith Motor Co. v Chaplin [1934] 2 KB 35 (CA)   144
Whitwell v Arthur (1863) 35 Beav 140   150
William S. Gordon & Co Ltd v Mrs Mary Thompson Partnership 1985 SLT 112   147
Williamson v Barbour (1877) 9 ChD 529   80
Winsor v Schroeder (1979) 129 WLJ 1266   7, 106
Wise v Perpetual Trustee Co [1903] AC 139 (HL)   8
Yenidje Tobacco Co Ltd, re [1916] 2 Ch 426   151

Table of Statutes

Age of Majority (Scotland) Act 1969   61
Agricultural Holdings Act 1948   142
Arbitration Act 1950   124
   s 4   117
Banking Act 1979
   s 46   65
Bankruptcy Act 1914   24
   s 33(6)   171
Betting and Gaming Act 1960   62
Business Names Act 1985   60, 66
   s 1   66
   s 2   66
   s 2(4)   67
   s 3   66
   s 4   67
   s 5   67
Civil Liability (Contribution) Act 1978   96
   s 3   101
Companies Act 1981   17–18, 44, 60, 66
Companies Act 1985   58
   s 34   66
   s 35   24, 73
   s 459   116, 151
   s 716   65
   s 717   65
Competition Act 1980   58
Consumer Credit Act 1974   66
Family Law Reform Act 1969   60
Finance Act 1972
   s 22   2
Finance Act 1985   68
   s 48   49, 52
Insolvency Act 1985   34, 171
Joint Stock Companies Act 1856   16
Landlord and Tenant Act 1954
   Part II   142, 143
Law of Property Act 1925   136–7
   s 61   125
   s 72   142
Law of Property Act 1969
   s 9   142

Limited Partnership Act 1907   1, 9, 17
   s 3   48
   s 4(1)   47
   s 4(2)   48
   s 6   11–12
   s 6(1)   11–12, 50, 51
   s 7   47
   s 8   48
   s 9   48
   s 13   48
   s 14   48
   s 16   48
Mental Health Act 1959   149
Misrepresentation Act 1967
   s 2(1)   152
   s 2(2)   152
National Health Service Act 1977
   s 54   63, 143
Partnership Act 1890
   s 1   12, 15, 22
   s 1(1)   1
   s 1(2)   1
   s 2   25, 33
   s 2(1)   8, 25, 139
   s 2(2)   14, 25, 34
   s 2(3)   3, 15, 25, 34, 35, 36, 52, 57
   s 2(3)(a)   38, 51
   s 2(3)(b)   37
   s 2(3)(c)   37
   s 2(3)(d)   38, 39, 40, 41, 42, 46, 47, 51, 171
   s 2(3)(e)   40, 41, 171
   s 3   33, 41, 42, 171
   s 4(1)   2
   s 4(2)   2
   ss 5–8   71
   ss 5–18   70
   s 5   3, 74, 76, 77, 78, 80, 81, 82, 83, 84, 85, 153
   s 6   75
   s 7   75, 76
   s 8   73, 76, 78

Table of Statutes

Partnership Act 1890—*continued*
  s 9   95, 96
  s 10   86, 88, 89, 90, 93, 95
  s 11   89, 90, 91, 92, 93, 94, 95
  s 12   95
  s 13   89, 94
  s 14   70, 72, 96, 100, 149, 160
  s 14(1) 42, 43, 44, 45, 51, 54, 101
  s 14(2) 46
  s 15   80
  s 16   80
  s 17   96
  s 17(1) 96, 97, 98
  s 17(2) 97, 98
  s 17(3) 98
  s 18   99
  s 19   3, 27, 103, 114
  s 20(1) 135-6, 137
  s 20(2) 136
  s 20(3) 139, 140
  s 21   138, 140
  s 22   136
  s 23   3, 131, 132, 147
  s 24   114
  s 24(1) 118, 119
  s 24(2) 121, 122
  s 24(3) 120
  s 24(4) 120
  s 24(5) 114, 115
  s 24(6) 115
  s 24(7) 122
  s 24(8) 115, 116, 122
  s 24(9) 117, 118
  s 25   114, 125
  s 25(3) 121
  s 26   147, 157
  s 26(1) 29, 30, 31

Partnership Act 1890—*continued*
  s 26(2) 31
  s 27   32
  ss 28-30 5
  s 29   107, 108, 113
  s 30   113
  s 31   128, 129, 133, 136
  s 31(1) 131
  s 32   29-30, 146-7, 157
  s 32(b) 30, 31
  s 32(c) 30, 31
  s 33(1) 147-8
  s 34   148, 149
  s 35   149-51
  s 36   44, 70, 96
  s 36(1) 99, 100, 101
  s 36(2) 99
  s 36(3) 99, 100
  s 38   153
  s 39   136, 158, 159
  s 40   157
  s 41   152
  s 42   155
  s 42(1) 163, 164, 165, 166
  s 42(2) 166
  s 43   164
  s 44   167, 168, 169
  s 46   3
Partnership Law Amendment Act 1965   3
Race Relations Act 1976
  s 10   60
Registration of Business Names Act 1916   66
Sex Discrimination Act 1975
  s 11   60
Solicitors Act 1974   149
  s 20   65

1

Partnerships and Partnership Law

What is a partnership?

A partnership is defined, with misleading simplicity, in s. 1(1) of the Partnership Act 1890 as 'the relation which subsists between persons carrying on a business in common with a view of profit'. All legal definitions have exceptions, however, and s. 1(2) is quick to exclude all forms of company (from ICI to Jones the Butchers Ltd) which would otherwise fall within the definition. The definition however, does provide the three essential ingredients for a partnership, namely, a business, carried on in common and with a view of profit, and we will return to those later on in this chapter. For the moment, however, the key word in the definition is the word 'relation'. Partnership is a relationship, it is not an organisation in its own right with a separate legal personality. Unlike a company, therefore a partnership cannot of itself make contracts, employ people, commit crimes or even be sued, any more than a marriage can. Where we talk of a partnership (or frequently of a firm) we simply mean the partners who comprise the partnership. Rather like a marriage, a partnership is simply a relationship which if established governs the rights and duties between the parties and their relationships *vis-à-vis* the rest of society.

The other key difference between a partnership and a company is that a partnership (like a marriage) does not confer any limited liability on the partners. Thus it is possible for each partner to be liable without limit for debts incurred by the other partners in the course of the partnership business. This is seen by the business community as an obvious drawback but an attempt in 1907 by the Limited Partnerships Act to create partnerships in which some of the partners would have limited liability was doomed to failure, partly because of the weaknesses of the form itself (if the limited partner for example interferes in the management of the firm he loses his immunity) but largely because private companies arrived at the same time, providing both limited liability and a separate legal personality to hide behind. The presumed advantages of Mr Salomon in the famous case of *Salomon* v *A. Salomon & Co. Ltd* (1897) would not have been available to him under either of the partnership forms available in the United Kingdom.

Many of the problems associated with partnership law which stem from this lack of legal personality are not helped by the fact that in common usage a partnership often looks like and is regarded as a separate entity. The words 'and Co.' are frequently found at the end of the name used by a firm. This signifies nothing in legal terms and does not make the firm into a company. Most private limited companies use the word 'limited' at the end of their names. Further, partners can sue and be sued in the firm's name, tax assessments are raised on the firm and indeed s. 4(1) of the Partnership Act itself provides that:

> Persons who have entered into partnership with one another are for the purposes of this Act called collectively a firm, and the name under which their business is carried on is called the firm-name.

If any further complication is required, in Scotland a partnership does have a separate legal personality but no limited liability by virtue of s. 4(2) of the 1890 Act. But all this is a smoke-screen designed to assist in commerce and the procedure of the courts. At all times remember that a partnership is in law a relationship which affects the rights and duties of those concerned and no more.

For a recent example of the confusion caused by this apparent separate identity of the firm we need look no further than that modern phenomenon, value added tax. Under s. 22 of the Finance Act 1972 (which introduced the tax), registration for VAT could be in the firm name and no account was to be taken of any change in the partnership. But Glidewell J in *Customs & Excise Commissioners* v *Evans* (1982) was forced to conclude that since a partnership was not a person but only a group of taxable persons trading jointly, an assessment could only be made against the individual partners and further that such assessments must be notified to each partner. Since the particular firm involved, which ran a wine bar known as the 'Grape Escape', had had a change of personnel during the year and not all the partners had been so notified, the assessment was, therefore, invalid. The authorities were forced to change the law in the Finance Act 1982 to cover the specific case.

I have made much of the analogy of a partnership and a marriage. It has often been said that one should choose one's partners as carefully as one's spouse (for the eminently practical reason that your partners may bankrupt you). But this analogy should not be carried too far. Partnerships can occur informally, i.e., without any express intention of the parties concerned, and, being essentially contractual in nature, can be started and finished in any way the partners decide. To a large extent partnership law is a voluntary code which can be varied by agreement.

Partnership law

Partnership Act 1890

Where then do we find the law relating to partnerships? Partnership law in fact developed in a very traditional way through the courts, both of common law and equity, particularly during the latter half of the 19th century. The Partnership Law Amendment Act 1865 (known as Bovill's Act) was a brief statutory incursion aimed at clarifying the distinction between partners and their creditors (of which much more in chapter 2) but in 1890 the Partnership Act was passed, based on a Bill drafted by Sir Frederick Pollock in 1879. This Act forms the basis of partnership law today and has remained virtually unscathed through a century of change. A copy of the Act is an essential aid for any student of partnership law — for one thing it is central to the subject, for another it is likely that you will be able to take a copy into the examination and finally it is, by today's standards, inexpensive.

But is far from being a straightforward Act in modern terms. It was, and is, largely declaratory of the law — there were virtually no 'new' rules (s. 23 is an exception to this). But it is neither a codifying nor a consolidating Act. Large areas of the subject remain open to the vagaries, or delights, according to taste, of case law. Section 46 preserves all equitable and common law rules 'except so far as they are inconsistent with the express provisions of this Act'. It is again, also by modern standards, a short Act with short sections (50 sections or 79 subsections in total) with a total lack of modern legislative jargon and cross-referencing. The draftsman rejected the temptation to define every conceivable concept and whilst this does occasionally cause difficulties (we shall for example agonise over ss. 2(3) and 5 later on) it makes the blighter readable. Turning from the Partnership Act 1890 to the Companies Act 1985 is to experience the culture shock of the time-traveller. Like man and the apes they are cousins but the relationship is difficult to imagine.

Comparing the Partnership Act to the Companies Act also demonstrates another facet of the 1890 Act. It is on the whole a voluntary code. Section 19 allows all its provisions as to the rights and duties of partners *vis-à-vis* each other to be varied by consent, express or implied (from a course of dealings). Other sections are also subject to contrary intention. This feature can be traced to the contractual nature of the relationship called a partnership. As with other contracts the parties can, within certain defined limits, agree to whatever terms they wish as between themselves (and thus the parts of the Act covering those areas are also subject to contrary agreement) but they cannot rely on any such agreement *vis-à-vis* third parties on the well known principles of privity of contract (and thus those of the Act relating to third parties are not voluntary). The third type of section in the Act, by which the courts are allowed to interfere in the relationship, either to establish liability or to end the partnership, are, of course, also non-negotiable.

Common law and equity

Since the 1890 Act is both declaratory in nature and partial in scope, it follows that the many cases decided before that date are relevant either to explain or amplify the Act itself or to cover areas outside its scope. It must be true that for a declaratory Act above all others, earlier cases can be relied on to clarify the draftsman's (and also Parliament's) intentions. It goes almost without saying that cases decided since 1890 are of great importance in deciphering the law. In this context, however, it is important to realise that the Partnership Act 1890 applies equally to Scotland and that cases decided in Edinburgh are of strong persuasive authority. The concept of partnership was also exported, among other countries, to Canada, Australia and New Zealand and their statutes bear a strong resemblance to our own. Cases decided in those jurisdictions are therefore also important (and in many instances of a more recent vintage).

The contractual basis of partnership has already been noted. The common law rules relating to formation, variation and vitiation of a contract all apply to partnerships (for example, the remedy of rescission of the agreement for misrepresentation is as comprehensive as any court order for a dissolution of the partnership). Tort also plays a part — in particular, the concepts of passing off and vicarious liability. But these are mainly areas where partnership is in one sense incidental — the problem arises from tort or contract not from the relationship between partners. In one area of the common law, however, the partnership concept is central. The liability of partners for partnership debts (the central issue of any firm) is based upon an understanding and specific application of the law of agency. Each partner is an agent of his fellow partners (and a principal in relation to the acts of his fellow partners). The application, not always consistent, of the agency concept to partnership is a problem that will be considered in chapter 4.

Yet partners are more than contracting parties — they had been established by the courts of equity as owing fiduciary duties to each other by the time of the Act, and developments in the law of equity in recent times have strengthened rather than diminished such duties. In other words, partners are expected to behave towards each other as if they were trustees for each other, making full disclosure and being scrupulously fair in their dealings. Equity does not require fault or dishonesty to establish a breach of such a duty (unlike the common law) and such duties can be enforced by the equitable remedy of account which simply requires proof of an inequitable retention of property. The Act merely cites three examples of these 'higher' duties (in ss. 28 to 30) and one of the untested areas in modern times is how some of the more venerable decisions on those and other duties should be read in the light of the recent expansion of the law of constructive trusts and fiduciary duties in other areas (see chapters 5 and 6).

Partners are, therefore, contractors, agents, principals, fiduciaries and beneficiaries all at the same time. The potential chaos suggested by such an analysis is, however, for the most part lacking. More difficulties arise from the lack of recent decisions on key areas — one reason for this being that most partnership agreements provide for arbitration in the case of a dispute.

Other relevant statutes

Although partnerships are for the most part exempt from those aspects of public and EEC control which have caused company law to expand in a geometrical progression since 1967 there are nevertheless areas where such control exists. Chapter 3 is concerned with such intrusions. The two most important for the purposes of this book, since they affect the creation and dissolution of partnerships *qua* partnerships, are the Business Names Act 1985, regulating the use and disclosure of firm-names, and the insolvency legislation concerning dissolution. There are many other cases, of course, where partnerships cannot avoid the complexities of modern life — employment law and taxation, for example — but in general the problems that arise in such cases are caused by adapting the complex provisions of those areas of the law to partnerships — problems not helped, as we have already seen, by the schizophrenic nature of the concept of partnership as a relationship which is dressed up to look like a separate being.

Having established that a partnership is a relationship and that we must find the laws relating to it from many sources, we must now turn to those three legal criteria we ran into at the beginning without which no partnership can exist — a business, carried on in common and with a profit motive.

Essentials of a partnership

Chapter 2 will deal in rather more detail with the rules governing precisely how and when a partnership is or is not established and the circumstances in which the question might be raised. For the moment it is sufficient to note that a partnership can arise by association of events as well as from a contractual agreement and that the question of whether or not a partnership has been established can crop up in such varied areas as taxation, insolvency, national insurance and the statutory powers of corporations as well as the more obvious example of making one person liable for the debts incurred by another. In all such cases, however, the courts must always bear in mind the three essential criteria contained in s. 1 of the Act without which there cannot be a partnership.

Business

Partnerships are business media — they cannot, unlike companies, be formed for benevolent or artistic purposes. Section 45 of the Act defines 'business' for this purpose as including every trade, occupation or profession, subject, of course, to those professions, such as the Bar, where a partnership is forbidden by professional rules. It was therefore established prior to the Act that the occupation of a landowner cannot form the basis of a partnership whereas that of a market gardener clearly can. In other words there must be some commercial venture — a selling of goods or services for a reward — before there can be a partnership. The concepts of trade and profession are well known to income tax lawyers and two difficulties which have arisen in that context have also arisen in partnership law, i.e., the distinction between the self-employed trader or professional man and an employee, and the status of a single commercial venture.

Partners are by definition self-employed. An employee is not a trader and thus cannot be a partner and the distinction is the common one between a contract of service and a contract for services. For example, the tax courts have had to decide whether an actress who undertakes several engagements on radio, film and the stage etc. is entering a series of employed posts or is simply carrying out her profession. The test evolved for tax purposes is whether the taxpayer has found a 'post' and stayed in it or was simply entering a series of engagements. Either conclusion is possible (see *Davies* v *Braithwaite* (1931) and *Fall* v *Hitchen* (1973)). There is no reason to suppose that the question is any different for partnerships but this is a complex issue which we will reserve for consideration in chapter 2. For the moment let us take an example to demonstrate a recent area where this issue has arisen.

In *E. Rennison & Son* v *Minister of Social Security* (1970) a firm of solicitors employed various clerical staff. In 1966 the staff entered into contracts with the firm which described them as self-employed, being paid at hourly rates and having the right to hire out their services elsewhere. In 1967 the staff entered into a written 'partnership' agreement, the partnership business to be carried out at the office or elsewhere, the profits and losses to be divided among them on terms to be agreed and with provision for other items such as the keeping of accounts and retirement. In fact the staff continued to work exactly as before at the same rate of hourly pay — payment being made in a weekly lump sum to one of the staff who then divided it out. The question arose as to whether the staff were employees for national insurance purposes, or in legal terms, whether they were employed under a contract of service. The judge, Bridge J, decided that the staff had never changed their original roles. The 1966 contracts were found to be contracts of service and the partnership agreement did not affect them. The method of paying a lump sum to the 'partnership' was no more than an agreement about the method of paying the amounts earned under the contracts of service.

The judge did not therefore have to decide whether a contract between two partnerships could be a contract of service or, in other words, whether one partnership can employ another partnership. Because partnerships can only exist to carry on a business the answer yes would have to imply that an employment could be contracted in the course of carrying on the business of the employee partnership. There is some support for that proposition in the tax case of *Fall* v *Hitchen* (1973), mentioned above, and it is accepted that, for example, a firm of accountants who act as auditors of companies are theoretically to be taxed on the receipts of such offices as employees.

For tax purposes a trade can include an adventure in the nature of a trade and it now seems to be accepted that for a partnership a business can exist even if it is only for a single commercial venture, for example, when a lady found herself contracted to purchase two houses without having sufficient funds and so agreed with a local property dealer to purchase the houses jointly and share the profits equally: *Winsor* v *Schroeder* (1979). Woolf J admitted that where there was only one transaction involved it was less likely to be regarded as a partnership but that this situation had all the elements of partnership. The emphasis must be, as in the tax cases, not on whether it is a single venture but whether it is a commercial venture and not, for example, simply realising an investment, e.g., buying a house, finding that one's spouse won't live there and having the property improved and sold at a profit: *Taylor* v *Good* (1974). Factors used in tax cases have included a profit motive, a commercial organisation, the subject-matter of the transaction (some things are more likely to be held as investments than others), repetition and the circumstances of the realisation (e.g., insolvency).

This need for a business has excluded several relationships which might otherwise have been construed as partnerships. For example, most members' clubs and other non-profit-making associations cannot be said to be carrying on a business and are thus not partnerships: see *Wise* v *Perpetual Trustee Co.* (1903). Nor does the simple co-ownership of property constitute partnership. One of the rules for determining the existence of a partnership in s. 2(1) of the Act provides that no form of co-ownership (both the English and Scottish forms are set out) shall 'of itself' create a partnership as to anything so held or owned *whether or not they share any profits made by the use of the property*. Co-ownership without a business attached does not create a partnership, it is simply co-ownership, which is, incidentally, not the position in most of our European neighbours. This distinction between co-ownership and partnership creates many problems in the field of partnership property and we will return to it in chapter 6.

A similar situation arises with an agreement for a joint purchase only of property (e.g., to achieve a discount). This equally cannot amount to a partnership. For example, if Mr Smith and Mr Jones agree to purchase a case of wine for their own consumption because it proves to be cheaper than buying six bottles each and Mr Smith sends in the order, intending to recover a share of the cost from Mr Jones, it is not suggested that they are thereby partners. It would, of course, be different if they intended to resell the wine at a profit. This basic distinction was made as early as 1788 in a case called *Coope* v *Eyre*. Mr Eyre purchased some oil on behalf of what we would now refer to as a syndicate, dividing it up after purchase. Eyre failed to pay and the seller sought to recover from the other members. Gould J said no, there was no community of profit. 'But in the present case there was no communication between the buyers as to profit or loss. Each party was to have a distinct share of the whole, the one having no interference with the share of the other, but each to manage his share as he judged best.'

Nearly 200 years later yet another relationship was excluded from a partnership by the Court of Appeal. It is not unusual for persons intending to set up a company to prepare the ground whilst waiting for the incorporation procedure to take place — in technical terms they are known as promoters. In *Keith Spicer Ltd* v *Mansell* (1970) the question was whether, in carrying out these preliminary activities, the promoters could be regarded as partners. In that case one of the promoters ordered goods from the plaintiff company intending them to be used by the proposed company and the goods were delivered to the other promoter's address. The promoters opened a bank account in the name of the proposed company, omitting the all-important 'Ltd' at the end. The bank account was never used and the promoter who had ordered the goods became insolvent. The county court judge found that there was insufficient evidence of partnership and this was upheld by the Court of Appeal. Harman LJ said that the promoters were merely working together to form a company, they had no intention of trading prior to incorporation — they could not be partners because they had never carried on business as such.

A word of caution should be given here, however, since the other members of the Court of Appeal simply agreed that on the facts of the case there was insufficient evidence to support a finding that a partnership existed and the decision does seem an extreme application of the business requirement so that perhaps on less extreme findings of fact a different result might have been achieved. In this respect Harman LJ himself pointed out that for the courts the question of the existence of a partnership is a mixed question of law and fact. It is an inference from the primary facts as found by the judge from which as a question of law one can say whether or not there is a partnership.

Carried on in common

A partnership of necessity requires the involvement of two or more persons in the business. With the singular exception of a limited partner under the Limited Partnerships Act 1907, it follows that the distinction in this context is between participation *in* the business and a connection *with* the business, such as that of a supplier of goods or services. In *Strathearn Gordon Associates Ltd* v *Commissioners of Customs & Excise* (1985), the company acted as a management consultant and was paid fees plus a share of the profits of seven separate developments. It argued that these were receipts of a partnership carrying out the various developments and that the company was not supplying services for the purposes of VAT. The VAT Tribunal rejected this argument. The parties had not made any agreement to carry on a business together. What the company had actually agreed to do was to supervise the carrying out of the work and in essence that was an agreement for the provision of services. The mere fact that the consideration was measured by reference to a share in the profits was not enough to convert it into a partnership. In other words they were not involved in the business, they simply provided services for the business. All such cases must at the end of the day depend upon their own facts.

If there is no participation in the business then it seems that even if there is an intention to draw up a partnership agreement and some discussion between the parties as to the consequences of it, the courts will not declare a partnership. In *Saywell* v *Pope* (1979), Mr Saywell and Mr Prentice were partners in a firm dealing in and repairing agricultural machinery. In January 1973 the firm obtained a marketing franchise from Fiat which expanded the work of the firm. Until that time Mrs Saywell and Mrs Prentice had been employed by the firm to do a small amount of work but they then began to take a more active part in the business. At the suggestion of the firm's accountant the four drew up a written partnership agreement but this was not signed until June 1975. The bank mandate in force before 1973 enabling Mr Saywell and Mr Prentice to sign cheques was, however, unchanged, and no notice of any change in the firm was given to the bank or the creditors or customers of the firm. Neither of the wives introduced any capital into the business and had no drawing facilities from the partnership bank account. A share of the profits was credited to them for 1973 and 1974 but they never drew on them. In April 1973 the wives had been informed that if they became partners they would become liable for the debts of the firm and they had not objected. The Inland Revenue refused to accept that the wives had become partners until 1975.

Slade J agreed with the Revenue. The written agreement could only apply from the date it was signed and even though it contained a statement that the partnership had actually begun earlier that could not make them partners during that period unless that was the true position. There was no evidence that in 1973 the parties had contemplated such an agreement and neither the partnership agreement nor the discussion of liability could be taken as creating an immediate partnership. There was no evidence that during the relevant time they did *anything in the capacity of partners*. The crediting of the net profits was of more significance and we shall return to this in the next heading. What is important is that despite the fact that there was a business and a 'sharing' of profits no partnership existed since in effect the wives had never been integrated into the firm.

It should perhaps be said at this stage that in both the examples above it was the partners themselves who were seeking to establish a partnership for tax purposes and the burden of proof was on them. The position may well be different if a third party is seeking to make a partner liable as such. One of the interesting things about partnerships is that one can be liable as a partner even if in law a partnership does not exist, for example if you allow yourself to be represented as such to the third party in question (see chapter 2).

Another way of making the distinction between a partner and a business 'contact', for want of a better word, is whether the alleged partner has any control over the property or ultimate management control. In one sense neither of the wives in *Saywell* v *Pope* had either of these. It is possible to enter into a business venture with another party without establishing a partnership, particularly if that other party is itself a separate business entity, whether incorporated or not.

In the Canadian case of *Canadian Pacific Ltd* v *Telesat Canada* (1982), the Telesat Canada Corporation had only those powers allowed to it by its founding statute and these did not permit it to enter into a partnership. A shareholder of the company sought to establish that an agreement between the corporation and the nine principal Canadian telephone companies setting up the Trans-Canada Telephone System had established just such a forbidden partnership. The Ontario Court of Appeal decided that since the arrangement did not involve the corporation's abandoning control over its property or delegating ultimate management control, it did not amount to a partnership. Similarly, in *Mann* v *D'Arcy* (1968), Megarry J held that an agreement between a firm of produce merchants and another merchant to go on a joint account on the sale of some potatoes did not amount to a new and separate partnership. It was a single venture controlled by the existing firm in the ordinary course of its existing business. 'The arrangement was merely one made of buying and selling what [the negotiating partner] was authorised to buy and sell.'

We saw at the beginning of this section that an exception to this requirement of participation is a limited partner. A limited partnership formed under the 1907 Act of that name must be registered as such and must have at least one general and one limited partner. A limited partner is defined as one who contributes to the partnership when he joins it a stated amount of capital in cash or in kind and whose liability is limited to the amount so contributed by him. A general partner is anyone who is not a limited partner and is fully liable for all the debts of the firm. Although the general rules of partnership apply, s. 6(1) of the 1907 Act expressly forbids a limited partner from taking any part in the management of the firm with the effective sanction that if he does so he will assume full liability for debts as if he were an ordinary partner.

This is an obvious drawback to limited partnerships since the temptation to interfere in the business will be greatest when affairs are going badly and the investment is at risk, and yet that is precisely the time when the greater general liability may become a reality. Neither is it clear either exactly what will amount to 'taking part in the management' for this purpose. Section 6 of the 1907 Act itself allows a limited partner to inspect the books of the firm and to 'advise with the partners' on the state of the firm. Perhaps the distinction will be between active and passive advice. In any event the private company offers the same advantages with none of the drawbacks.

With a view of profit

Most of the problems concerning the existence of a partnership revolve around the concept of profit-sharing. It is impossible to establish a partnership if there is no financial return from the business — it would hardly be a business if no financial return was contemplated. Far more problems arise in practice in the reverse situation — i.e., when a financial return from a business is argued *not* to constitute the recipient a partner because, for example, it is really a wage paid to an employee, or interest paid to a creditor or a contractual return for the supply of goods or services rendered. At one time a mere receipt of a share of the profits established a partnership: *Waugh* v *Carver* (1793); but this was repudiated by the House of Lords in *Cox* v *Hickman* (1860) and the repudiation was codified into s. 2(3) of the 1890 Act. It is now well-established that mere receipt of a share of the profits of a business does not automatically make the recipient a partner. Thus the VAT Tribunal in *Strathearn Gordon Associates Ltd* v *Commissioners of Customs & Excise* (1985) were able to declare in a sentence that: 'The mere fact that this consideration was measured by reference to a share of the net profit does not in our judgment convert the agreement into a partnership'. An agreement for the supply of services was exactly that and no more. The precise circumstances under which the receipt of a share of the profits will turn an employee, creditor or supplier into a partner are discussed in chapter 2.

There must, however, be a profit motive — but then all businesses are designed to make money and a simple requirement of a profit motive might not seem to add anything to the business criterion already discussed. It has been argued, however, that that is the only requirement as to profit imposed by s. 1 of the 1890 Act. Returning to the words of that section, there must be a 'business carried on in common with a view of profit'. These words, so the argument goes, require only a profit motive and not necessarily a *share* in the profits for each partner; i.e., only the business need be carried on 'in common', not necessarily the profits. Another, equally appropriate interpretation, however, is that it is a business with a view to profit which must be carried on in common. A share of the profits must on that basis be contemplated for a partnership to be established.

Some support for this view can be found in the recent Australian case of *United Dominions Corporation Ltd* v *Brian Pty Ltd* (1985), where the court was concerned to distinguish a partnership from a joint venture which did not amount to a partnership. Dawson J regarded the important distinction as being between the sharing of profits which would indicate a partnership and the sharing of a product generated by the joint venture. Enterprises of the latter kind are common in the exploration and exploitation of mineral resources in that country.

Further support can be found in the English case of *Saywell* v *Pope* (1979) discussed above in relation to participation in the business. One of the factors relied on by the taxpayers in that case to establish a partnership was that the wives of the two admitted partners had been credited with a share of the profits in the firm's accounts. Slade J, accepting the proposition that receipt of a share of profits was not conclusive in any event, went on to state that these book entries were never accompanied by any actual drawing out of the share of profits credited to the two wives. In other words, since there was no evidence of any actual receipt of a share of the profits during the relevant period, a partnership could not be said to exist on the basis of the accounts. Receipt or at least a genuine entitlement to receipt would seem to be necessary.

In yet another tax case one of the issues raised was whether the activities could amount to a partnership on the basis that the making of a profit was not the primary motive of the parties. This arose in the case of *Newstead* v *Frost* (1980). David Frost, the seemingly perennial television personality, formed a partnership with a Bahamian company to exploit his highly profitable activities in the United States. The major purpose behind this was the common one of tax avoidance, the general idea being to isolate the income produced from the individual and thus from the United Kingdom and the Inland Revenue. The latter attacked this partnership on two fronts — one, as to the capacity of the company to enter into such a partnership (of which more anon) and two, as to the existence of the partnership itself. The Revenue argued that this agreement was designed largely as a tax avoidance scheme and so did not constitute carrying on a business with a view of profit. The House of Lords, however, disagreed. The partnership was in fact formed to create a profit from the exploitation of the entertainer's activities and the fact that it was hoped such profits would avoid tax did not affect that basic idea.

The use of partnerships as a vehicle for tax avoidance or what is more euphemistically called 'tax planning' is a modern phenomenon. The decision in *Newstead* v *Frost* merely reflected the then current judicial attitude to tax avoidance — i.e., that the form of a transaction had to be given effect to whatever the motives involved unless it was an absolute sham. Since that case was decided, however, the House of Lords, in a series of cases beginning with *W.T. Ramsay Ltd* v *IRC* (1982) and culminating in *Furniss* v *Dawson* (1984), has established that where there is a pre-ordained series of transactions (or a single composite step) and the insertion of artificial steps (i.e., those which have no business purpose as distinct from a business effect) then for tax purposes those intermediate steps can be discounted. Despite subsequent sniping at the decision by one or two Chancery judges, those principles have had a dramatic effect on the tax-avoidance industry as a whole, which will inevitably reflect on the use of partnerships in such schemes. It will now have to be shown that the partnership was introduced other than for purely tax-avoidance reasons. In future cases, therefore, the question of primary motive or reasons may be of somewhat greater significance than it has been up to now.

So far we have been discussing the question of the intention to create and share in *profits*. In one sense that is not entirely accurate since it has long been clear that the profits in question must be *net* profits — i.e., those calculated after accounting for the expenses incurred in making them. Another of the rules for establishing the existence of partnership, in s. 2(2) of the 1890 Act, makes this clear: 'The sharing of gross returns does not of itself create a partnership, whether the persons sharing such returns have or have not a joint or common right or interest in any property from which . . . the returns are derived'. Thus an author who is paid 10% royalty (at the least, one hopes) on the published price of his book is not a partner with his publisher — duties of good faith might well be stretched otherwise!

Another example can be found in the case of *Cox* v *Coulson* (1916). Mr Coulson was a theatre manager who agreed with Mr Mill to provide his theatre for one of Mill's productions. Mr Coulson was to pay for the lighting and the posters etc., Mr Mill to provide the company and the scenery. Under the agreement Mr Coulson was to receive 60% of the gross takings and Mr Mill the other 40%. The play must have been heady stuff since the plaintiff in the case was shot by one of the actors during a performance. She sought to make Mr Coulson liable on the basis that he and Mr Mill were partners and so responsible for the outrage. The Court of Appeal had little difficulty in rejecting any claim based on partnership since s. 2(2) made it quite clear that the sharing of gross returns did not create such a partnership.

Implicit in the idea of sharing net profits is the sharing of expenses and thus if necessary in net losses (except for our friend the limited partner of course). Sharing gross returns, as in the two examples above, cannot fall into this category since it is implicit in such agreements that each party has to bear his own separate liabilities in respect of the undertaking. It would be very rare for a publisher, for example, to share in the costs of writing and even rarer for an author jointly to sponsor the activities of his publisher.

Partnerships, therefore, are about businesses carried on by persons who intend to share in the net profits of that business. Two points should now be borne in mind. First that there are in addition to the concepts just discussed the provisions of s. 2(3) of the 1890 Act which were intended to draw the often fine distinctions between a partner and a creditor where a share of the profits is undoubtedly being received. These provisions form the basis of part of chapter 2 but they must always be read subject to s. 1 of the Act and the essentials of a partnership. Second, it may perhaps occur to the reader that in this general area, as with others in the law, the result often seems to depend upon the question being asked and the consequences of the answer. It may well be that the emphasis may vary between, say, one case where the parties are trying to convince a doubting Inland Revenue of the existence of a partnership, and another where an unpaid supplier is seeking to make someone liable as a partner of the person who ordered the goods.

Partnerships then and now

Before embarking on a more detailed study of the creation, operation and extinction of partnerships it is useful to have some idea of the changing role of partnerships in the commercial life of the country. The 19th century, which saw the establishment of the partnership as a popular business medium, culminated in the Act of 1890 and the basic partnership rules which still apply today. By the turn of the century, however, the demise of the partnership as the common form for small businesses was well under way, whilst in more recent times the development of professional partnerships, especially those of accountants, and the influence of taxation have presented new challenges and brought new uses for the partnership form. Looking to the future, there are already two known areas of possible development for partnerships. This continuing change in the way partnerships have been and are being used help to put the law and its development in context.

Partnerships up to 1890

Partnerships, as we have seen, developed naturally (in the sense of slowly through the case-law system) out of the laws of contract, agency and equity. They were hedged in with few compulsory rules and since they conferred neither legal personality nor limited liability they rarely raised issues of a sufficient concern to merit the interference of Parliament. They provided freedom to operate on any terms which could be agreed and did not allow those responsible to avoid the consequences of their actions. The courts responded to any problem with an ease and calm assurance which typifies the so-called 'golden era' of English law. Only rarely did they cause confusion — Bovill's Act of 1865 being the exception, since it was deemed necessary to clarify the distinction between partners and creditors following the *volte face*, already mentioned, about whether simply taking a share of the profits meant an automatic partnership or not. But in general the fact that in 1890 only one real change was made by the Act to the existing case-law rules is a testimony to the 19th-century judges who created much of the present law.

Partnerships thrived and multiplied. This was due in part to their compatibility with utilitarian philosophy, much in evidence in the early 19th century, as anyone with even a passing acquaintance with the novels of Charles Dickens must be aware. But it was also due to the fact that in the early part of the century there were really no alternatives for the small or medium-sized business. Companies could be formed with both legal personality and limited liability but only by a royal charter or a private Act of Parliament. This may have been ideal for the East India Company or the canal and railway companies and other vast enterprises but it was slow and very expensive and not at all in tune with the growing needs of the age. The earlier problems of the South Sea Bubble and other fiascos, however, prevented any easier form of incorporation. At common law, companies, known as deed of settlement companies, were in effect merely large partnerships.

The expansion of industrial and commercial life during that period, however, soon provided the pressure for legislation to provide a cheaper and quicker access to the twin benefits of incorporation and limited liability. Partnerships were inappropriate for entrepreneurs turning their attention to world markets. By 1855 the modern concept of the registered limited company was possible and the Joint Stock Companies Act 1856 allowed promoters to register and thus create a company simply by filing the requisite documents — a process still in force today. Decisions such as *Salomon* v *A. Salomon & Co. Ltd* (1897) pressed home the benefits of limited liability; the concept entered into popular mythology, as can be discovered from listening to the Company Promoter's song from the Gilbert and Sullivan comic opera, *Utopia Ltd*. To explain the distinction between a company and its members, Gilbert invented the story of a monarch whose rule was absolute except that he could at any time be exploded by the 'Public Exploder' on the word of two 'Wise Men'. To avoid this the King turned himself into a limited company and confronted his tormentors with the thought that although they could wind up a company they could not blow it up!

The registered company was to be the business medium from then on. Administratively and economically it was more attractive than a partnership and by the time of the Partnership Act itself partnerships were on the decline. There were, however, still some disadvantages for the small business in selecting the corporate form, such as increased formality and less flexibility, especially if a dispute arose, but company law itself was to develop so as to negative most, if not all, of them.

The growth and development of private companies

One of the consequences of this growth in companies was the limited partnership, introduced by the Limited Partnerships Act 1907. We have already come across this 'commercial mongrel' and more will be said in the next chapter. As an attempt to revive the partnership form, however, it was a dismal failure. By the Companies Act 1907 the private company was introduced and sank its rival almost without trace. A private company allowed management participation by the director-shareholders without loss of limited liability and it could raise money by means of a floating charge (i.e., a charge over all its assets, which can nevertheless be utilised by the company until disaster strikes) — a method of finance which for technical reasons has always been denied to partnerships.

As company law became more complex and above all more interventionist so that greater public disclosure was demanded of such things as accounts and exactly who owned what, it might have been expected that small businesses would return to the partnership fold. But this never happened — partly at least because company law itself sought to protect the small private company from the more embarrassing aspects of this policy. In recent years the attractiveness of the small private company has been enhanced by two important developments. The first is a consequence of our membership of the EEC. Most of our European 'partners' differentiate between the public and private company form to a far greater extent than we do — for example, they have separate codes for each form. The vast majority of EEC-inspired changes to company law therefore have been applicable only to public companies and to accommodate this approach the 1980 Companies Act created a much clearer distinction between public and private companies in the UK — one visible effect of which is the use of a different abbreviation at the end of a company's name. When writing a cheque for Marks & Spencer for example, the ending is no longer 'Ltd' but 'plc'. Many of the more Draconian rules are only applicable to public companies and the 1981 Companies Act excused 'small' and 'medium'-sized companies from many of the accounting disclosure rules. Even those disclosure requirements which still exist are currently under review.

At the same time the courts evolved the concept of the 'quasi-partnership' company, that is, a company which, although legally a company, is in economic and management terms a partnership, or more precisely where there is an underlying right for the shareholder-directors to take part in the management of the company. In *Ebrahimi* v *Westbourne Galleries Ltd* (1973), the House of Lords decided that a breach of that underlying obligation, typically a dismissal of one of the directors, although perfectly in accord with the formal procedures of the Companies Act could lead to a winding up of the company on the just and equitable ground. (Incidentally Lord Wilberforce in that case rejected the term 'quasi-partnership' as being misleading but the term has stuck and provided it is used only as a general description little harm will be done.) Small companies are therefore protected one way or another from most of those areas of company law which would otherwise prove to be a drawback.

Partnerships today

The rise and rise of the private company has left the partnership today as the chosen medium mainly for those professions which are prevented by their professional rules from forming companies — solicitors, accountants, doctors and surveyors spring to mind as obvious examples. But there have been genuine growth areas of activity in recent times which have themselves given rise to developments in the uses of the partnership form. The influence of taxation on choice of business medium can be much exaggerated and it is doubtful whether it should actually prompt a decision one way or the other. Partnerships are liable to income tax on their profits but assessed by reference to the total incomes of the partners. Companies are subject to corporation tax as a separate entity with a further charge on the distribution of those profits to the shareholders. Under the imputation system of corporation tax, introduced in 1973, however, the overall rate remains the same whether the profits are distributed or not. Any advantages in cash-flow terms, from the fact that partnerships are taxed on last year's profits whereas companies on those of the current year, are on the whole balanced by other aspects of corporation tax.

Taxation does, however, play a part in modern partnership usage. As indicated earlier, partnerships have been used as tax avoidance vehicles, and even the 'simple' process of assimilating partnerships into the tax

Partnerships and Partnership Law

system throws up areas of general importance (remember the VAT case earlier). Yet another recent development has been the joint use of companies and partnerships — giving rise to the concept of the corporate partner — and after a brief look into our crystal ball we will conclude this chapter with a look at the way partnerships have been adapted to the various demands of the late 20th century.

Partnerships tomorrow

One of the less appealing consequences of the growth of the private company has been the vastly increased administrative burden they have placed on the Register of Companies. It is also a well known fact that many such companies honour their continuing registration obligations largely in the breach. In 1981 therefore the Government issued a Green Paper (a consultative document) called *A New Form of Incorporation for Small Firms* (Cmnd 8171), which was designed partly to encourage the continued development of small businesses and partly to reduce the number of private companies by providing a realistic alternative. Little has been heard of it since, although it contained the seeds of many new ideas. The most popular proved to be the provision of an incorporated unlimited firm — in effect a partnership with legal personality which appealed to those professions currently using the partnership form since it would simplify many of the internal problems associated with partnerships which are caused by the lack of such personality. But this would hardly reduce the number of private companies or stimulate the business side of the economy.

A more radical proposal (by Professor Gower in an annex to the paper) would be for an incorporated limited firm, a hybrid form using the Partnership Act management, agency and internal structure but allowing the use of a floating charge to raise money and requiring limited registration and disclosure obligations (e.g., an annual auditor's certificate of solvency). The most difficult area would be the protection of creditors who would lose their recourse to the partners themselves to recover their debts. This problem could, however, be overcome and the whole concept of limited liability for small businesses can be overstated since the largest creditors, the banks, usually insist on a personal guarantee from the directors. As in other areas of life it is the little man who will suffer. If such a proposal ever comes to fruition it will probably also require a 'stick' to reduce the number of private companies — a minimum capital requirement is the most obvious method.

The European Community is dedicated to integrating business structures within its area. With this in mind it has recently adopted a

19

regulation (which is *ipso facto* part of UK law) providing for the creation of European Economic Interest Groupings (EEIG). Based on a French model this is a loose cooperation grouping of several businesses in different Member States. Its purpose is to facilitate and assist the business of its members and it cannot retain its profits — they must be distributed to the members. This new concept will be created by contract but has some of the aspects of a separate legal person through not limited liability in itself. It is obviously far too early to say whether much, if any, use will be made of this new form but it is clearly available for partnerships to expand across frontiers if they so wish. Much will depend upon the attitude of the various professional bodies to the use of this new and, as yet, little understood concept.

Partnerships: variations on a theme

Group partnerships

Partnerships today, therefore, serve a very different economic function from that at the time of the 1890 Act. So flexible and successful are the provisions of that Act, however, that legal draftsmen have been able to adopt the form to meet the new demands of both the professions and taxation. For many years partnerships have been limited in size — the current limit is 20, but this limit has been waived since 1967 for most of the professional partnerships, including solicitors and accountants. Accountants in particular often now combine together in very large economic and often international units; some firms, like the multiple retail stores, seem to have a branch in every town in the country. Clearly a single partnership of three or four-figure numbers is possible but not very workable and these firms often organise themselves into group partnerships, which is in essence nothing more than a partnership between partnerships. In this way each branch office is in effect a semi-autonomous partnership but each one is linked by a partnership deed to the 'head' office, usually in London.

Much care must be taken, of course, in the drafting of the two agreements — the head partnership agreement and the branch partnership agreement: voting and financial matters are obvious areas of concern. But it is essentially a matter for agreement. There are potential problems: for example, as to the liability of a partner in one branch for the debts incurred by the head office or by another branch, but many of them will be capable of solutions based on the ordinary principles of agency. Similarly internal problems can be left to the ever-developing law on constructive trusts and fiduciary duties. It is firms such as these, however, which have the most to gain from the introduction of the incorporated firm suggested by the 1981 Green Paper. In one respect at least this is an area where company law is coming back to meet partnerships — a proposed EEC directive suggests that a holding company should be liable for the debts of its subsidiary.

Subpartnerships

A similar variation on the partnership theme is the subpartnership, that is, a partnership where one of the partners agrees to divide his share of the main partnership profits and losses with others. There are in effect two partnerships, one of which is a partner of a 'head partnership' together with individual partners. Thus a partnership of A, B and C can have a subpartnership if C agrees to subcontract his profit and losses from the head partnership with D and E. The questions which arise are whether this is possible; if it is, what are the liabilities of D and E with respect to the debts of the head partnership, and what are the fiduciary duties of A, B and C towards D and E? Rather surprisingly the answer to the first question is yes. Whilst it might at one time have been possible to argue that C, D and E are not actually carrying on a *business* (whereas in a group partnership it is envisaged that each 'branch office' will be doing so), such arrangements have been accepted by the courts of England, Scotland and Australia. Presumably the business is the management of the interest in the principal partnership.

The answer to the second question was given by Connolly J in the Queensland case of *Australia & New Zealand Banking Group Ltd* v *Richardson* (1980). The bank had lent $A30,000 to a newsagents' firm of which Mr Gary and Mr Richardson were partners. They later discovered that a Mrs Vernon had an association with the business in that she had advanced $A25,000 to Richardson, her son-in-law, to fund his half share of the partnership. In 1976 Mrs Vernon and Richardson agreed in writing that they would be equal partners in the half-share and were each entitled to withdraw $A200 per week from the business so long as the cash flow of the business allowed. She played very little part in the affairs of the business itself. The bank now sought to recover the debt directly from Mrs Vernon. The judge, having ruled that in no way could she be regarded as a full partner in the business, had to decide whether her subpartnership with Richardson nevertheless made her fully liable for the debts of the head partnership.

In short the judge's answer was no. The liability of a subpartner is limited to the extent of his subcontract with the subpartner who is also a full partner in the head partnership:

[A] subpartner's only interest in and relationship with the partnership lies in his right to a share of such of its profits as reach his partner. He has no rights against the partnership and can only enforce his right to profits which have actually been received by his subpartner.... He has no say in the running of the business for that would involve rights which cannot be conferred on him by one partner alone. It follows that he cannot be liable for the partnership debts on the footing that they were authorised by him.

In effect, therefore, a subpartner will simply suffer loss in revenue arising from main partnership losses but if the principal partner is liable to contribute further to the debts he may be able to call on a contribution from the subpartner.

Since the only conceivable business of the subpartnership is the management of the interest in the main partnership, few fiduciary problems will arise as between the subpartners since their interests are solely financial, consequential on the success or failure of the main partnerships. On the other hand it is possible that if the main partner were to involve the subpartners in the management of the main firm he would be in breach of his duties to the other main partners. At least on a formal level, therefore, the subpartnership will simply be a vehicle for the economic consequences of the share in the main partnership.

By way of postscript it should, however, be remembered that if the subpartner is regarded as a full partner by a third party, such as the bank in this case, he will be liable as such whatever the agreements involved. It is significant that in this case the bank had no knowledge of Mrs Vernon's existence until they commenced the proceedings. At no time did they rely on her being a partner when the credit was being extended.

Companies as partners

It is perfectly possible for a company to be a partner. (s. 1 of the Partnership Act relates to persons and the Interpretation Acts have always defined a person as including a company unless the contrary is provided). There is in fact nothing to prevent a partnership being composed entirely of companies. Companies as partners can fulfil many roles. For example, they enable the size limits of a partnership to be overcome — those partnerships which are still limited to 20 may thus have 20 companies as partners, each company having as many members as it wishes. Companies also provide some means of limited liability for partnerships since although the company partner would be liable for all the partnership debts without limit, the partnership creditors in pursuing their debts could only recover from the company's own resources and not those of its members. Tax planning has also involved the use of such corporate partners and even those professions which cannot form a company to practice their profession can involve a corporate partner as a service company. This ingenuity of the partnership draftsman is one of the reasons why there has been little pressure for the reform of partnership law itself and is yet another example of the flexibility achieved by the 19th-century law-makers.

There are problems, however, as always. Companies are artificial legal persons and there are two limits on their ability to do things. As an eminent judge once remarked, 'A company cannot eat nor sleep'; or, in other words, there are those physical things which a company simply cannot do. In addition they are limited by their objects and powers as expressed in the objects clause which every company must include in its memorandum of association. If a company enters into a contract (of which a partnership agreement is one) which is outside the terms of those objects and powers then such a contract is void, even if all the members of the company ratify the contract (*Ashbury Railway Carriage & Iron Co Ltd* v *Riche* (1875)). Such a contract is said to be *ultra vires* the company (literally outside its powers). If an agent acts outside the scope of his authority his acts can nevertheless be ratified by his principal (thus a company may ratify the acts of a director, or a partner the acts of another partner) but this cannot apply to *ultra vires* contracts.

In *Newstead* v *Frost* (1980) the Revenue attacked the partnership between David Frost and the Bahamian company on both of these grounds. Mr Frost and the company formed the partnership to exploit 'the activities of television and film consultants and advisers . . . and of producers, actors, directors, writers and artistes'. In fact the only entertainer so exploited was Mr Frost himself. The first argument put forward by the Revenue, who needed to negative the partnership, was that physically a company cannot be a television entertainer or an author and so could not form a partnership for such purposes since the only other partner could not exploit his own skills. The House of Lords rejected this. There was nothing in the agreement which required the company to entertain or write books and there was nothing to prevent the company and the individual jointly agreeing to exploit the individual's skills. The Court of Appeal had earlier commented that even if a company cannot 'do' the act in question, if the partnership as a whole could do it then it would be part of the partnership business and would have to be brought into account between the partners accordingly.

The objects clause of the company authorised it to carry on 'all kinds of financial commercial trading or other operations'. The second argument of the Revenue was that this did not include entering into a partnership of this nature. The House of Lords was rather more taken with this argument but since the trial judge and the Court of Appeal had all rejected it, they were not prepared to dissent. The importance of this point is not, of course, the detailed construction of a particular clause but the general question of *ultra vires*. If the company has an express power to enter into a partnership as a means of carrying on any of its authorised businesses then that will settle the question. If it is not an authorised business (on construction of the objects clause) than it is *ultra vires*, however conducted, whether in partnership or not. What was not raised in the case was whether, assuming the business to be an authorised business, the company has an *implied* power to carry it on in partnership. The answer will be yes if it is 'reasonably incidental' to such a business (*Deuchar* v *Imperial Gas Light & Coke Co Ltd* (1925).

The law of *ultra vires* as applied in *Newstead* v *Frost* has in fact since been developed in two ways. First it is now clear that provided the company has the express authority to do something in its objects clause (e.g., to give guarantees, make loans etc.) then no question of *ultra vires* can arise even if that authority is used otherwise than for the benefit or purposes of the company — disputes of that nature are as to the authority of those acting for the company and not the capacity of the company itself and so can be ratified by the company. It is always a question of simply construing the objects clause and no more: *Rolled Steel Products (Holdings) Ltd* v *British Steel Corporation* (1984). Second, even if the transaction is *ultra vires*, it will not be void as against a person dealing with the company in good faith as the result of what has become s. 35 of the Companies Act 1985. Whether this will apply in a corporate partnership will depend in each case upon its facts and the interpretation of the obscure wording of that section.

Other problems have and will arise with corporate partners. We mentioned above the question of liability and a recent example of such a problem in this context arose in the case of *Re Rudd & Sons Ltd* (1984). In this case the partnership consisted of just two companies. Both companies went into liquidation and so the partnership had to be wound up. Nourse J was faced with organising the creditors of the partnership and of each company. He decided that in so far as the partnership assets were concerned, the partnership creditors ranked equally since the companies legislation could not apply to partnerships and the Bankruptcy Act 1914, which applies preferential claims to partnerships, only applies as against the assets of individuals. There was, in effect, a gap in the legislation.

2

Establishing a Partnership

Questions and answers

A partnership is therefore a relationship between persons carrying on a business in common with a view of profit. Having digested that, the next question for a lawyer is how such a relationship can be established. In this respect s. 1 of the Act is not a great deal of help since it merely lays down minimum criteria and it is to s. 2 of the Act that we must turn for more detailed guidance. This section, according to the marginal note, contains rules for determining the existence of a partnership and they are intended to be of practical assistance in dealing with specific situations. In effect s. 2 is intended to assist in the quest for the criteria required by s. 1. We have already mentioned the rules as to co-ownership (s. 2(1)) and the sharing of gross returns (s. 2(2)) in the hope of shedding some light on the concepts of business and profit as required by s. 1. The main force of s. 2 is, however, in s. 2(3), which deals with the relationship between receiving a financial return from a business and the creation of a partnership — whether, indeed, the recipient is involved simply in a debtor-creditor relationship or is involved in risk-taking.

The question of establishing a partnership arises in three main areas. First, when a person who has dealt with a business seeks to make another person liable as a partner in that business — sometimes this is called in Americanese the 'outsider question'. It is usually about recovery of a debt or other liability from a person on the basis that he is a partner — if he is not a partner he will not be liable and so the issue is crucial. There are in fact two aspects of this particular question, since such a person may be a partner either because of his financial and managerial interest in the business or because without any such interest he has been represented as a partner to the third party. A partnership by association can be achieved either way.

The second area arises when one person seeks to enforce a duty or obligation from another on the basis that they are partners with each other and such duties or obligations will not apply if there is no partnership — this can be called the 'insider question'. Since partners owe fiduciary duties to each other (over and above the common law duties of reasonable care etc.) this is often very important. The third case is in the field of taxation and associated areas since it may be in the parties' interest to establish a partnership for tax purposes (or even sometimes for the Revenue to establish one). There are no special rules in the tax legislation to determine the existence of a partnership and the general law applies.

Sometimes the difficulties become clearer if the question asked is: if they are not partners, what are they? The answer will almost invariably be either debtor and creditor or employer and employee. In essence, therefore, many of the disputes as to the existence of a partnership resolve themselves into a distinction between either a partner and a creditor or a partner and an employee, although it is perfectly possible for a person to be both a creditor and an employee of a business without being a partner. There are no absolutes in this area, simply rules and guidelines which can bend with the facts. One essential factor is the burden of proof and in general this is, of course, on the person alleging that a partnership exists. This is particularly relevant in tax cases where the taxpayers are seeking to establish a partnership. In *Saywell* v *Pope* (1979) for example, Slade J placed the burden of proof fairly and squarely on the taxpayer, an obligation which can be traced to the Scottish case of *IRC* v *Williamson* (1928).

One note of caution when reading tax cases as to the existence of a partnership for those uninitiated in the mysteries of taxation: tax cases are first heard by commissioners and only proceed to the courts on an appeal by way of case stated. It is for the commissioners to establish the facts and the court will only reverse their decision if either the law as applied to those facts is wrong or if the commissioners could not reasonably have come to the conclusion which they reached: see *Edwards* v *Bairstow* (1956). This can be a nuisance for those seeking to build elaborate arguments on tax cases since in many instances the courts will simply be saying that the commissioners were not so obviously wrong that their conclusions should be overruled. Thus at the end of his judgment in *Saywell* v *Pope* Slade J concludes:

> On the basis of such evidence I cannot hold that the commissioners, in deciding that [a partnership] had not been proved, reached a decision such as no person acting judicially and properly instructed as to the relevant law could have reached . . . It is not for me to speculate as to the decision which I might have reached if, like the commissioners, I had the benefit of hearing all the oral evidence and seeing the witnesses cross-examined.

Inherent in all these questions is the assumption, quite rightly, that partnerships, being largely unregulated by the law in modern terms, can arise informally — in effect by association and even by accident or carelessness. But most partnerships today are professional partnerships entered into in a formal and careful manner, usually with a complex partnership agreement or deed. These do not arise otherwise than by intention and it would present a false picture to assume that partnerships by association form the majority. It is simply that the latter give rise to far more difficulties, for obvious reasons, in the particular area of formation. Before we proceed to those difficulties, however, a word or two about formal partnerships would seem to be in order.

Formal partnerships

The partnership agreement or deed

In this respect a partnership agreement or deed is no different from any other contract. There are no formalities arising from the fact that it is a partnership agreement and the general rules as to the formation of contract apply. Thus a partnership agreement can arise from a course of dealings provided that the courts can discover a *consensus ad idem*. In *Jackson* v *White* (1967) the court refused to hold that there had been a partnership agreement since no particular contractual intention could be attributed to the parties, whereas in *Dungate* v *Lee* (1967) such an agreement was inferred. Being a contract, the partnership agreement is also subject to various contractual rules such as those relating to capacity, illegality, misrepresentation and mistake which apply to all contracts. Those with a particular application to partnership are considered in the next chapter; for example, the validity of restraint-of-trade clauses in partnership agreements has been the subject of recent litigation.

Usually, however, the partnership agreement takes the form of a deed setting out the conditions of the partnership and the terms upon which it is to be conducted. Standard forms of partnership deeds are included in many of the larger works on partnership and in books of precedents. Within very few limits, such as the restraint-of-trade issues mentioned above, partners may include whatever terms they wish. In fact the Partnership Act itself encourages this. Section 19 provides that:

> The mutual rights and duties of partners, whether ascertained by agreement or defined by this Act, may be varied by the consent of all the

partners, and such consent may be either express or inferred from a course of dealing.

Thus the implied terms as to management, accounts, indemnity etc. found in the Act can be varied by the partnership deed. Further, it envisages that the express terms of the deed itself can be varied by consent and that such consent can be 'inferred from a course of dealing'. At the end of the day each case will thus depend upon the particular contractual agreement.

This freedom to contract is, however, just that. It is subject to the restrictions placed by UK law on the scope of contract and in particular by the doctrine of privity of contract. Thus although A and B may agree as to restrictions as to who may do what etc. as between themselves, this clearly cannot affect a third party who has no notice of their terms. Section 8 of the Act provides indirect statutory confirmation of this:

> If it has been agreed between the partners that any restriction shall be placed on the power of any one or more of them to bind the firm, no act done in contravention of the agreement is binding on the firm with *respect to persons having notice* of the agreement.

Since there is no central registry of partnership deeds (as there is with a company's constitutional documents) there is no general concept of constructive notice in this context and although it is possible to think of situations where a third party could have constructive notice they are unlikely and the usual requirement will be one of actual notice.

It is not within the scope of a book of this size or purpose to analyse a specimen partnership deed. There are, however, two areas where the agreement will usually touch on matters relating to the establishment of the partnership itself. First it will purport to give a starting date to the partnership and second it may well make some provision for the duration of the agreement and thus of the partnership and it seems appropriate to consider these topics at this point.

Commencement

'You do not constitute or create or form a partnership by saying that there is one', said Lord President Clyde in *IRC* v *Williamson* (1928). Thus any statement in the partnership agreement as to the date when the partnership commenced is always subject to contrary proof if the circumstances show that the date is incorrect. Sometimes, therefore, the courts have declared that the execution of a partnership deed will not even operate to create a partnership from the date of the deed if the external evidence clearly shows that there is no partnership in fact: *Dickenson* v *Gross* (1927). Usually, however, the problem arises when the deed declares that a partnership has existed from a date preceding the execution of the deed itself. Such a statement cannot in law operate retrospectively. At best it may accurately reflect the past position but if in fact there was no partnership during that period such a statement in the deed cannot retrospectively alter the situation: *Waddington* v *O'Callaghan* (1931). Thus in *Saywell* v *Pope* (1979) a partnership agreement signed in June 1975 which stated that the partnership had commenced in April 1973 was held to be of 'little assistance' in establishing the existence of a partnership at the earlier date. It is, of course, equally possible for a partnership to exist prior to the date specified in the deed if the circumstances so dictate.

Duration

Whilst it may seem unduly pessimistic, most partnership agreements provide for some method of ending the partnership or at least some time span by which the partnership is to be measured. These clauses vary tremendously in nature, some providing an ending on certain dates or events whilst others use more uncertain or variable criteria. Some partnerships have no such provision at all. In general for the purposes of duration the Act divides partnerships into those entered into for a fixed term and others. The latter are known as partnerships at will. The distinction is of some importance since a partnership for a fixed term can only be ended in accordance with the terms of the agreement or the express provisions of the Partnership Act (e.g., death or bankruptcy of a partner) or by a court order if there is a serious dispute. A partnership at will, on the other hand, can be ended at any time by one partner giving notice to his other partners to that effect.

The right to dissolve a partnership at will by notice is contained in s. 26(1) of the Act. This provides that:

Where no fixed term has been agreed upon for the duration of the partnership, any partner may determine the partnership at any time on giving notice of his intention so to do to all the other partners.

It is important to note that the Act uses the expression 'no fixed term' rather than talking of a 'partnership at will'. Section 26(1) cannot, however, be read in isolation since s. 32 of the Act provides, *subject to contrary*

Establishing a Partnership

intention, that a partnership is dissolved (a) if entered into for a *fixed term*, by the expiration of that term; (b) if entered into for a single adventure or undertaking, by the termination of that adventure or undertaking; (c) if entered into for an *undefined time*, by any partner giving notice to the other or others of his intention to dissolve the partnership; and in that case the partnership is dissolved from the date mentioned in this notice as the date of dissolution or, if no date is mentioned, as from the date of the communication of the notice.

Section 32(c), therefore, like s. 26(1), also provides for dissolution at any time by one partner giving notice to that effect, but unlike s. 26(1) it applies to partnerships for an *undefined time* rather than to partnerships with *no fixed term*. There is another difference in that s. 32 is subject to contrary agreement whereas s. 26(1) appears to be mandatory (unless it could be regarded as a right or duty of a partner and so subject to contrary agreement by virtue of s. 19 mentioned above). However, it has been possible to reconcile these two sections by a particular construction of the phrases 'no fixed term' and 'undefined term'. This is made somewhat easier by the fact that s. 32(a) speaks of a partnership for 'a fixed term' and it would be strange therefore if an 'undefined term' in s. 32(c) meant anything other than the opposite, i.e., a partnership with no 'fixed term'. (Section 32(b) is fortunately *sui generis* and can be left out of this particular construction game.)

This miraculous balancing act was achieved by the Court of Appeal in *Moss* v *Elphick* (1910). The facts were very simple in that the partnership agreement between the two partners contained no mention of any time-limit or other limiting factor except to provide that it could be terminated 'by mutual arrangement only'. Moss gave Elphick a notice of his intention to dissolve the partnership and the question was whether he had the right to do so under either s. 26(1) or s. 32(c). The Court of Appeal had little difficulty in rejecting his right under s. 32(c) since, although this was a partnership for an undefined time the provision as to mutual consent was a clear contrary intention which the Act provided for. What then of s. 26(1) where such contrary intention was (it was apparently accepted in that case) not provided for? The argument that 'no fixed term' simply meant a partnership with no definite term in the deed was rejected. Instead the section was construed as applying only 'to cases in which the partnership deed is silent as to terms with regard to the duration of the partnership', or in other words to those for 'an undefined time'. The deed was far from silent in this case and s. 26(1) could not therefore apply.

The practical consequence of this decision is that any provision in the **agreement** as to termination, however vague or tenuous, will prevent

s. 26(1) applying since it will not be for 'no fixed term' (apologies for the double negative but it makes the position clearer) and will also amount to a contrary intention for the purposes of s. 32(c), so that neither section will be available for a dissolution by notice. It presumably follows that a provision such as the one in *Moss* v *Elphick* will make the partnership one for a fixed term under s. 32(a), although that would seem to be a generous interpretation of the phrase and perhaps render s. 32(b) redundant. The Court of Appeal in coming to their decision were much concerned that s. 26 should not conflict with freedom of contract in partnership matters. It should be realised that if s. 26(1) had applied in that case the provision as to mutual consent would have been meaningless.

The law on partnerships at will and dissolution by notice is therefore in a reasonable state of order despite the difficulties of the wording in the two sections. Problems remain, of course, as to whether in any particular agreement there is a provision limiting the right to dissolve by notice. (If anyone is still confused, the result of *Moss* v *Elphick* is that if there is such a provision it will take the partnership out of s. 26(1) since it will not be one 'not for a fixed term' and it will also be contrary intention for the purpose of s. 32(c).) An example of whether such a limitation exists or not can be found in *Abbott* v *Abbott* (1936).

If the right to dissolve or terminate a partnership by notice does exist, the next question is as to what form of notice will be sufficient. Section 32(c), as we have seen, states that the notice takes effect either from the date specified in the notice or from the date of communication. Section 26(2) provides that in a partnership constituted by a deed any form of written notice will suffice, which allows for other forms of notice for less formally constituted firms. Both sections therefore allow for written or other forms of notices, but is it permissible to dissolve a partnership set up by deed otherwise than by written notice if it is served under s. 32(c) and not s. 26(1)? Alternatively do the rules as to the effect of the notice under s. 32(c) have any effect on a notice served under s. 26(2)? Unfortunately there are no answers to these questions but the wording used in s. 26(2) being permissive in nature would hardly seem to negative s. 32(c).

There are, however, examples of what can amount to a notice and when a written notice is communicated. To take one example of the former it appears that simply denying the existence of a partnership at will in the course of legal proceedings can amount to a notice of dissolution if the court actually finds that one exists. This was recognised in the New Zealand case of *Smith* v *Baker* (1977) which was based on UK authorities. Mere denial of a partnership's existence may, however, prove less effective as a notice. As to the form of communication it appears that a written notice

Establishing a Partnership

which does not itself specify a date of dissolution will only be effective at the time it is received rather than at the time it is posted, thus reversing the usual contractual postal rules. This was the decision in *McLeod* v *Dowling* (1927) where the partner sending the notice dies between the posting and receipt of the notice. The judge decided that the partnership had in fact been dissolved by the death before it had been dissolved by the notice.

One final point on duration. If there is a partnership for a fixed term (presumably as construed in *Moss* v *Elphick*) and after that has expired the partners continue the partnership then the partnership will be automatically converted into a partnership at will. This was the position prior to the Act: see *Neilson* v *Mossend Iron Co* (1886); and it is now expressed in s. 27 as follows:

> Where a partnership entered into for a fixed term is continued after the term has expired, and without any express new agreement, the rights and duties of the partners remain the same as they were at the expiration of the term, so far as is consistent with the incidents of a partnership at will.

The difficulties presented by this section are not so much as to whether a partnership at will exists or not but as to which of the terms of the original agreement will apply.

For an original provision to continue in force, therefore, it must (a) have been in existence at the *expiration* of the fixed term and (b) be consistent with a partnership at will. The former is a question of fact and it must be borne in mind that the original written terms may have been varied by a course of dealing or other agreement. The latter depends upon its consistency with the concept of dissolution by notice since that is the hallmark of a partnership at will. Thus it is impossible for any term which restricts that right (and as we have seen that means any term as to the ending of a partnership at all) to continue into a partnership at will. On the other hand, terms as to the consequences of a dissolution may well be consistent with a partnership at will. In particular it seems that a provision allowing one partner to purchase the share of another at a valuation within a certain time-limit is perfectly acceptable — see, for example, *Daw* v *Herring* (1892) and *Brooks* v *Brooks* (1901). An arbitration clause has been allowed to continue and it is also clear that the fiduciary and agency rules continue to apply.

Partnerships by association

Children, and others, are frequently told that if they play with fire they

Establishing a Partnership

might expect to be burned. The same is true of partnerships. Someone who takes part in the running of a business and receives a share of the net profits cannot expect to avoid the consequences of his acts. Equally a person who allows himself to be represented or represents himself to another as a partner cannot then escape liability on the basis that he is only an employee or a consultant etc. There are in fact two distinct strands. In the first case the person involved will be a partner in the full sense of the word, whereas in the second the person will only be liable *as if he were* a partner, he will have no rights *as a* partner. In the first case the law has to distinguish between the genuine creditor or outsider on the one hand and a partner who simply wishes to take the benefit of partnership without accepting the burden on the other. The second case is basically an example of estoppel and designed to protect persons extending credit or making supplies on the strength of the representation. For the sake of convenience we can divide this topic into associations by financial involvement and associations by representation, provided these labels are not regarded as tablets of stone.

Association by financial involvement

In the early days the courts took the view that participation in the profits of a business created a partnership so that a creditor who was to be repaid out of the profits of a business automatically became a partner and was liable as such: see, e.g., *Waugh* v *Carver* (1793). In 1860 this idea was rejected by the House of Lords in *Cox* v *Hickman*. In that case a partnership business which was in financial difficulties was transferred by the original partners to trustees who were to run the business and to divide the profits between the various creditors. If the creditors were repaid in full the business was to be transferred back to the original partners. Two of the creditors acted as trustees and Hickman now sought to make them liable as partners. The House of Lords decided that since they had not been represented as partners the mere fact that they were sharing in the profits of the business did not of itself make them partners. Thus there was neither association by representation nor by financial involvement.

Cox v *Hickman* established that the sharing of profits, although in certain cases strong evidence of the existence of a partnership, does not raise the irrebuttable presumption of its existence. This major change in the law caused some confusion and led to Bovill's Act of 1865 which to all intents and purposes is now ss. 2 and 3 of the 1890 Act. As Lindley LJ remarked in *Badeley* v *Consolidated Bank* (1888) the former rule was artificial in that it took only one term of the contract and raised a whole presumption on it. From 1860 onwards, therefore, the courts have refused to be bound by a rigid application of the profit-sharing concept. It is a question of looking at all the facts and terms of the agreement. *Cox* v *Hickman* concerned a deed of arrangement with creditors — in effect a very early form of the administration procedure introduced for companies by the Insolvency Act 1985, i.e., an attempt to save the concern by continuing the business and if successful handling it back to the original controllers. The creditors remained creditors.

The current position is set out in s. 2(3) of the 1890 Act which provides:

> The receipt by a person of a share of the profits of a business is prima facie evidence that he is a partner in the business, but the receipt of such a share, or of a payment contingent on or varying with the profits of a business, does not of itself make him a partner in the business.

The section then goes on to provide five specific cases to which the first half of that sentence does not apply. In those cases receipt of a share of the profits does not of itself make the recipient a partner. Before examining the effects of this somewhat contradictory section we should perhaps remind ourselves that we are dealing with net profits in this context (remember s. 2(2) makes it clear that a share of gross receipts is no evidence of partnership).

By way of introduction to s. 2(3) it must be said at once that the wording could have been better. In particular the use of the words 'prima facie' is unfortunate since one interpretation of the phrase is that since a receipt of a share of profits is prima facie evidence of a partnership, if there is no other evidence at all then a partnership exists. On the other hand the second part of the section makes it quite clear that such a receipt does not *of itself* make the recipient a partner, i.e., exactly the opposite of such an interpretation of the first part. Either 'prima facie' must mean something else (e.g., evidence upon which the court *may* act) or the section cancels itself out by providing conflicting burdens of proof: the first part suggesting that if evidence of profit-sharing is produced it must be rebutted and the second part suggesting that additional supporting evidence of a partnership is required. One simple (perhaps too simple) way out of that impasse is to apply the basic rule that he who alleges must prove. Since in 99 cases out of 100 this is a third party seeking to establish a partnership so as to create a liability, supporting evidence will be required.

However that may be, the courts have treated s. 2(3) as simply re-enacting the original test in *Cox* v *Hickman*. The classic statement of the effect of s. 2(3), which is still used by judges, was given by North J in *Davis* v *Davis* (1894):

Adopting then the rule of law which was laid down before the Act, and which seems to me to be precisely what is intended by s. 2(3) of the Act, the receipt by a person of a share of the profits of a business is prima facie evidence that he is a partner in it, and, if the matter stops there, it is evidence upon which the court must act. But, if there are other circumstances to be considered, they ought to be considered fairly together; not holding that a partnership is proved by the receipt of a share of profits, unless it is rebutted by something else; but taking all the circumstances together, not attaching undue weight to any of them, but drawing an inference from the whole.

Whilst this statement seems to suggest that evidence of receipt of a share of the profits, if it is the only evidence, requires the courts to find that a partnership exists, it should be pointed out that the courts have always found other evidence to consider, if only from the circumstances by which the profits came to be shared, so that it is the last sentence of that quotation which is relevant and applied today. North J also quoted with approval the somewhat shorter test of Lindley LJ in *Badeley* v *Consolidated Bank* (1888): 'I take it that it is quite plain now, ever since *Cox* v *Hickman*, that what we have to get at is the real agreement between the parties'. In discovering this the courts have refused to be dogmatic or to lay down universal rules so that ultimately each case must depend upon its facts — it is a partnership agreement or some other form of contract such as one of loan, employment or a joint venture between two separate businesses? The following examples may, however, give some indication of the factors involved.

One of the most persuasive factors in establishing a partnership by financial association is an agreement to share losses as well as profits, for that is an indication of the true participation in a business — the so-called risk factor. The strength of this factor is illustrated by the Canadian case of *Northern Sales (1963) Ltd* v *Ministry of National Revenue* (1973). Three companies made an agreement for the marketing of a rape-seed for the 'crop year' 1960–61, each being entitled to a share of the profits. Collier J, after stating that a share in the profits was not conclusive evidence, turned to examining the surrounding circumstances. He found that the agreement provided for the sharing of losses as well as profits, which he regarded as characteristic of a partnership contract. He also relied on the fact that the agreement provided for consultation between the parties and there had been some consultation. The judge therefore found the companies to be carrying on a partnership even though there was 'no contribution of capital, no common management, no common assets, no common facilities, no common bank account and no common firm-name'. Such features were not essential for the existence of a partnership.

But the sharing of losses is not conclusive — remember there are no absolutes in this area. For example, in *Walker* v *Hirsch* (1884), Walker was employed as a clerk by two partners and he agreed with them that in return for his advancing £1,500 to the firm he was to be paid a fixed salary for his work in the business and to be entitled to one-eighth of the net profits and be liable for one-eighth of any losses. The agreement could be determined by four months' notice on either side. Walker continued to work exactly as he had done before the agreement and was never represented to the customers as a partner. The partners determined the agreement and excluded him from the premises. He now asked for a dissolution of the firm on the basis that he was a partner. The Court of Appeal decided by reference to the agreement and those famous surrounding circumstances that this was not a partnership agreement but simply a contract of loan repayable where he left the firm's employment.

In *Davis* v *Davis* (1894), North J was persuaded to discover a partnership by the fact that the parties drew exactly similar sums from the business and had represented themselves as partners to outsiders. In *Walker West Development Ltd* v *F J Emmett Ltd* (1979), the Court of Appeal, faced with a complex agreement between property developers and builders in relation to a housing development did not consider the absence of joint liability for losses as crucial. Rather they approached the issue by asking whether there was in reality one business carried on in common or two separate businesses, the one employing the other. Since the agreement referred to 'the project', to be advertised as a joint project of the two companies and the net profits were to be divided in equal shares, the Court of Appeal felt able to conclude that a partnership existed although both Goff LJ and Buckley LJ admitted to some amount of indecision.

Having established this basic rule as to the sharing of profits, s. 2(3) goes on to specify five particular instances in which such a receipt 'does not of itself' make the recipient a partner. In these cases such a receipt is not even prima facie evidence of partnership, although, as we have seen, even in the general cases subject to this section, those words have very little force. The practical difference between a specific receipt within one of these heads and a receipt subject to the general wording of the section is in reality small except that it is quite clear that the burden of proof will in the specific cases always be firmly on those alleging that a partnership does exist to adduce additional evidence; conflicting burdens of proof clearly cannot exist in these cases. With due respect to the draftsman of the Act it will be easier if we leave paragraph (a) of the section until we come to paragraph (d) since they are related.

Establishing a Partnership

The first specific receipt covered is therefore in s. 2(3)(b):

> A contract for the remuneration of a servant or agent of a person engaged in a business by a share of the profits of the business does not of itself make the servant or agent a partner in the business or liable as such.

This provision is quite self-evident, for, as we have seen, the relationship of employer and employee is inconsistent with partnership, and that of an independent agent (e.g., an estate agent engaged to sell the partnership offices) is clearly distinguishable on the basis that there is no involvement in the business. What this paragraph does, therefore, is to make it quite clear that if such a relationship has been established by other factors suggesting either a contract of service or an independent contractor, the mere fact that he is to be paid out of the net profits of the business will not make him a partner. The major question remains — is he an employee or a partner? We shall return to that question at the end of this chapter.

Nor need we dwell long on s. 2(3)(c), although it applies to a common situation. It provides that:

> A person being the widow or child of a deceased partner, and receiving by way of annuity a portion of the profits made in the business in which the deceased person was a partner, is not by reason only of such receipt a partner in the business or liable as such.

It is not unusual for partners to make provision for their dependants in the event of their death and one way is to provide in the partnership agreement that a partner's widow or children are to receive a specified proportion of the profits of the business after his death. Such a receipt is clearly no evidence of partnership. In practice the agreement might also provide that a proportion is payable to the partner after his retirement, but this may well be regarded as the purchase price of his share of the business or as his 'remuneration' as a consultant partner and is not within this paragraph.

For tax reasons, however, it is now equally sensible for each partner to participate in a Revenue-approved pension scheme during his working life. This will involve each partner entering into a contract with a life assurance company which in return for annual contributions by each partner will provide him with immediate life assurance cover and a lump sum on his retirement. This lump sum must, under the approved scheme rules, be used to purchase an annuity for himself and dependants. A partner may invest up to 17% of his taxable partnership income in such schemes and deduct

Establishing a Partnership

such payments from that income before tax is payable. Such schemes enable provision to be made for a partner's dependants with the maximum tax advantages. On another contemporary note we should remember that when the Act became law widows for the purpose of this paragraph would rarely have included widowers and children would have been legitimate ones only. There is little doubt that a modern court would apply the paragraph widely to include anyone who was dependant on the deceased partner, including former spouses (of either sex) and children, however acquired. The important point is that the provision of an annuity for a dependant after a partner's death does not make him or her a partner.

The central issue in s. 2(3) is, however, the distinction between a partner and a creditor. As we have seen, it was this issue in *Cox v Hickman (1860)* which led to the section being passed at all. Two paragraphs, (a) and (d), provide more specific guidance on this issue. Section 2(3)(a) states that:

> The receipt by a person of a debt or other liquidated amount by instalments, or otherwise out of the accruing profits of a business does not of itself make him a partner in the business or liable as such.

Section 2(3)(d) continues:

> The advance of money by way of loan to a person engaged or about to engage in any business on a contract with that person that the lender shall receive a rate of interest varying with the profits, or shall receive a share of the profits arising from carrying on the business, does not of itself make the lender a partner with the person or persons carrying on the business or liable as such. Provided that the contract is in writing, and signed by or on behalf of all the parties thereto.

Paragraph (a) therefore relates to the repayment of the loan itself out of profits whereas paragraph (d) applies to the payment of interest on a loan out of profits. In practice the former presents few problems and is in effect no more than a statutory version of the actual decision in *Cox v Hickman*. If the trick is to distinguish between a creditor and a partner, it is unlikely that the latter would require capital repayments out of profits; it is much more likely that this will be a compromise method of paying off a creditor and so avoiding an insolvency, as in fact happened in this case. On the other hand, if there are other factors not present in that decision then a partnership can exist, e.g., if the creditors take over the business completely and are not obliged to return it to the original partners when their debts have been satisfied.

An income return by reference to the profits of a business is a different matter entirely. A person wishing to invest in a business would take a share of the profits as his return and the fact that this can be called 'interest' does not turn an investment into a loan. The tax courts have spent many complex hours distinguishing between genuine and false 'interest' payments. If we remember s. 1 of the Act it is the hallmark of a partnership that those involved are running a business together for an income return based on net profits. The courts approach this problem by ascertaining the intention of those involved. Did they intend to form a partnership and to avoid the consequences of being partners or did they always envisage only a debtor–creditor relationship? In answering this question s. 2(3)(d) seems to have been of little practical assistance — it will always be a question of ascertaining the intention of the partners although, of course, this must be gleaned objectively from all the facts and not necessarily the expressed intention of the parties.

In *Re Megavand (ex parte Delhasse)* (1878), Delhasse lent £10,000 to a business run by two partners. The agreement provided that this was to be a loan and was not to make Delhasse a partner. On the other hand he was to receive a fixed proportion of the profits and was given rights to inspect the accounts and, if necessary, to dissolve the firm. This 'loan' was not repayable until after a dissolution and in fact the £10,000 formed the basis of the partnership's capital. The court had little difficulty in holding that Delhasse was indeed a partner despite the express wording to the contrary. In effect he was the classic sleeping partner or 'banker' who puts up the money for others to exploit their skills. Section 2(3)(d) (already in existence in Bovill's Act) could not save him since the surrounding circumstances, objectively construed, indicated the intention to set up a partnership.

The leading case in this area is still, however, *Pooley* v *Driver* (1877). In that case the loan agreement contained a covenant by the admitted partners that they would observe all the covenants in their own partnership agreement. In effect this gave the 'lender' an equal right with the partners to enforce the partnership agreement. The partnership agreement itself provided strong evidence against this being a loan. For example 20 parts of the 60 equal parts of capital were to be allocated to persons advancing money by way of loan and the profits were to be divided amongst the holders of capital in proportion to their capital holding. This combined evidence of profit-sharing and control convinced the court that this was a clear case of a partnership and that the parties intended to be partners. 'What they did not intend to do was to incur the liabilities of partners', said Jessell MR.

No doubt both these cases are an example of partnership draftsmen being carried away with the forerunner of s. 2(3)(d) and giving that paragraph far more strength than it in fact has. In *Pooley* v *Driver* Jessell MR put paragraph (d) firmly in its place:

> I take it to mean this, that the person advancing must be a real lender; that the advance must not only profess to be by way of loan, but must be a real loan; and consequently you come back to the question whether the persons who entered into the contract of association are really in the position of creditor and debtor, or in the position of partners . . . But the Act does not decide that for you. You must decide that without the Act; and when you have decided that the relation is that of creditor and debtor, then all the Act does is this: it says that a creditor may take a share of the profits, but . . . if you have once decided that the parties are in the position of creditor and debtor you do not want the Act at all, because the inference of partnership derived from the mere taking a share of profits, not being irrebuttable, is rebutted by your having come to the conclusion that they are in the position of debtor and creditor.

It should perhaps be noted that whatever benefit is conferred by s. 2(3)(d) it cannot apply if the loan is made under an oral rather than a written agreement since the proviso to the paragraph is quite clear: 'Provided that the contract is in writing, and signed by or on behalf of all the parties thereto'. Confirmation that this means what it says was given by Smith LJ in *Re Fort (ex parte Schofield)* (1897), although the reader may feel that the benefit of the paragraph is somewhat tenuous in any event.

Section 2(3) concludes with paragraph (e):

> A person receiving by way of annuity or otherwise a portion of the profits of a business in consideration of the sale by him of the goodwill of the business is not by reason only of such receipt a partner in the business or liable as such.

The intention is clear: to protect the vendor of a business who, as is quite common, agrees to sell the goodwill of that business by reference to the future profits of the business. Since goodwill is notoriously difficult to value except by reference to profits this is a sensible provision. Like the other paragraphs in s. 2(3), however, it really adds little to the realities of any decision. The courts will be concerned to see whether or not this is the relationship of vendor and purchaser. If it is then there will be no partnership. On the other hand, if the reality is that one partner is taking on another active partner who is buying his way into the business nothing in s. 2(3)(e) will save him.

Establishing a Partnership

Section 2(3) taken as a whole, therefore, merely states rather than solves the problems associated with the financial returns from a partnership and adds little to *Cox* v *Hickman*. Ironically the only time when the wording of at least part of it has been crucial has arisen not in relation to the existence of a partnership but in connection with s. 3 of the Act. This section provides that a person who has lent money to a business 'upon such a contract as is mentioned' in s. 2(3)(d) or who has sold the goodwill 'in consideration of a share of the profits of the business' (i.e., within s. 2(3)(e)) is postponed to (will only be paid after) all the other creditors of the business. In other words such a lender or seller will only be able to recover his debt if the partnership is dissolved after all the other partnership creditors have been paid in full. It can therefore be important to decide whether a particular loan or sale is within s. 2(3)(d) or (e) simply for repayment purposes.

Two cases illustrate the importance of such matters. In *Re Fort (ex parte Schofield)* (1897), Schofield lent £3,000 to Fort on an oral agreement that they should share in net profits until the loan was repaid. On Fort's insolvency Schofield asked for repayment. The issue was simple. Was this loan within s. 2(3)(d) and so caught by s. 3 so that Schofield would come last in the queue of creditors (and so receive nothing in practice). Schofield argued that since this was an oral and not a written agreement it was within the proviso to s. 2(3)(d) (i.e., that the contract must be in writing and signed by the parties) and so outside the terms of that paragraph and naturally therefore outside s. 3. The Court of Appeal rejected this argument. Section 3 applies to 'such a contract' as is specified by s. 2(3)(d) and this was taken to refer to any contract of loan providing for a return out of net profits. The proviso related only to those wishing to take advantage of s. 2(3)(d) to avoid being partners.

In *Re Gieve (ex parte Shaw)* (1899), the widow of a businessman sold the business to Gieve and Wills under an agreement by which she was to be paid an annuity of £2,650. They carried on the business. Gieve died and Wills became insolvent. Could the widow sue for the annuity (which would be capitalised for the purposes of a claim in bankruptcy) or was she subject to s. 3? In this case the Court of Appeal found that she could sue. Section 2(3)(e) requires a person to be receiving, by way of annuity, 'a portion of the profits of a business' in return for the sale of the goodwill. On the facts she had simply required that an annuity be paid to her, there was nothing in the agreement that it should be paid out of the profits of the business. The fact that without the business the purchasers could not have paid the annuity was irrelevant. In reality this agreement was neither one of partnership nor the sale of the goodwill in return for a share of the profits but a sale coupled with an annuity.

Establishing a Partnership

Although s. 3 is a penal section in that it deprives a creditor of his rights, it has limits. In *Re Lonergan (ex parte Sheil)* (1877) the Court of Appeal made it clear that although the section postponed the debt it had no effect on any security the creditor might have, such as a mortgage over the partnership property. As a mortgagee such a creditor retained his full rights. The opposite conclusion was said to be equivalent to confiscating the property of the mortgagee and there was nothing in this section to suggest that.

By way of postscript it could have been argued that the mere presence of s. 3 might have lent more weight to s. 2(3)(d) in cases such as *Pooley* v *Driver* in that such a creditor although having the benefits of s. 2(3)(d) would suffer the burden of s. 3. The current state of play is that s. 2(3)(d) confers precious few benefits whereas s. 3 remains a real burden.

Partnerships by representation

Partnerships which arise as the result of financial involvement are true partnerships in that the relationship is established both within and outside the firm. But it is equally possible for a person to be liable *as if he was* a partner even though he is in no way carrying on a business in common with a view of profit. This liability is known variously as a partnership by holding out, partnership by estoppel or a quasi-partnership. In fact it is not a partnership at all and our heading is equally misleading in that respect. The liability arises where a person by words or conduct represents to another that he is a partner, on the strength of which that other person incurs a liability, believing the representation to be true. Whether this is phrased as an action for misrepresentation, breach of warranty of authority or fraud, the significance is that such a person cannot turn round and claim that he is in fact not a partner and so should not be liable as such. He is estopped by his actions from denying that he is a partner and so is liable as such. This doctrine has no other consequences, however, and cannot make him a partner for purposes other than his liability to another.

All this is contained in s. 14(1) of the Act:

Every one who by words spoken or written or by conduct represents himself, or who knowingly suffers himself to be represented, as a partner in a particular firm, is liable as a partner to any one who has on the faith of any such representation given credit to the firm, whether the representation has or has not been made or communicated to the person so giving credit by or with the knowledge of the apparent partner making the representation or suffering it to be made.

Central to this concept, therefore, is the representation that he is a partner. Whether there has been such a representation by the person concerned is a question of fact of each case. It is irrelevant whether he is pretending to be a partner in an actual firm or in a firm which does not exist. To illustrate this we can use the Australian case of *D & H Bunny Pty Ltd* v *Atkins* (1961) where two men, Atkins and Naughton, approached the credit manager of the company and asked for extended credit facilities, stating that they had agreed to become partners with each other. Goods were supplied to Naughton on credit debited to an account opened in their joint names. Atkins was held liable for the purchase price on the basis of his representation of partnership even where no such firm existed. The fact that the section refers to the representation being as to a partner 'in a particular firm' was held not to require the evidence of an actual firm.

Problems are much more likely to arise, however, over the liability of someone who does not actually make the representation himself but is represented by another as being a partner. In such cases the section requires that he has *knowingly* suffered himself to be so represented. Three separate factual situations can arise here: one where the person concerned knows of the misrepresentation before it is made and knows that it is going to be made; another where he has no actual knowledge of the misrepresentation but a reasonable man would have known of it; and yet another where he has failed to take steps to correct a misrepresentation which he has since discovered. The first case produces no problems except of fact, but what is the position with regard to negligence in either of the other two? Does negligently failing to realise that a misrepresentation is being made or negligently failing to correct a misrepresentation once known, amount to 'knowingly' suffering the representation for the purposes of s. 14(1)?

Some assistance can be gained from the decision of Lynskey J in *Tower Cabinet Co Ltd* v *Ingram* (1949). Christmas and Ingram carried on a partnership business selling household furniture under the name 'Merry's' (unlikely as that may seem). The partnership was dissolved by mutual agreement in 1947. Christmas continued to run the business and ordered several suites of furniture from the plaintiffs. By mistake he confirmed the order on old notepaper which had Ingram's name on it. The plaintiff not having been paid by the business sought to make Ingram liable under s. 14(1). The plaintiff had never dealt with the firm before and apart from the notepaper had no knowledge of Ingram's existence. The judge held that it was impossible to conclude that Christmas had knowingly suffered himself to be represented as a partner since he neither knew of nor authorised the use of the old notepaper. The fact that he might have been negligent or careless in not seeing that all the old notepaper had been destroyed when he left was not sufficient. (Since this case involved the liability of a former partner for debts incurred after he ceased to be a partner s. 36 of the Act was also relevant and we shall return to the case in chapter 4).

Negligently allowing a misrepresentation is not therefore the same as knowingly allowing it. This decision would seem to prevent any problems likely to be associated with the provisions first introduced by the Companies Act 1981 that the names of all the partners should be included on all business correspondence (see chapter 3). If a partner on retirement fails to destroy all the notepaper bearing his name, is he now within s. 14(1) of the 1890 Act? There may well be a distinction between negligence and recklessness in such a case, i.e., the difference between not realising the consequences and realising but not caring about the consequences. It is possible to argue that the latter does amount to an implied authorisation to use his name. There is no authority as to the failure to correct an unauthorised misrepresentation once known but again the distinction may be between negligence and recklessness in such failures. It is a question of achieving a balance between the person so represented and the person being misled. In cases such as *Ingram's* case the position will often be solved by reference to s. 36 of the Act (see chapter 4) but that section does not apply where the persons concerned have never been partners.

Section 14(1) requires the person misled to have 'given credit'. In practice this means incurring any liability and no technical use of the word 'credit' has been applied. Finally the person misled must have acted on the strength of the representation and implicit in that, of course, is that he must believe it to be true. But that is all the person misled need show — he does not have to prove that he would not have given credit if he had known it to be untrue. Reliance and belief are necessary but not exclusive. Once again this is best illustrated by an Australian case, *Lynch* v *Stiff* (1944). Mr Lynch was employed as a solicitor in a practice. Although his name appeared as a partner in the heading of the firm's notepaper, he remained at all times an employee of the firm. He had previously been employed by the employer's father and had always been Mr Stiff's solicitor, handling his business on behalf of the firm. When the son took over the business he assured Mr Stiff that his affairs would continue to be handled by Mr Lynch and it was clear that Mr Stiff kept his business there at least partly because of that statement and the apparent statement on the new notepaper that Mr Lynch was now a partner. Mr Stiff gave the firm money for investment which the son misappropriated and Mr Stiff now sued Mr Lynch under a provision identical to s. 14(1). One point that arose was whether it made any difference that Mr Stiff had entrusted his affairs to the firm because of his confidence in Mr Lynch prior to the representation being made in the notepaper and thus may well have done so even if no such representation had been made. The Court held that so long as Mr Stiff could prove reliance and belief he need show no more.

But reliance is necessary and without it there can be no liability under the doctrine of holding out. An unusual example of this arose in the case of *Hudgell Yeates & Co* v *Watson* (1978). In January 1973 Mr Watson instructed one of the partners in the plaintiff firm of solicitors to act for him in a case. This work was passed to another partner, Miss Griffiths, who together with a managing clerk (who appears to have done most of the actual work) acted for Mr Watson in 1973. There was a third partner, a Mr Smith, who worked in a different office and took no part at all in Mr Watson's case. Mr Smith forgot to renew his solicitor's practising certificate for 1973 until 2 May and so was disqualified for acting as a solicitor from 1 January to 2 May 1973. When Mr Watson was sued for failure to pay his bill for legal costs he argued that since for part of that time Mr Smith had been disqualified from acting as a solicitor the whole firm was precluded from acting as such, since work done by one partner was done as an agent for the others. Accordingly the charges for work done during that period could not be enforced.

The Court of Appeal by a majority dismissed this argument finding that on Mr Smith's disqualification the partnership between himself and the other two partners was automatically dissolved (under s. 34 of the Act — see chapter 7) and reconstituted as between the two qualified partners who could thus sue for the money used. For present purposes, however, the important point is that this was not affected by the doctrine of holding out since at no time did Mr Watson give any credit on the basis that Mr Smith was at any time a partner in the firm.

Both these cases also show the clear distinction between liability on the holding-out ground and the creation of a true partnership. In *Lynch* v *Stiff*, Mr Lynch remained at all times an employee and in *Hudgell Yeates & Co* v *Watson*, it was precisely because Mr Smith was not at the relevant time a partner that there was no viability in Mr Watson's defence. It should be remembered that if there is a holding out under s. 14(1), not only will the person so represented be liable as if he were a partner, those actually making the representation will also be liable for the consequences of making that representation. It is less clear, however, if A holds B out as being a partner of A and C, what the precise circumstances are in which C will be liable. Section 14(1) has no direct application and thus presumably the basic rules of estoppel will apply.

For the present, however, the situation remains as expressed by

Establishing a Partnership

Waller LJ in the *Hudgell Yeates* case:

'The doctrine of holding out only applies in favour of persons who have dealt with a firm on the faith that the person whom they seek to make liable is a member of it.' [*Lindley on the Law of Partnership* (13th ed, 1971), p. 108.] The fact, if it be the fact, that Mr Smith was held out as being a partner might well make the other partners liable for his actions in contract because they were holding him out as a partner. Similarly, in so far as he was holding himself out as a partner he would be making himself liable for the debts of the firm. But in each case this would not be because he was a partner but because on the facts he was being held out. When the different question is asked, was there a partnership so that the acts of the others must have been the acts of Mr Smith, my answer is no.

(It was because Bridge LJ in that case failed to make this distinction that he disagreed with the other two judges.)

Before leaving partnerships by representation we should mention s. 14(2) of the Act. This provides that:

[W]here after a partner's death the partnership business is continued in the old firm-name, the continued use of that name or of the deceased partner's name as part thereof shall not of itself make his executors or administrators estate or effects liable for any partnership debts contracted after his death.

Since other provisions of the Act provide that a deceased partner's estate is only liable for debts accrued or liabilities incurred prior to his death there seems little point in this section — indeed if anything it can only do harm since it suggests that there might be other circumstances in which such a liability might arise.

Investing in a partnership

We have seen, therefore, that, under the general law of partnership, it is virtually impossible to invest in a business (in the sense of putting money into a business which is run for your benefit and from which you expect to benefit by way of a share in the profits) without becoming a partner and thus fully liable for the debts of the firm. The courts' construction of s. 2(3)(d) of the Act, discussed above, shows that if anything other than a straight debtor–creditor relationship can be discovered then a partnership will exist. Any attempt to control the business will usually be fatal. Even if a loan within s. 2(3)(d) is achieved the lender can be penalised by s. 3 in that his debt will be paid last on any insolvency. This may, however, not be as drastic as it first appears. For a start the lender will be able to sue not only the firm but also the personal estate of each partner to recover his debt since by the very nature of a partnership it cannot be truly insolvent until all the partners are also insolvent. Second, we have already seen that any security remains valid despite the postponement of the debt.

It is clear, therefore, that it is generally impossible to create the partnership equivalent of the equity shareholding in a small private company. Limited liability can be achieved through corporate partners but this is a cumbersome device — why not simply run the whole thing as a company in the first place? Yet another outside factor has recently discriminated against partnerships in this respect. Under the Business Expansion Scheme very generous tax relief is available to those wealthier taxpayers who invest in new equity shares in companies carrying on qualifying trades. Thus not only the mechanism but also the motive exists for a genuine venture capital investment into a small company which cannot apply to partnerships. It is not surprising therefore that partnerships play little part in the general commercial world.

One possible solution is the limited partnership created in 1907 which we have come across before and, as we have seen, proved to be a failure in providing the answer. It is time to clear the air, however, and to take a slightly longer look at this interesting but inevitably underused form of business association.

Limited partnerships

Unlike partnerships in general, limited partnerships are entirely the creation of statute — there are no common law or equitable rules to explain their existence. They are formed and regulated by the Limited Partnerships Act 1907, s. 4(1) of which makes this quite clear: 'limited partnerships may be formed in the manner and subject to the conditions by this Act provided'. However, much of the law applicable to ordinary partnerships applies and s. 7 of the 1907 Act provides that the Act of 1890 and the rules of equity and common law applicable to all partnerships shall apply 'subject to the provisions of this Act'. Limited partnerships are therefore in effect a gloss on ordinary partnership law and their problems are to be solved by reference to that law unless the 1907 Act provides otherwise. There are three major differences between limited and ordinary partnerships. First as to the method of formation, second as to the financial position of the limited partner and third as to the detailed changes to the internal rules of partnerships as provided by the 1890 Act.

Before examining the differences, however, it is important to stress two points of similarity. First, a limited partnership is also simply a relationship — it is no more a separate legal person than an ordinary partnership. Second, those partners who are not limited partners are in exactly the same position *vis-à-vis* liability as an ordinary partner. Such partners are referred to as general partners by the 1907 Act (s. 3). In the words of Farwell J in *Re Barnard* (1932), a limited partnership is 'merely a combination of persons for the purpose of carrying on a particular trade or trades, and is in no sense strictly speaking a legal entity' and as he made clear in that case, a general partner, even a sole general partner, is personally liable for all the firm's debts.

Limited partnerships can only be formed by registration — there is no such thing as an unintentional limited partnership. Registration is to be with the Registrar of Companies by a statement signed by all the partners which contains the firm's name, the general nature of the business, the principal place of business, the full name of each partner, the date of formation and the term if any, for which the partnership is entered into, and, in addition, a statement that it is a limited partnership and of the limited partners' identities, the sum contributed by each limited partner and the method of contribution (s. 8). A change in any of these particulars must be registered within seven days (s. 9). The Registrar keeps an index of all limited partnerships on the register and having filed the statement or any changes in it he must acknowledge receipt by letter (ss. 13 and 14). The file of each limited partnership is open to public inspection (s. 16). Like a private company, therefore, formation is by a set administrative procedure with public notice of the firm's basic constitution. Unlike a private company, however, it is not bound by any doctrine of *ultra vires* nor need it disclose its internal rules of conduct. Above all, of course, it is not *incorporated* by registration.

Every limited partnership so formed must contain at least one general and one limited partner. A limited partner is defined in s. 4(2) as someone 'who shall at the time of entering such partnership contribute thereto a sum or sums as capital or property valued at a stated amount, and who shall not be liable for the debts or obligations of the firm beyond the amount so contributed'. A limited partner therefore is someone who contributes a fixed amount of capital, which is the most he can lose if the firm is unsuccessful. Though, of course, he may lose more in income terms from loss of profits if the losses are so apportioned within the firm. A company may be a limited or general partner. If a limited company is the sole general partner everybody's liability is limited. If a limited partner withdraws any

Establishing a Partnership

part of his contributed capital he nevertheless remains liable for the full stated amount. It is clear, therefore, that there is a substantial distinction between general and limited partners in terms of financial commitment.

One of the purposes of public registration is that any creditor of the firm can discover the identity and liability of the limited partners, so if there is a change of status by a partner either way this must not only be notified to the Registrar within seven days, but if either a general partner is to be made a limited partner or a limited partner's share is to be assigned, this fact must also be notified in the *London* (or *Edinburgh*) *Gazette*. (Since the *Gazette* is full of equally riveting topics it is only marginally more readable than a telephone directory.) Failure to do this renders such a change or assignment null and void for the purpose of avoiding liability.

The Act limits a limited partner's liability in respect of his capital investment, it does not, however, limit his liability to bear losses out of his entitlement to a share of the profits. In *Reed* v *Young* (1984), Nourse J drew a clear distinction between these two types of liability. It means that if the firm as a whole suffers a loss no creditor can sue the limited partner for a new contribution to the firm's assets, but within the firm's accounts he may lose his right to undrawn or future profits by virtue of the agreement itself. In such cases, therefore, the partner has suffered a loss of the whole amount although he has not increased his capital liability. The tax advantages of thus claiming an allowable loss of the whole for tax purposes was negatived by s. 48 of the Finance Act 1985.

Since limited partners have this declared limited liability and any wider liability falls upon the general partners, what is the position if the sole, or all of the general partners become insolvent? The general partner will have his own private creditors (i.e., those whose debts have nothing whatsoever to do with the firm). Are they entitled to pursue their debts against the firm's assets (including the contribution of the limited partners) in priority to the limited partners' rights to recover their contributions? Such a problem faced Farwell J in *Re Barnard (Martins Bank* v *the Trustee*) (1932). His actual decision was no more than that in such circumstances the creditors have a right to claim a contribution (in technical terms to prove) from the assets of the firm but he made it quite clear that the firm's assets must first be applied in satisfying the firm's creditors (and the general partner's own personal assets must first be applied for his own creditors). Any surplus of the firm's assets must then be applied in repaying the limited partners their actual contributions. Only then will the balance be available for the private creditors.

A limited partner's protection is therefore substantial, provided he complies with the 1907 Act. Failure to comply will simply make him a general partner—s. 5 is quite clear. There are two major ways in which such failure can arise. First, a limited partner is required to contribute the capital as quantified in the registration statement. In *Rayner & Co.* v *Rhodes* (1926), the plaintiffs were owed money by the limited partnership of Jones & Co. When Mr Rhodes was sued for his amount he claimed to be a limited partner and that he had already contributed the £5,000 he had agreed to contribute to the firm. In fact he had given a running guarantee for that amount to the firm's bankers for any overdraft and had deposited securities with the bank for that amount. Wright J decided that the 1907 Act required that money or its equivalent be transferred to the firm for its use. A guarantee was in no sense of the word a payment in cash or its equivalent—the firm had no access to the securities deposited with the bank nor could it enforce the guarantee. Mr Rhodes had merely assumed a future contingent liability. The registration statement had stated that Mr Rhodes had contributed £5,000 in cash and since that was wrong the Act had not been complied with and so there was no registration of Mr Rhodes as a limited partner. He had to be regarded as a general partner and treated as such.

The second way of failing to comply with the 1907 Act derives from s. 6(1). It is worthwhile setting this part of the Act out in full:

> A limited partner shall not take part in the management of the partnership business, and shall not have power to bind the firm: Provided that a limited partner may by himself or his agent at any time inspect the books of the firm and examine into the state and prospects of the partnership business, and may advise with the partners thereon.
>
> If a limited partner takes part in the management of the partnership business he shall be liable for all debts and obligations of the firm incurred while he so takes part in the management as though he were a general partner.

This section provides an insight into the policy of the Act. A limited partner is to invest his capital and leave the running of the business to the general partners—a concept totally alien to the concept of an ordinary partnership (and even to some companies since *Ebrahimi* v *Westbourne Galleries Ltd* (1973)). He is to be given only those rights necessary to protect his investment. If he goes beyond those rights he ceases to be a limited partner.

The policy may in fact be easier to ascertain than the reality. Clearly, examining the books and looking into the state and prospects of the partnership business and, if necessary, even advising the partners on such matters will not usually be regarded as takng part in the management of the business. But there must be many fine distinctions to be drawn between the two in practice and these may be even more crucial since the most likely time for a limited partner to cross the dividing line is when the business is going downhill and it is at precisely that time that the potential liabilities as a general partner will be very real. One possibility is that the court may ask whether he is doing more than is necessary simply to protect his investment. If *Cox* v *Hickman* had involved a limited partnership, however, it is hard to imagine that those taking over the business on a caretaker basis would have escaped liability as general partners. It is perhaps ironic that such creditors, protected by s. 2(3)(a) or (d) of the 1890 Act, are in a potentially better position than a limited partner in this respect.

Section 6(1) is the first 'modification' of the general law of partnership. It should be noted that in addition to management it also provides that a limited partner has no power to bind the firm. That has no relevance, of course, to his liability by representation under s. 14(1) of the 1890 Act nor the liability of the firm so representing him as a general partner. All it means is that he has no implied authority to bind the firm but he may well have actual or apparent authority to do so. These terms may well be confusing at this stage of our journey but all will be revealed in chapter 4. For the moment it is sufficient to note that s. 6(1) of the 1907 Act does not necessarily prevent a limited partner binding the firm to a contract.

The remainder of s. 6 is also concerned with modifications of the Partnership Act 1890 for the purpose of the limited partnership. These can be divided into four areas. First, following on the management restrictions in s. 6(1), it is provided that any differences arising as to the ordinary matters connected with the partnership business can be decided by a majority of the general partners (in other partnerships the implied term of the agreement provides for a decision by a majority of all the partners). Second, as to the composition of the partnership, it is provided that another person may be introduced as a partner without the consent of the limited partner (in other partnerships there is an implied term that unanimity of all the partners is required for this but since a new partner cannot, in theory, bankrupt a limited partner by his deeds his consent is not thought necessary). Third, a limited partner may, with the consent of the general partners (and a notice in the *Gazette*), assign his share to another who then becomes a full limited partner with all the assignor's rights. In ordinary partnerships an assignee of a partner's shares does not become a partner and has only a right to the income from it: he has no right even to inspect the books. These three topics will all be considered so far as ordinary partnerships are concerned in chapter 5.

The fourth area where the statutory rules are different concerns the grounds upon which a dissolution is presumed to have occurred. A limited

Establishing a Partnership

partner has no right to dissolve the partnership by notice even if it is a partnership at will. He can only escape from the firm by assigning his share and then only with the consent of his fellow partners. His capital cannot therefore be suddenly withdrawn at the first sign of trouble and in this respect at least a limited partner is like a shareholder in a private company. A creditor under s. 2(3) of the 1890 Act is not necessarily subject to such restraints. Further there is no implied dissolution on any of the following events, although there would be for an ordinary partnership: a charge on the limited partner's share in the firm in satisfaction of a private debt; the death of a limited partner or the insolvency of a limited partner. Insanity of a limited partner is only a ground for dissolution if his share cannot otherwise be realised. All these variations reflect the limited partner's status as an outside investor.

In essence, therefore, a limited partnership, although in some respects affording the possibility of allowing an investor the protection of limited liability rather like that of a company shareholder, suffers from the major drawback that such an investment and management are incompatible. In many companies, however, the shareholders and directors are the same people, thus merging the two functions, and this is particularly so in the type of companies which could function as limited partnerships. There is therefore no incentive at present for the choice of a limited partnership as a business medium. Where they are still used, e.g., in speculative film ventures, the potential tax advantage by notionally debiting a partner's share of the losses against his right to future profits, and so creating a larger taxable loss than he is actually liable to outsiders for was, as we have seen, stopped by s. 48 of the Finance Act 1985, reversing the decision of Nourse J in *Reed* v *Young* (1984).

Partners and employees

As we have already mentioned, the concept of partnership and employment are mutually exclusive. Because a partnership is simply the relationship between partners no partner can be employed in the business since he cannot employ himself. This contrasts with the position of a 'one-man' company where it is quite possible for the sole director as the authorised agent of the company to employ himself in the company's business in some capacity or other (see, e.g., *Lee* v *Lee's Air Farming Ltd* (1961)). Of course, it is perfectly possible, and very common, for a partnership to employ people. All the partners have authority to make contracts in the course of the partnership business and employing people is clearly such a contract (see chapter 4); although it is usual, and safer, bearing in mind the modern legislation on employment protection, to include a term in the agreement that questions of employment and dismissal should be a matter for all the partners to discuss. The important thing is that a partner cannot employ himself—a person involved in the work of a business is either a partner (and so self-employed and taxed as such) or an employee (and taxed as such).

Before turning to the special case of 'salaried partners' we should recall three cases already discussed where the courts had to distinguish between partners and employees. Partnership is the relation which exists between persons carrying on a business in common with a view of profit. In *Walker West Development Ltd* v *F.J. Emmett Ltd* (1979) the decision was that on the facts a property developer and a builder were in fact partners in a joint project and that the developer had not employed the builder. In *E. Rennison & Son* v *Minister of Social Security* (1971), some former employees of a solicitors' firm who formed a 'partnership' and purported to hire themselves out to the firm were held to be still employees—their original contracts of service remained unaltered and had not become a contract for services. Nor does it matter that the persons are described as partners if they are in truth employees—thus the wives of the partners in *Saywell* v *Pope* (1979) remained employees despite the endeavours of all concerned.

The importance of the distinction between partners and employees is evident in relation to their rights as against each other. An employee is entitled to the protection of the law in relation to such things as redundancy and unfair or wrongful dismissal, whereas a partner enjoys no such protection. Not surprisingly therefore the question does come up before the Employment Appeal Tribunal and other industrial tribunals. In *Palumbo* v *Stylianou* (1966), for instance, a hairdresser who opened a new shop left his assistant in charge of the old one, allowing him to keep the net profits (after deducting his 'wage' of £3 per week). When the assistant was dismissed the tribunal held that he was a partner and so unable to claim any redundancy payment. The result of such a finding is, of course, that the partnership had been dissolved by the dismissal and the assistant could have asked for a winding up. It is generally a question of swings and roundabouts in such situations. The setting may be different: it may be a national insurance or tax problem, but the question remains the same—is the recipient a partner under the general law of partnership—is he carrying on a business in common with a view of profit?

On the other hand, the distinction so far as persons dealing with the partnership is concerned may be far less relevant, since a person who is in law an employee may nevertheless be represented to an outsider as a partner and liable as such under s. 14(1) of the Act. So that although an employee does not enjoy the implied authority of partner to bind the firm he can easily acquire apparent authority as the result of a representation and make the whole firm liable for his acts. There are occasions, however, when the distinction is vital. In *Bennett* v *Richardson* (1980), for instance, Mr Richardson, who was blind, was sitting in the rear of a van hired by a partnership which consisted of himself and the person driving the van. The van 'had certain defects' and was uninsured. Mr Richardson was charged with using the van in contravention of various road traffic regulations all of which referred to his using, causing or permitting the use on a road of a vehicle defective in various ways. He was acquitted by the magistrates and on appeal to the Divisional Court that acquittal was upheld. That court decided that where a person was charged with using, or causing or permitting the use of a defective vehicle which he was not actually driving, he could not be convicted unless he was the driver's employee. The fact that he was in partnership with the driver was irrelevant.

Salaried partners

The growth in recent times of professional partnerships with their elaborate structures and agreements, has led to a greater number of persons being involved in those concerns under the general label of 'salaried partners'. The typical case is the ambitious and clever young professional who has served his apprenticeship and wants the status and prestige of being a partner without having the capital or experience to become a full partner. He will be represented to the world as a partner, his name will appear on the notepaper etc., but his rights within the partnership may be restricted in various ways—in particular he will be limited to a fixed sum by way of payment which will be described as a 'salary' but will usually be payable out of *net* profits so that he takes the risk of the outgoings of any year preventing him being paid. (In most cases this is of course entirely illusory since the larger firms are well insulated from such things. In the larger firms of solicitors in the City, for example, such salaried 'junior' partners can expect £40,000 p.a. in this way, so perhaps it is worthwhile continuing to read this book and to work hard for a 'good' degree.)

A judicial description of a salaried partner and the legal issues raised by such a person was given by Megarry J in *Stekel* v *Ellice* (1973):

> Certain aspects of a salaried partnership were not disputed. The term 'salaried partner' is not a term of art, and to some extent it may be said to be a contradiction in terms. However, it is a convenient expression which

is widely used to denote a person who is held out to the world as being a partner, with his name appearing as partner on the notepaper of the firm and so on. At the same time, he receives a salary as remuneration, rather than a share of the profits, though he may, in addition to his salary, receive some bonus or other sum of money dependent upon the profits. *Quoad* the outside world it often will matter little whether a man is a full partner or a salaried partner; for a salaried partner is held out as being a partner, and the partners will be liable for his acts accordingly. But within the partnership it may be important to know whether a salaried partner is truly to be classified as a mere employee, or as a partner.

Prior to *Stekel* v *Ellice* there was little authority as to the criteria by which to draw the distinction between an employed salaried partner and a full salaried partner. In *Re Hill* (1934), the issue arose only peripherally in connection with the equitable rule that a trustee who is a solicitor cannot make a profit from acting as a solicitor for the trust. Such a person may employ his partner as the solicitor provided it has been expressly agreed between the partners that the trustee shall himself derive no benefit from the charges made. In this case, however, there was no such agreement, but the trustee argued that since he was, by virtue of a general agreement with his partners, limited to a 'salary' of £600 a year out of the profits, and the profits without the trust work would easily cover that amount, he was not benefiting from the trust work undertaken by his partners. In deciding that the exception would not be extended so far, the Court of Appeal clearly regarded the trustee as a partner and not as an employee even though he was to do only a limited amount of work in connection with the business and take a small salary out of the profits (small compared with the firm's profits that is).

Re Hill was of course concerned with the case of a salaried partner at the opposite end of the spectrum from most modern examples since the partner was semi-retired rather than aspiring to greatness. The issues are the same (i.e., is the individual a partner or an employee) but it is more likely perhaps that he will be regarded as a partner since he will usually have negotiated his agreement from a position of strength as a senior partner. Such partners are frequently described as 'consultants' to outsiders.

In *Marsh* v *Stacey* (1963), however, it is far from clear what the semi-retired partner became. One of two partners, by agreement between them, reduced his activities and instead of taking a percentage of the profits (indicative perhaps of a full partner) he agreed to accept 'a fixed salary' of £1,200 a year 'as a first charge on the profits'. In the course of his judgment in the Court of Appeal, Upjohn LJ said that he 'really became a salaried partner, as it is called, that is to say an employee of the partnership'. On the other hand the Court of Appeal held that this 'employee' could wind up the firm provided the profits amounted to more than £1,200. Employees clearly have no such rights so he must have been more than an employee. One possible explanation for this decision is that the court treated him as a creditor who was entitled to recover his debt.

Not surprisingly therefore when Megarry J in *Stekel* v *Ellice* (1973) was faced with deciding whether a salaried partner in the modern sense was really a partner or an employee he reverted to basic principles rather than legal precedents: 'I have found it impossible to deduce any real rules from the authorities before me, and I think that, while paying due regard to those authorities, I must look at the matter on principle'. The facts of the case are illustrative of the modern salaried partner. Ellice was an accountant and in partnership when his partner died. He then agreed to employ Stekel, another accountant, at a salary of £2,000 'with a view to partnership'. In August 1968 Stekel asked about a partnership, but Ellice preferred to wait until the final account with his deceased partner's executors had been agreed and so he suggested that Stekel become a salaried partner. An agreement was signed to this effect on 1 October 1968 which was to last until 5 April 1969 when Stekel was to be entitled to a deed making him a full partner. Amongst the terms of this agreement, which continued the salary provision, was one that either 'partner' should be able to give a notice determining the partnership for specified breaches of the partnership agreement and another that all the capital, except for a few items, was to belong to Ellice. Stekel's name appeared on the firm's notepaper and he acted as a partner within the firm. His salary, however, was paid without deduction of tax (an employee's tax is deducted before payment under a system known as Pay As You Earn or PAYE whereas self-employed persons pay later directly to the Revenue, which has the merit of delay but the pain of actually signing a cheque). In the event no new agreement was made in April 1969 and by August 1970 the two had separated.

Stekel now sought a dissolution and winding up of the firm. His argument was that the 1968 agreement had simply amounted to a contract of employment which had been replaced as from April 1969 by a partnership at will and, as we have seen, under such a partnership any partner may dissolve the partnership at any time by simply serving a notice on the other partners, which he had duly done. Ellice, on the other hand, argued that the 1968 agreement had set up a full partnership agreement between them and that this had been implicitly renewed in April 1969 by the conduct of the parties. Under that agreement there could only be a dissolution on certain specified grounds and no possibility of a general right to dissolve by notice existed. The issue was clear—did the 1968 agreement make Stekel a partner or an employee?

Having decided to revert to matters of principle, Megarry J admitted that:

> It seems to me impossible to say that as a matter of law a salaried partner is or is not necessarily a partner in the true sense. He may or may not be a partner, depending on the facts.

It is a question of looking at the substance of the relationship between the parties and not necessarily the labels used. Whilst he thought that many salaried partners would in fact be employees held out as being partners it was quite possible for a salaried partner to be a true partner, in particular if he was entitled to share in the profits in a winding up. On the facts of this case the terms of the agreement as to capital, dissolution, management and accounting, indicated the existence of a partnership and the conduct of the parties and the tax position all pointed in that direction. The judge, therefore concluded that the 1968 agreement had constituted a full partnership which continued to apply.

To decide this, Megarry J had to consider s. 2(3) of the Act since Mr Stekel had no 'share of the profits' within that section. But he decided that this simply meant that there was no 'prima facie' evidence of a partnership under that particular head; it did not negative the other evidence of partnership. The provisions relating to salary and capital were unusual but the remainder of the evidence pointed towards a contract of partnership and not a contract of employment. 'If it is merely a contract for employment, then it is one of the most remarkable contracts for employment that I have seen', he confirmed.

3

Legal Controls on Partnerships

Public and private controls

I have already stressed the essentially *laissez-faire* attitude adopted by the courts and the 1890 Act itself to partnerships. This is not surprising in that the major formative developments took place in a *laissez-faire* age, but what is rather more surprising is that to a large extent that attitude still applies today. Reading the Act is almost like stepping back in time, especially if the reader has just come from even a random attempt to penetrate the Companies Act 1985 (for anyone in doubt I suggest the provisions, originally in the 1980 and 1981 Acts, on the treatment of shares in a public company which come to be held by that company). But company law is not simply more technical than it was 40 years ago, it has also become more pervasive and inquisitive. Companies are regarded as part of the public domain, so that not only is there compulsory registration of information on formation (which is then open to all who take the trouble to look), but a continuing and ever-expanding disclosure requirement whilst the company is a going concern. If public investment is required there are also all the rules for admission to listing on the Stock Exchange to be complied with. There are provisions for instigating both company and Department of Trade and Industry enquiries into the ownership or conduct of companies. Even such historically unregulated areas as take-overs are now governed by a complex code of self-regulatory rules devised by the City itself.

Partnerships, on the other hand, have for the main avoided such restrictions—there is no public disclosure (a weak form of registration if a business name was used disappeared after 1981) and no machinery for publc inquiries into their activities. This is due partly to their size (in economic terms) and partly to the fact that the major partnerships today are those of professional people who have their own professional codes of conduct and disciplinary bodies. Thus provisions such as the Competition Act 1980 and restrictions on competition enforced by the European Commission under article 85 of the EEC Treaty are unlikely in practice to apply to partnerships, either because the threshold is too high or a 'dominant' position is not really feasible. In short partnerships rarely enter the public domain and their regulation is largely left to the settlement of private disputes either between partners *inter se* or between partners and those who deal with them. In such cases, of course, the law is called upon to resolve those disputes, but these usually involve the application of accepted private law concepts such as agency and constructive trusts.

There are nevertheless three general areas where the public interest, either directly by legislation or through the doctrine of public policy worked out by the courts, does limit partnership activities and it is with those areas that this chapter is principally concerned. In addition there are areas where the State or its institutions, having devised a system for a particular purpose, for example, to collect taxes or national insurance, has to assimilate partnerships into such a system. One example is the judicial system which requires a set form of procedure for litigation and has to include partnerships; and it has long been established that the fact of an insolvency requires intervention in an attempt to provide an orderly and civilised compromise between the defrauding of creditors and the debtors' prison—again partnerships have to be incorporated into the system. In fact it is in this general area, the assimilation of partnerships into systems designed for individuals, that their lack of legal personality has caused most problems (companies, being separate legal persons present far fewer problems—they are either regarded as individuals for this purpose, e.g., the legal system, or an entirely different system is evolved for them, e.g., corporation tax). Such problems of assimilation are dealt with at the end of this chapter.

As mentioned above there are public controls on three general areas of partnership life. The first of these is the area of freedom of contract. Partnerships are in essence a rarefied form of contract and thus require all the elements needed for a contract (above all an offer and acceptance or *consensus ad idem*). In addition, however, they are subject to those restrictions on the power to contract which apply generally–questions such as capacity, undue influence and illegality. They are also subject to the control of the courts if the terms of the agreement are contrary to public policy—this is particularly true of restraint-of-trade clauses in professional partnership agreements. These are clauses which attempt to limit a partner's business activities both in area and scope if he leaves the firm. They seem in recent times to have caused particular problems for doctors and solicitors. Another common clause, an arbitration clause, is also regulated in the sense that if arbitration is desired it becomes subject to the specialised laws on arbitration and its procedures, especially the recent attempt by the Arbitration Act 1979 to limit any subsequent appeal to the courts.

The second area of control relates to the freedom of association. Partnerships have for a long time been limited in size (usually by provisions in the Companies Acts—an anomaly that was perpetuated by the 1948 and 1985 consolidations) although it is true that such limitations have been relaxed considerably in recent years. Other restrictions relate to the composition of particular professional partnerships. The third area of control is a mixed area of legislation and caselaw. It applies to the freedom to trade under a chosen business name. This freedom is now restricted by the Business Names Act 1985 (based on provisions introduced by the Companies Act 1981) in that certain names are prohibited, others need permission and most require disclosure of the partners' names on relevant documents and buildings. It is also restricted by the common law tort of passing off whereby one trader is prevented from diverting trade from another by the use of a similar name. This action is also available to companies but since registration of a company name is protection against another company using that name it is more usual if a partnership or other unincorporated business is involved.

Restrictions on the freedom to contract

Capacity

Capacity used to be a more dominant issue than it is today. One of the reasons for this is that two of the potential categories of parties who had limited capacity to contract, namely married women and companies, now have full capacity (subject to very limited exceptions in the case of a company which we saw at the end of chapter 1). In fact the pendulum has now moved the other way in that it is unlawful under s. 11 of the Sex Discrimination Act 1975 for any partnership having more than six members to discriminate against a potential partner on the grounds of sex. There is a similar provision relating to discrimination on the grounds of race etc. under s. 10 of the Race Relations Act 1976. The remaining categories of limited capacity are minors, enemy aliens and persons of unsound mind. The latter have capacity, it seems, so long as they are capable of appreciating the nature of the agreement. Great care is needed in such cases, however, since intervening insanity no longer automatically dissolves a partnership. The modern law, quite rightly, is concerned to protect the mental patient and not his partners.

Since the Family Law Reform Act 1969 and the Age of Majority

(Scotland) Act 1969, the age of majority in the UK has been 18, so that on attaining that age an individual attains full legal capacity. Until that age he is no longer referred to as an infant but as a minor. A minor does have the capacity to become a partner—the law is still very much as laid down by the House of Lords in *Lovell and Christmas* v *Beauchamp* (1894). That case established that although a minor can become a partner and be entitled to a share in the profits of a firm he cannot be personally sued for the firm's debts, whereas the adult partners are fully liable for debts incurred by the minor on behalf of the firm. The adult partners are, however, entitled to have any capital contributed by the minor applied in satisfaction of the firm's debts and to deduct any losses from his undrawn or future share of the profits. It is not possible, however, for the adult partners to hide behind the minor in order to evade responsibility for partnership debts.

Prior to reaching 18 a minor may repudiate the partnership agreement but once he has reached that age he must decide within a reasonable time whether to do so. By simply carrying on he will automatically become a full partner although he will still not be liable for debts incurred during his infancy: *Goode* v *Harrison* (1821). If he repudiates a contract to enter into a partnership he can recover any premiums paid on the basis that there has been a total failure of consideration: *Steinberg* v *Scala (Leeds) Ltd* (1923).

Closely linked to questions of capacity is the equitable concept of undue influence. If it can be established that a person entered into a partnership contract on unfavourable terms due to the undue influence of the other party, the court may declare the agreement to be void and order the return of any property and award damages. It seems, however, that in some cases the other partners may be able to retain part of the firm's profits—see *O'Sullivan* v *Management Agency & Music Ltd* (1985).

Illegality

A partnership is illegal if it exceeds the numerical limits imposed by law but this arises from the restriction on the freedom to associate. Similarly the professions maintain the purity of the professional partnerships by making impure partnerships illegal—but again this is better regarded as a restriction on the freedom of association. In general terms a partnership is illegal if it is formed for a purpose prohibited by statute or at common law. The latter relates to the upholding of current ideas of morality, religion or public policy. Clearly such grounds are continuously shifting and the older cases should be read with some care. In times of war it is illegal for a person resident in one country to form a partnership with a person resident in an enemy country. A partnership formed to commit or assist in or benefit from a criminal offence is equally obviously illegal. (If you dig back through the old cases you can find a partnership dispute involving two highwaymen—much good it did them for it appears that they were both hanged!).

A partnership agreement is illegal not only if the purpose for which the partnership is intended to be formed is illegal but also, although the purpose is one which could be attained by legal means, it is the intention of the parties that it should be attained in an illegal way. If a partnership is illegal in either way it will be void and the parties will have no rights as against each other or against anyone else. On the other hand in the second case an innocent third party may be able to enforce his rights against an illegal partnership if he was unaware of the illegality. The partners cannot rely on their own illegality to defeat a claim by an innocent third party if the transaction he is relying on was not itself illegal. This is the clue to illegality—there may well be legal transaction wrapped up in an illegal partnership and care must be taken to unravel the various strands. Illegality can be subsequent to the formation of a partnership, e.g., because an outbreak of war makes one partner an enemy alien. In such cases the Act provides for automatic dissolution of the firm.

A modern example of the concept of illegality is the case of *Dungate* v *Lee* (1967). Dungate and Lee agreed to set up a bookmaking business at Newhaven, contributing £500 each to the business. Lee obtained a betting licence. Dungate had no bookmaker's permit. Although there was no written agreement it was orally agreed that only Lee was to deal directly with customers over the counter and that in fact became the practice. Dungate handled credit betting on the telephone. Following a dispute Dungate brought an action for dissolution of the partnership and Lee argued that the partnership was in any event illegal under the Betting and Gaming Act 1960 which required every bookmaker to have a permit. Buckley J refused to allow this argument since the 1960 Act did not require every *partner* to have a permit and since the agreement did not require Dungate to carry on the practice of bookmaking himself it could not be said that the partnership was formed for an illegal purpose.

Restraint-of-trade clauses

Many partnerships contain a clause prohibiting a partner who leaves the firm from subsequently competing with it, usually within a stated area and for a specified time. If such a clause is regarded as unreasonable by the courts it will be void as being in restraint of trade. The basic presumption is that such clauses are unreasonable as being in breach of the public's interest in everyone being able to carry on his trade or profession freely, so that if the remaining partners wish to enforce it they must show that the clause is reasonable both as between the parties and also in the interests of the public. The courts have, in deciding what is reasonable, paid great attention to the type of contract involved and the relative bargaining strength of the parties. Thus they are highly suspicious of any such clause in a contract of employment but much more lenient with regard to a clause inserted by the purchaser of a business and its goodwill on the vendor. Restraint-of-trade clauses in partnership agreements are usually akin to the latter type in that a retiring partner will have transferred his share of the goodwill to remaining partners who may well then have an interest in protecting their purchase, but it may well be that a restriction on a 'salaried' partner who is just about a partner would be rather more strictly viewed.

In *Deacons* v *Bridge* (1984) Lord Fraser of Tullybelton suggested that it was pointless to equate partnership clauses with either the vendor-purchaser or employer-employee categories, and that the courts should simply ascertain what the legitimate interests of the remaining partners are which they are entitled to protect, and then see whether the proposed restraints are more than adequate for that purpose. As to the ascertainment of these 'legitimate interests', that, he said, will depend largely on the nature of the firm and the position of the former partner within that firm. If to this test is added the criterion of a possible public interest in the prevention of a monopoly in a particular area then the test would appear to be complete. It should be stressed that if the clause is wider than is reasonable in such circumstances it will be cut down entirely and not simply made reasonable. Most of the modern cases in this area concern doctors and solicitors so that these two types of partnership provide the most recent illustrations.

A medical partnership may have two different types of goodwill to protect—that attaching to its National Health Service practice and that attaching to its private practice. In *Hensman* v *Traill* (1980), Bristow J decided that no restriction at all could be taken by the remaining partners in relation to the National Health Service since any restriction on a doctor from complying with his obligations to care for patients under the National Health Service Act 1977 is contrary both to the Act (s. 54 of which prohibits the 'sale' of such goodwill) and public policy. If that is correct then the main general test of reasonableness as between the parties and the public interest in monopolies can only apply to private medical practices. For an example of the public interest in a country without the NHS see the Canadian case of *Baker* v *Lintott* (1982).

The test of reasonableness with respect to medical partnerships has not been applied uniformly over the years. In *Whitehill* v *Bradford* (1952) a covenant not to 'carry on or be interested or concerned in carrying on the business or profession of medicine, surgery, midwifery or pharmacy or any branch thereof' within 10 miles and for 21 years was upheld, whereas in *Lyne-Pirkis* v *Jones* (1969) the Court of Appeal rejected a clause which required the former parties 'not to engage in practice as a medical practitioner' as being too wide. This approach was approved by Plowman J in *Peyton* v *Mindham* (1972) when he rejected a clause that the outgoing doctor should not 'advise, attend, prescribe for or treat any person who is or has during the subsistence of the partnership been a patient of the partnership'. The reason given was that this could preclude consultancy work and such a prohibition was unnecessary to protect the remaining partner, who therefore lost his entire protection for the goodwill of the practice.

In the case of solicitors, the Court of Appeal, in *Oswald Hickson Collier & Co* v *Carter-Ruck* (1982), stated that it is contrary to public policy for a solicitor to be prevented from acting for a client when that client wants him to act, particularly in litigation. It followed, therefore, that a restraint-of-trade clause in a partnership deed which prevents one of the partners acting for a client in the future is also contrary to public policy since there is a fiduciary relationship between a solicitor and his client and the client ought reasonably to be entitled to the sevices of whichever solicitor he wishes. However, the same court in *Edwards* v *Worboys* (1983) refused to regard this as a matter of general principle and the Privy Council in *Deacons* v *Bridge* (1984) 'respectfully and emphatically' declined to agree with it. It was said to be unjustified either on the authorities or in principle.

Deacons v *Bridge* is in fact also an interesting example of the application of the reasonableness test in relation to solicitors. The firm, established in Hong Kong, had 27 partners and 49 assistant solicitors. It worked through self-contained specialist departments. Mr Bridge became a full partner in 1974 in charge of the intellectual property division (about 10% of the total work of the firm). He was charged a nominal amount for goodwill. In 1982 he resigned from the firm and received a substantial amount for his share in the firm although only a nominal amount for his goodwill. He then set up practice on his own account in Hong Kong. The firm now sought to enforce a clause in the partnership agreement that no former partners should act as a solicitor in Hong Kong for five years for any client of the firm or any person who had been a client in the three years before he left. Applying the test of legitimate protection of the remaining partners, the Privy Council regarded this clause as being reasonable both in scope and time. In particular they rejected Mr Bridge's argument that since he had only been concerned with 10% of the firm's clients he was being unreasonably restricted in respect of the other 90%. The firm was a single practice for the mutual benefit of all the partners—whilst a partner he had enjoyed the protection of this clause. The low nominal value paid for the goodwill was irrelevant since he had paid a nominal amount for it. The court not only rejected the argument that such clauses were always void for public policy reasons but in fact regarded this clause as being in the public interest since it encouraged younger people to join the firm and also tended to secure continuity of the firm which was beneficial to clients.

Restrictions on freedom of association

People are restricted from forming partnerships in two ways. First for most partnerships there is a maximum number of partners allowed by law. The current limit of 20 can be found in s. 716 of the Companies Act 1985 (for limited partnerships it is in s. 717). Until 1982 banking partnerships were limited to 10 but this lower limit was repealed when s. 46 of the Banking Act 1979 was brought into force. There is no limit, however, for specified partnerships. The section itself exempts solicitors, accountants and stockbrokers (and has in fact done so since 1967), and by virtue of five statutory instruments issued under the section (all are called the Partnerships (Unrestricted Size) Regulations with a number and the year) the limits no longer apply to patent agents, surveyors, estate agents, valuers, actuaries, consulting engineers, building designers and loss adjusters. These exceptions are carefully drafted so as to define exactly the professional qualification required of the partners before the firm itself can be exempt from the restriction. Some require that all the partners be professionally qualified, others, such as estate agents and loss adjusters, require that three-quarters of the partners are so qualified, whilst for consulting engineers only a majority need to be professionally qualified. Similar restrictions on limited partnerships do not appy to solicitors, accountants or stockbrokers and, by a single statutory instrument, to surveyors, auctioneers, valuers or estate agents.

The second restriction on association stems from the regulation of individual professions. Thus under s. 20 of the Solicitors Act 1974 it is unlawful for a solicitor to form a partnership with someone who is not a solicitor. Under the Banking Act 1979 no banking business may be carried on without either recognition from the Bank of England as a bank or a licence to carry on a deposit-taking buiness. Partnerships may be licensed or recognised as banks but not if all the assets belong to a single individual. There are similar restrictions for firms carrying on a consumer credit business under the Consumer Credit Act 1974. Barristers are prohibited from forming partnerships at all.

Restrictions on choice of business name

Until 1982 all business names used by firms had to be registered under the Registration of Business Names Act 1916 at a central registry. Registration was of little legal significance since, unlike registration at the companies registry, it did not lead to constructive notice of the facts so registered. The 1916 Act and the register were abolished by the Companies Act 1981. The 1981 Act replaced the old system with a new one which is designed to control the use of certain words or expressions in business names and to require disclosure of the partners' names to potential customers and suppliers. These provisions can now be found in the Business Names Act 1985 (compare its legislative style with that of the Partnership Act 1890).

The 1985 Act applies by virtue of s. 1 to all partnerships in Great Britain which carry on a business here under a name which does not consist only of the surnames of all individual partners and corporate names of all the corporate partners and certain 'permitted additions'. These additions are the forenames or initials of the partners, the letter 's' at the end of a surname which belongs to two or more of the partners, and anything which merely indicates that the business is being carried on in succession to a former owner of the business. Thus any partnership which is of any size must be caught by the Act together with any firm using a trade name rather than the surnames of the partners. It is an interesting question as to whether a group partnership is a separate partnership for this purpose. Most medium and large firms of solicitors, architects, accountants etc. will be included. Even the addition of '& Co.' at the end will render the firm liable to the provisions of the Act. (It is a criminal offence for a partnership to use the abbreviation 'Ltd' by virtue of s. 34 of the Companies Act 1985.)

If the Business Names Act applies, then ss. 2 and 3 provide limitations on the choice of business name. The written approval of the Secretary of State for Trade and Industry is needed before a business can use any name which is likely to give the impression that the business is connected with the Government or any local authority. In addition, for certain other words and expressions, such approval is required and, if appropriate, a written request must first be made to 'the relevant body' for their comments which must then be forwarded to the Department of Trade and Industry. These words and expressions and the relevant body, if any, can be found in the Company and Business Names Regulations 1981 as amended by the 1982 regulations of that name. These words or expressions run from 'abortion' to 'Windsor' through such words as 'European', 'midwife' and 'polytechnic'. To take one practical example of how the system works, any firm wanting to use the phrase 'district nurse' in its name must ask the Panel of Assessors in District Nurse Training for its opinion which must then be sent on to the Department of Trade and Industry (who must have been informed that such an opinion has been sought) for its decision. Unapproved use of any such names is a criminal offence under s. 2(4) of the Act.

The Business Names Act also provides, in s. 4, that a partnership subject to the Act must disclose the name of each partner, and an address for each of them at which service of a writ or similar document will be effective, on all its business documents (letters, orders, receipts, invoices etc.) and at its business premises by a notice displayed in a prominent place. Business premises for this purpose include premises to which suppliers as well as customers have access. The obligation to list each partner on a business document would clearly be inconvenient for a very large firm and so if there are more than 20 partners that requirement will be satisfied by the keeping of a list of the partners at the firm's principal place of buiness and a statement in the document of the existence and location of such a list and of its availability for public inspection. The list must be so available during office hours—refusal of inspection is a criminal offence. Such firms must, however, comply with the display requirement at their premises and in addition any partner must produce a written list of the partners 'immediately' on a request from 'any person with whom anything is done or discussed in the course of the business'.

Failure to comply with these disclosure requirements may have civil consequences for the firm. Section 5 of the Business Names Act provides that the firm cannot enforce an action based on any contract made whilst it was in breach of s. 4 if the defendant has shown either that he could not pursue a claim against the partnership because of the breach or that he has suffered financial loss as a result of it. This protection is only available to the other party as a defendant, however, and lapses if he brings a counter-claim.

The Business Names Act does not therefore prevent more than one firm from using the same or a similar name nor does it prevent a firm from using a name similar to that of a registered company or vice versa. To protect the goodwill and reputation of the firm, therefore, the partners may be forced to rely on the tort of passing off. This is designed to provide a remedy by way of damages or, more usefully, by way of injunction for an injury to the legitimate trading reputation of a company, partnership or other business. This rationale was expressed by Astbury J in *Ewing* v *Buttercup Margarine Co. Ltd* (1917):

The ground of interference by the court in these name cases is that the use of the defendant['s] name, or intended name, is calculated to deceive, and 'so to divert business from the plaintiff to the defendant', or 'to occasion a confusion between the two businesses': *Kerly on Trade Marks*, 4th ed., p. 568.

It is not entirely clear whether the defendant must intend to deceive or cause confusion. Clearly if fraud can be shown there is no problem (see *Croft* v *Day* (1843) but Lord Halsbury in *North Cheshire & Manchester Brewery Co. Ltd* v *Manchester Brewery Co. Ltd* (1899) indicated that if there was an injury then intention was irrelevant. Particular problems may occur if the defendant firm is simply using the surnames of the partners and has no intention to cause injury.

Partnerships and the public domain

Partnerships do not operate in a vacuum. They pay taxes, rates and national insurance and they use the legal system. Because they do not have a separate personality their assimilation into these State systems is not always easy. We have already seen the teething problems encountered with VAT, and the complexities of fitting partnerships into the income tax system have filled many weighty publications. The basic solution for income tax is to regard the partnership as one person for the purposes of an assessment but to calculate the assessment according to the tax position of each partner. Since a change in the membership of the firm is technically a cessation of the old firm's business and the commencement of the new firm's trade or profession this can have far-reaching consequences for tax assessment. In fact partners may elect to regard the old and new firm as continuing the same business and the Finance Act 1985 stopped most tax advantages from such a change of partners.

Insolvency is also an area where partnerships present special problems. Either one partner may be insolvent or all the partners, with the consequence that the firm is insolvent, and rules have had to be worked out whereby the firm's creditors and the individual partners' creditors are dealt with as fairly as possible. A further description of insolvency can be found at the end of this book.

The legal system has also assimilated the partnership into its procedure. Order 81 of the Rules of the Supreme Court provides that 'any two or more persons claiming to be entitled, or alleged to be liable, as partners' may sue or be sued in the firm-name (if any) at the time the cause of action accrued. But, when suing, the partners must give the defendants on request the

Legal Controls on Partnerships

names and addresses of all the partners at the time of the action accruing, and, if they are being sued, they must each enter an appearance individually. Judgment can be given for or against the firm but execution can be levied on all the partners, even one not a party to the proceedings if it turns out that he was a partner (or liable as such) at the time when the judgment debt was incurred. The legal system itself therefore pretends that a partnership exists on its own account but this is eminently practical. For example, in the case of *Deacons* v *Bridge* (1984), mentioned earlier, the firm sued as 'Deacons (a firm)' rather than in the names of the 27 partners.

Having disposed of this modern, public legislation we must return to the Partnership Act itself and its provisions relating to the settlement of private disputes involving partners. It will be a relief to return to its more graceful and understandable style—it does not, for example, provide such things as a list of 'permitted additions' as the 1985 legislation feels compelled to!

4

Partners and Outsiders

Potential problem areas

Sections 5 to 18 of the Partnership Act 1890 are included in that Act under the heading: 'Relations of partners to persons dealing with them'. The title of this chapter, 'Partners and outsiders', is simply a more modern (and less attractive) way of saying much but not quite the same thing. To be strictly accurate we are concerned here with the effect of the partnership relationship on the partners *vis-à-vis* their individual and collective liability to those who are outside that relationship. Such people are usually referred to as 'outsiders' or 'third parties' and in fact they may not actually be 'dealing' with the partnership at all. For example, someone who is injured by one partner driving his car on partnership business may well seek to make the other partners liable, but he can hardly be said to have been dealing with the firm as the Act impliedly requires. In fact, however, the Act does provide for liability in two areas, contracts and other civil wrongs, and we can establish the scope of the liability of one partner for the acts of his fellow partners under those two general heads.

But it is not enough to know the basic scope of this liability. Assuming that a partner is liable for a particular breach the next question is how and to what extent will he be liable? Until recently, English (but not Scots) law maintained a fatuous distinction in this respect between contracts and other wrongs. Finally because partnership is a potentially fluid form of business medium it is important to know for how long a partner may be liable; e.g., if he retires is he liable for debts incurred before and after he retires? In seeking the answers to these questions we need to consider ss. 5 to 18 of the Act (with the exception of s. 14 which we have already discussed in chapter 2 in relation to a partnership by representation) and s. 36 which applies in practice in this context and so may be allowed to trepass from the part of the Act dealing with dissolution. In fact, however, the majority of these sections add little to the common law and one or two actually confuse what would otherwise be a reasonably straightforward common law position.

Liability of partners for contracts

Agency concepts

Of one thing there is absolutely no doubt whatever — each partner is an agent of his fellow partners simply by virtue of the relationship. Unlike other agency relationships, however, that same partner is also a principal with regard to his other partners who are also his agents. Thus each partner is an agent and a principal at the same time. This rather confusing position may explain why the application of the law of agency to partnerships is not always straightforward. The basic position can, however, be simply stated in the form of a question and answer. If A, B and C are partners and A orders goods from X, which X delivers but has not been paid for, in what circumstances can X recover the purchase price from B and C? Since A is an agent of B and C, who are his principals, he can bind them to any contract provided that he is acting *within his authority*. This is no more than an application of the basic concept of agency — if an agent makes a contract on behalf of his principal then, provided the agent is acting within his authority, the contract is binding on the principal, who can then sue and be sued on it by the third party without reference to the agent — it is a clear and well established exception to the doctrine of privity of contract.

That such a relationship exists between partners has been stated many times in the courts. The common law position was explained by James LJ in *Re Agriculturist Cattle Insurance Co (Baird's case)* (1890) and this has been substantially codified by ss. 5 to 8 of the 1890 Act. Section 5 itself confirms the position quite clearly: 'Every partner is an agent of the firm and his other partners for the purpose of the business of the partnership'. We shall return again to that phrase 'business of the partnership' but it is in one sense misleading, for it is possible for a partner to bind his copartners for acts entirely unconnected with the firm's business if he has the authority to do so. A partner is an agent and if he has the requisite authority his principals (the other partners) will be bound by his acts. It is time, therefore, that we looked at exactly what can amount to authority for this purpose and thus have such drastic and far-reaching effects on the liability of others.

There are three ways in which an agent (or partner) can have this authority. Confusion arises not from any doubts as to the nature of these three types of authority but simply as to what each type should be called. Judges and writers disagree with each other and there is little point in worrying about the correct titles. For our purposes we can divide authority into actual, implied and apparent authority. Implied authority is sometimes referred to as usual or presumed authority and apparent authority as ostensible authority, although the terms apparent or ostensible can be used to mean implied or usual authority — see what I mean?

Actual authority is the easiest to grasp — an agent may bind his principal to any act which he is expressly authorised by his principal to do. Thus if a principal authorises his agent to buy 100 tons of wheat and the agent does so the principal will be bound by the contract. Implied or usual authority is the authority which arises from the status of the particular type of agent involved. If an agent does an act which the third party would regard as a normal thing for the type of agent to do then the principal will be bound by it. Apparent or ostensible authority arises where the principal has held out the agent as having authority to do a particular thing so that the third party relies on the representation. It is another example of the doctrine of estoppel — the principal cannot in such circumstances deny the agent's authority.

Both implied and apparent authority, therefore, are based on the idea that the agent looks as though he has authority to do the particular thing and the third party should be able to rely on appearances. It is also implicit in both these ideas that, even though the agent has no actual authority from his principal, the principal will still be bound. The difference is that implied authority arises from the nature of the agency (e.g., what it is usual for an estate agent to do) whereas apparent authority arises from a representation by the principal (e.g., if the agent has in fact made such contracts with the third party before and the principal has always honoured them). In both cases, of course, the third party cannot rely on the authority if he knows that the agent has no actual authority. These rules are based on commercial realities and the necessities of trade. The third party cannot be expected to check every item with the principal to see if the agent has authority.

Applying these concepts to partnership it is clear that actual authority is a question of fact in each case. One partner may be given actual authority either by the terms of the partnership agreement (e.g., to contract debts up to a limited amount) or by the oral or written agreement of the other partners. Apparent authority is also largely a question of fact — did the other partners by words or conduct represent that one partner had the authority to enter into the particular transaction? The law is the same as that applicable to persons being held out as partners under s. 14 of the Act, which we came across in chapter 2. The only difference is that it is not a question of whether the representation was that X was a partner, but whether X has the authority to act on behalf of the partnership. (Of course, if the representation is that X is a partner, X will also then have the implied authority of such a partner.) Implied authority, on the other hand, is a question of law to be ascertained in respect of each type of agent — what exactly is it usual for a particular partner to be able to do? The answer depends upon an examination of various sections of the Act and the relevant cases.

Because a partner's implied and apparent authority will usually be much wider than a partner's actual authority there will often be provisions in the partnership agreement seeking to limit any given partner's activities. But since such authority is, as we have seen, based on the idea that the third party can rely on appearances, no internal agreement between the partners can affect him unless he knows of the restriction, and he has no duty to inspect or check the partnership agreement. Restrictions on company agents in the company's articles of association will, of course, be registered in the companies registry which, prima facie, gives constructive notice to all. There is no such registration for partnerships and they have thus avoided all the problems of *Turquand's* case (*Royal British Bank* v *Turquand* (1856)) and s. 35 of the Companies Act 1985 as to external and internal restrictions. For partnerships the position is the same as for any other agency relationship and is codified in s. 8 of the 1980 Act:

> If it has been agreed between the partners that any restriction shall be placed on the power of any one or more of them to bind the firm, no act done in contravention of the agreement is binding on the firm with respect to persons having notice of the agreement.

There is one other agency concept which applies in a straightforward way to partnerships, although it causes problems with companies. If the partner making the contract has no authority under any of the three heads then the other partners may nevertheless ratify the contract and thus adopt it as binding on all concerned. Ratification may be express or implied by words or conduct but if it is effective no problems arise simply because a partnership is involved. This is because there are no limits as to the capacity of the firm: it may do anything it likes, whether or not it has anything to do with the usual business of the firm. Provided the partners agree, the firm can do anything. Companies are not yet so fortunate — they have a limited capacity according to their objects clause in the memorandum of association and clearly a company cannot ratify a contract made by an agent if the company itself cannot make such a contract. Recent case law suggests that this is a complex and fluid area which partnerships have fortunately avoided.

Partners and Outsiders

The implied or usual authority of a partner

As we have seen, the implied authority of any agent depends upon the status of the agent giving rise to the presumption that he has the authority to carry out the transaction. For partnerships this authority stems from s. 5 of the Act:

> Every partner is an agent of the firm and his other partners for the purpose of the business of the partnership; and the acts of every partner who does any act for carrying on in the usual way business of the kind carried on by the firm of which he is a member bind the firm and his partners, unless the partner so acting has in fact no authority to act for the firm in the particular matter, and the person with whom he is dealing either knows that he has no authority, or does not know or believe him to be a partner.

The implied authority of a partner therefore depends upon the answer to three questions: (a) does the act relate to the kind of business carried on by the firm; (b) if so, was it the usual way of carrying on that business; and (c) did the third party either know that the partner had no actual authority or believe that he was not a partner?

'Kind of business' Whether a particular activity is or is not related to the business of the firm is a question of fact and clearly depends upon the type of business involved. In many cases the answer will be obvious. For example, a contract by A to buy 100 tons of wheat from X will not bind A, B and C as partners in a firm of patent agents — there can be no sense in which X has been misled. In other cases it may be less obvious. What exactly is the scope of the business of a firm of stockbrokers, surveyors or solicitors? For an example relating to the last of these, we can use the Australian case of *Polkinghorne* v *Holland* (1934). Mrs Polkinghorne dealt with Mr Holland who was one of three partners in a firm of solicitors. After consulting him she altered her investments as a result of which she lost a great deal of money, and acted as a guarantor of a bank overdraft of a company in which she was a shareholder and Mr Holland was a director. She sought to make the other partners liable for the loss on the investment and, when forced to pay the bank on the guarantee, for that amount as well. The question was whether the investment advice and the guarantee were part of the firm's business. The court took the view that, although investment analysis was not part of the firm's business, when a solicitor is approached on such questions he is required by the nature of his office to

make enquiries and suggest where competent advice may be obtained. Thus his failure to do this was related to the business of the firm. On the other hand, the guarantee, although arising from her confidence in him as a solicitor, had nothing to do with the firm's business. He gave her no advice as a solicitor not did he act on her behalf — it was a business engagement between them as contracting parties, not as solicitor and client.

Two sections of the Act are relevant here. Section 6 provides that:

> An act or instrument relating to the business of the firm and done or executed in the firm-name, or in any other manner showing an intention to bind the firm, by any person thereto authorised, whether a partner or not, is binding on the firm and all the partners.
>
> Provided that this section shall not affect any general rule of law relating to the execution of deeds or negotiable instruments.

Clearly this applies mainly to the specific problem of negotiable instruments and deeds and the problem usually resolves itself into a question of whether the partner signing the deed etc. intended to act on his own account or on account of the firm. The basic position is, however, the same as for the general law; has the third party the right to rely on the appearance of the deed as being that of the firm? Thus in *Re Briggs & Co.* (1906), where a two-partner firm of father and son were being pressed by a creditor, the son agreed to assign the book debts (money owed to the firm) to the creditor in order to play for time. The father knew nothing of this. The deed of assignment stated that it was to be made between 'R.B. Briggs and H.R. Briggs, trading under the style or firm of Briggs & Co.', but the father's name was forged by the son. The question arose as to whether the father was liable on this deed. The court applied s. 6 since it related to the business of the firm and was done in a manner showing an intention to bind the firm and executed by a partner. It is implicit in this decision that the son had authority to do this *qua* partner (he clearly had no actual authority) and that the phrase 'thereto authorised' in s. 6 must be read accordingly. Read as such, s. 6 adds little to s. 5 of the Act.

Section 7 of the 1890 Act deals with another specific activity:

> Where one partner pledges the credit of the firm for a purpose apparently not connected with the firm's ordinary course of business, the firm is not bound, unless he is in fact specially authorised by the other partners; but this section does not affect any personal liability incurred by an individual partner.

In reality this is again simply declaratory of what we have already said in that a person who deals with a firm can only make the firm liable for that debt if the partner with whom he dealt had authority to contract it. Two phrases, however, could give rise to concern. First, it appears that for implied authority to exist the purpose need only be 'connected with the firm's ordinary course of business' rather than actually being in the course of the business (as is required by ss. 5, 6 and 8). Is there a difference so that implied authority in this case is wider than in the general areas under s. 5? If these sections are construed literally it might on one level be so — to take a New Zealand example, it has been held in *Kennedy* v *Malcolm Bros* (1909) that, whilst the purchase of a new farm is not within the ordinary course of business of a farming partnership, if it is an adjoining farm to be used with the existing farm then it is connected with that business. In reality, however, that is simply an example of apparent authority since the partners showed by their conduct that it was to be acquired as part of the business and so in effect held each other out as having authority to bind the firm to the transaction.

The second problem arises from the curious use of the word 'specially' in relation to the authority given by the other partners which will make them liable. Clearly this will include express authority but if that was meant why was the word 'specially' used? Does it therefore include something other than express (or actual) authority? The answer must surely be yes, since all the basic concepts of agency and commercial reality point to the fact that the other partners can be liable if they have represented the partner as having that authority. Prior to the Act there was a judicial disagreement in the case of *Kendal* v *Wood* (1871) but a majority of 2 to 1 took the view that in such cases apparent authority would suffice and this was followed in Australia. In *Kennedy* v *Malcolm Bros* itself, decided after the Act, it is clear that this was also regarded as the position and in the absence of any UK cases to the contrary it can be assumed to be the position here.

In short, therefore, ss. 6 and 7 add little to what has already been said. For implied authority to exist the act must relate to the business of the firm — how else can an impression of authority be given simply by the partner's status as a partner? But there is no such requirement if the third party is relying on either actual or apparent authority where authority stems from actual permission or words or conduct by the other partners. It is not enough, however, for implied authority, simply for the act to relate to the business — it must also be a 'usual' act within that context.

'In the usual way' This area raises such questions as does one partner have the implied authority to borrow money, insure the premises, convey land, give guarantees, sack employees etc. in the course of the firm's business?

What amounts to carrying on the business 'in the usual way'? Remember it must look all right to the third party if he is to take advantage of a partner's implied authority and this must stem from the act itself in the context of the particular business. What is it usual for one partner to do on his own? The answer can be gleaned from several cases decided both before and after the 1890 Act. The distinction seems to be between general commercial or trading partnerships on the one hand and non-trading partnerships on the other. The former enjoy a much wider implied authority than the latter, particularly with respect to the borrowing of money.

A trading partnership was defined by Ridley J in *Wheatley* v *Smithers* (1906) as one that required the buying and selling of goods. Applying that test he was able to decide that an autioneer's partnership was not a trading partnership — an auctioneer does not buy anything. This test was followed by Lush J in *Higgins* v *Beauchamp* (1914) in relation to a partnership carrying on a cinema house business 'and all other forms of entertainment'. Giving the judgment of the Divisional Court, Lush J, noting that Ridley J's test was approved by the Court of Appeal in that case, continued:

> In my opinion it would be wrong to say that every business which involves the spending of money is a trading business. To my mind a trading business is one which involves the purchase of goods and the selling of goods.

The cinema business could not come under that head so that it seems that the purchase of goods and the selling of service will not suffice — thus excluding most, if not all, modern professional partnerships.

The actual decision in *Higgins* v *Beauchamp* was that since the firm was not a trading partnership one partner could not bind his fellow partner to a debt incurred by him without any other authority. The other partner was in fact a dormant partner (i.e., one who takes no active interest in the firm's business) and as we shall see it is these partners who feature heavily in the case law on this topic and create special problems with regard to the final part of s. 5. In practice many of the problems relating to implied authority for professional firms relate to the other form of liability (for misapplication of clients' funds etc.) and we shall return to those later. Their implied authority otherwise is quite limited as the law stands, although, since many of the cases are quite old, it may be that the modern judges could extend this authority in the light of commercial developments.

For the moment, however, let us concentrate on trading partnerships. Partners in such firms do have implied authority to borrow money and to buy and sell trading stock in connection with the firm's business. They can also incur debts on account of the firm, instigate civil proceedings on its behalf and even lend money to outsiders. To take one example of these — selling goods — this can apparently apply to selling goods which don't belong to the firm. In *Mercantile Credit Co. Ltd* v *Garrod* (1962), Parkin was the active and Garrod the dormant partner in a business mainly concerned with the letting of lock-up garages and repairing cars. The partnership agreement prohibited the buying and selling of cars but Parkin, without any express authority, sold a car to the credit company so that it could be let on a hire-purchase contract to a customer. It then appeared that Parkin did not own the car and the company claimed the £700 paid for it from Garrod. Applying s. 5 of the Act, Mocatta J held that Parkin did have implied authority to sell the car. In coming to this decision the judge stressed the central concept of implied authority:

> I must have regard in deciding this matter to what was apparent to the outside world in general and Mr Bone [the company's representative] in particular, and to the facts relevant to business of a like kind to that of the business of this partnership so far as it appeared to the outside world.

Judged on those criteria it was a usual way of carrying on the business of the firm. It should be noted that the provision of the partnership agreement to the contrary was of no avail — the company had no notice of it and, as we have seen, s. 8 makes it clear that in such circumstances such limitations do not apply.

It is less clear what the implied authority of a trading partner is with respect to insurance, deeds and conveyances. Modern practice may here outweigh established and venerable cases. There is no implied authority, however, to give guarantees or enter into arbitration on behalf of the firm and it is equally clear that one partner has no such authority to bind his fellow partners into a partnership with other persons in another business. This is an obvious conseqeunce of the nature of partnership as a relationship involving mutual trust. Since any partner may bankrupt another by his actions it would be ridiculous if one partner could simply on his own initiative bind his fellow partners to another partnership, so that they could be liable for debts incurred by those other partners. Thus if A, B and C are partners, A has no implied authority to make D a partner, nor has he the authority to involve A, B and C with a firm of D, E and F in a new business venture.

But this restriction does not apply if the agreement between A and D, E and F does not amount to another business but simply amounts to a single joint trading venture between the two firms which is simply one method of carrying out the business of A, B and C, even though that venture may amount to a partnership for its duration. This is the result of the decision of Megarry J in *Mann* v *D'Arcy* (1968). D'Arcy & Co. was a partnership, consisting of three partners of which only D'Arcy was an active partner, carrying on a business as produce merchants. D'Arcy made an agreement with Mann to go on a joint account as to the purchase and resale of some 350 tons of potatoes on board a particular ship. It was clear that buying and selling potatoes was part of the ordinary business of the firm and that control of the venture remained with D'Arcy. In the event the venture produced a profit of about £2,410 but Mann had never received anything. He now sued one of the sleeping partners for his share (D'Arcy and the other partner no longer being 'men of substance') whose defence was that he had no knowledge of anything to do with this affair and that D'Arcy had no implied authority to make him a partner with Mann in this joint-venture partnership.

After examining the authorities Megarry J upheld the basic rule that in general there is no implied authority so as to make one firm liable as partners in another business concern but that this did not apply on the facts of the case. He emphasised that the existing prohibition only applied to 'another business' and this could not be said to be another business since it remained under D'Arcy's control, and was in any event part of the existing business of the firm. The fact that the venture was a partnership in its own right did not automatically prevent authority from being implied — there are partnerships and partnerships, and a single-venture agreement was different from a general partnership for a longer period. Turning to s. 5 the judge decided that the venture was related to the ordinary business of the firm and could be related to that business being carried out 'in the usual way', even though there was no evidence relating to produce merchants generally or this firm's previous conduct in particular.

In effect the judge regarded the whole transaction as a method of buying and selling potatoes so as to minimise potential losses (the market was, as ever, uncertain), i.e., as a form of insurance underpinning a commercial venture which was within the ordinary business of the firm:

> In my judgment the reality of the matter is that what in substance D'Arcy & Co. were doing through [D'Arcy] was to buy and sell potatoes; and this was plainly carrying on business 'in the usual way'. The terms on which [D'Arcy] bought and sold the potatoes were also plainly matters within his authority. Clearly he could agree the prices and other terms both for purchases and sales. Equally, I think, it was within his implied authority to insure the goods, whether during transit or otherwise. In my

judgment the arrangement for sharing the profit and the loss which he made with [Mann] falls within this sphere of authority. The arrangement was merely one mode of buying and selling what he was authorised to buy and sell on behalf of the partnership; and he was mitigating the risk at the expense of reducing the profit. Accordingly, it was within his authority.

I have analysed this case not just because it provides an example of the general concept of implied authority but because it perhaps indicates a modern judicial approach to the whole issue. The judge was faced with a general rule enunciated in cases decided before the Act and enshrined in legal folklore ever since. What he did was to apply the wording of s. 5 to the problem rather than to rely on general principles as to the nature of partnership. The result was to provide a pragmatic solution on the particular facts rather than to provide such general rules — perhaps the only real general principle now is the wording of the section itself. In this area, as in other fields of law, the answer may well depend upon the approach to the particular questions asked.

Two sections of the Act provide illustrations of the implied authority of a partner in this area and they apply to all firms, trading or otherwise. Section 15 provides that: 'An admission or representation made by any partner concerning the partnership affairs, and in the ordinary course of its business, is evidence against the firm'. Thus one partner has implied authority to make such admissions, e.g., as to liability, provided they relate to the ordinary course of the partnership business. Because s. 15 states that such admissions are admissible as evidence against the firm they must be 'usual' for the purpose of s. 5. Note that such admissions are not conclusive merely admissible. It is not within the ordinary course of the business, however, for a partner to represent that he has more authority than his actual or implied authority would suggest. Section 15 cannot be used by a partner to give himself apparent authority.

Section 16 provides that: 'Notice to any partner who habitually acts in the partnership business of any matter relating to partnership affairs operates as notice to the firm, except in the case of a fraud on the firm committed by or with the consent of that partner'. This is an example of the common law concept of 'imputed' notice and is declaratory of the pre-existing common law. The notice must be given to a partner at a time when he is a partner so that notice to a person who subsequently becomes a partner is not within the section — that was also the position prior to the Act: *Williamson* v *Barbour* (1877). This may be important, for example, where an employee becomes a partner. The notice must also relate to the affairs of the firm so that notice to one firm cannot be transferred to another even when there is common membership: see *Campbell* v *McCreath* (1975).

Implied authority exists, therefore, if a partner is doing something which is usual in the context of carrying on the firm's business. However, s. 5 does not stop there for it has a proviso that the third party cannot rely on this implied authority if either he knows of the partner's lack of actual authority (which is straightforward) or does not 'know or believe him to be a partner' (which is not).

Knowledge and belief   Section 5 of the Act, having established that an act done in the usual way and in the ordinary course of business of the firm will be within a partner's implied authority, then proceeds to exclude such authority in two situations. The first is unexceptional: where the partner has no actual authority and the third party knows that he has no such authority. Knowledge of lack of authority destroys the essence of implied authority since the third party cannot then be said to be relying on appearances. The second situation, however, presents some problems: where the partner has no actual authority and the third party 'does not know or believe him to be a partner'. Taken at face value this could suggest that if A, without any actual authority, orders 100 tons of wheat from X on behalf of a partnership of A and B, X will only be able to rely on s. 5 to make B liable for the contract if he knew or believed that A was a partner with B. Various permutations could also arise. For instance, what if X knew that A was a partner with someone but had no idea with whom? Again, suppose A has two partners, B and C, and X knows that A is a partner with C but has no idea of B's existence — can X sue B under s. 5?

Construing this last part of s. 5 is in fact far from easy. Does the third party simply have to know that A is a partner with some person or persons unknown, as they say, or does he have to know the identity of some or all of the other partners? Is there any validity in drawing a distinction between the case where X thinks that A is a sole trader but in fact he has a partner, B, and where X thinks that A is a partner with C, but has no knowledge of partner B? Why should B be liable in the second case and not in the first? Before we can even attempt to solve these problems thrown up by the wording of s. 5 we must first take on board a doctrine of the law of agency which further complicates matters in this area — the doctrine of the undisclosed principal.

This doctrine states that where an agent has authority to act for a principal but does not tell the third party that he is acting as an agent, the third party may sue either the agent or the principal, if and when it is discovered who he is, and either the agent or the principal may sue the third party on the contract. This rather surprising doctrine has never been very popular in the business world — it means, of course, that the third party can sue or be sued by someone of whose existence he was totally unaware. The justification for it is said to be the injustice that would otherwise be caused, i.e., if the third party has sold goods to an agent acting for an undisclosed principal and delivers the goods to the agent and, before the price is paid, the agent becomes insolvent the goods could be taken by the agent's creditors to pay for his debts unless the principal can demand their return. This has always seemed a rather thin basis for such a strong departure from the rules that only a party to a contract can enforce it. It is not inconceivable that the third party might not have entered into the contract at all if he had known the true identity of the principal involved.

There are, however, some limitations on this doctrine. First, the agent must have had authority at the time of the contract, otherwise anyone could later adopt the agent's contract and claim that the agent was acting on his behalf. Second, if the contract shows either expressly or by implication that it is to be confined in its operation to the parties (i.e., the agent and the third party) themselves, the possibility of agency is negatived and no one else can intervene as a principal. This is a question of construction of the contract in each case. For example, where the alleged agent was described as the 'owner' of a ship it was held that evidence was not admissible to show that he was in fact acting as agent for the real owner; the agent appeared to be the sole owner of the subject-matter of the contract: *Humble* v *Hunter* (1848). However, in a similar case where the alleged agent was described as the 'charterer' (hirer) of a ship, evidence was allowed to show who the principal was. To describe oneself as owner precludes the existence of another owner, but 'charterer' simply means no more than a contracting party and does not therefore preclude the existence of another owner: *Fred. Drughorn Ltd* v *Rederiaktiebolaget Transatlantic* (1919).

Ignoring s. 5 of the Act for the moment, the doctrine of the undisclosed principal, if applied to partnerships, would mean that any partner could sue or be sued on a contract made by another partner within the scope of his implied authority, even though his existence was unknown to the third party. Since each partner is a principal of his fellow partners he could equally well be an undisclosed principal. The wording of s. 5, however, suggests that this cannot be so, for if the third party does not know or believe that the contracting partner is a partner he cannot rely on that partner's implied authority so as to bind the other partners. This whole problem therefore resolves itself into two questions. Does s. 5 of the

Partnership Act 1890 negate the doctrine of the undisclosed principal so far as partnership law is concerned? If it does, then in what circumstances will an unknown partner be liable under the section itself?

In answering the first question it is clear that s. 5 operates equally in relation to the unknown partner suing the third party as it does in the more usual reverse situation of the third party suing the unknown partner. Judicial authority, such as it is, suggests that in fact s. 5 does *not* prevent the general rule from applying. In *Watteau* v *Fenwick* (1893), a hotel manager appointed by the brewers ordered certain goods from the plaintiff in breach of his agreement with the brewers. The plaintiff believed the manager to be the owner of the hotel (the hotel licence was in his name and his name appeared over the hotel door) but was nevertheless allowed to sue the brewers under the doctrine of the undisclosed principal. For our purposes the significance of this case is what the position would have been if the manager and the brewers had been partners. The plaintiff clearly did not know or believe the manager to be an agent (or partner in our scenario). The judge, Wills J, suggested that the result would have been the same:

> But in the case of a dormant partner it is clear law that no limitation of authority as between the dormant and active partner will avail the dormant partner as to things within the ordinary authority of a partner. The law of partnership is, on such a question, nothing but a branch of the general law of principal and agent.

But how can this possibly be reconciled with the actual wording of s. 5? Professor J.L. Montrose, in a well-known article, 'Liability of principal for acts exceeding actual and apparent authority' (1939) 17 Can Bar Rev 693 points out that the application of any of the possible meanings of the words 'does not know or believe him to be a partner' would have produced an entirely different result on the facts of *Watteau* v *Fenwick* as applied to a partnership. He also makes the point that, unless there was an intention to protect unknown (or dormant) partners in such circumstances, why was this part of s. 5 added in 1890? To follow Wills J is to ignore this part of the section entirely. The judge's views can of course be technically dismissed as an *obiter dictum* since the case was not in fact about partnerships but an ordinary case of agency. Further he does not actually refer to s. 5 and declare it to have no such effect. In UK law therefore we can start with a clean sheet on s. 5 if we wish, but there is a far more recent decision in the Supreme Court of New South Wales which adopts the same stance as Wills J and which is neither *obiter* nor oblique.

In *Hexyl Pty Ltd* v *Construction Engineering (Aust.) Pty Ltd* (1983), Hexyl and another company, Tambel, were partners in a land development and management scheme. Tambel entered into a building contract with the defendants which described Tambel as the 'proprietor' of the land (though in fact it had been purchased by Hexyl and Tambel in equal shares). This building contract contained a provision for arbitration in the case of a dispute and the defendants gave notice of a dispute and referred the matter to arbitration. The defendants sought to make Hexyl liable in the arbitration and Hexyl applied to the court for a declaration that since it was not a party to the building contract it could not be joined in the arbitration as a party to the arbitration proceedings. The defendants relied on the doctrine of the undisclosed principal to make Hexyl liable, Tambel being Hexyl's agents for this purpose. Hexyl raised several arguments against this, including one that the use of the word 'proprietor' to describe Tambel in the building contract precluded the doctrine applying on the authority of the 'owner' cases mentioned above. Construing the contract, Kearney J rejected that argument.

The main argument, however, centred on the effect of s. 5 of the New South Wales Partnership Act 1892 which is identical with the UK provision. Hexyl argued that since the building contract was made without any reference to the partnership, s. 5 prevented the defendants from involving them as partners. Section 5 was designed, they argued, to ensure the accountability of every partner for matters undertaken by or on behalf of the partnership where the other party is dealing with, or believes he is dealing with, the partnership. Kearney J, found on the facts that Tambel had in fact been acting within its actual authority but he rejected *Hexyl's* general argument as follows (emphasis added):

> I do not see any proper ground to confine the operation of s. 5 to a case where either the engagement is entered into the name of the partnership or it is entered into with a third party who has knowledge of the partnership and treats the transaction as a partnership transaction. *I regard s. 5 as being no more than a restatement, in the context of a partnership, of the general principle whereby undisclosed principals are affected with liability in respect of contracts made by and in the name of their agents.*

There is little escape from the force of such a judicial statement except to say that either it is wrong or that this part of s. 5 has no meaning. If there was no s. 5 then the decision would be unexceptional. The doctrine of the undisclosed principal is in many ways illogical. (If implied authority is based on appearances to the third party then the appearance in such cases is that the agent or partner is acting on his own behalf and the third party, having given credit etc. accordingly, has little room to complain — why should he have an alternative source of redress?) If the doctrine is applied to partnerships it puts dormant partners in a vulnerable position. On the other hand, partnership is all about mutual trust and liability and why should dormant partners be any less liable than active partners? In any event the doctrine of the undisclosed principal is 200 years old and unlikely to suffer an early demise.

But s. 5 does exist and it would be strange indeed if the last line, unlike the rest of the section, is to have no effect. We must therefore assume that the views of Professor Montrose as to its effect on *Watteau* v *Fenwick*, and the rejected plea of *Hexyl* in their recent case are correct. This does not, however, solve the problem. If the end of s. 5 does mean something, what exactly does it mean? Remember the words: 'does not know or believe him to be a partner'. It seems clear that in both the *Watteau* v *Fenwick* and *Hexyl* situations this should negative the application of the doctrine of the undisclosed principal. Thus if A, without any express authority, contracts with X, apparently on his own account, X cannot sue any of A's undisclosed partners since X did not know or believe A to be a partner. The position is also clear if A, again without express authority, contracts with X who knows that A has a partner or partners although he has no idea of their actual identity. Since A is contracting as an agent, the fact that X does not know the actual identity of the other partners is of no consequence: X does know or believe that A is a partner.

Suppose, however, that in such a case X knew that A and B were partners but had no idea of the existence of C, another partner. In such a case Professor Montrose suggests that if X is contracting with A and B jointly, C will not be liable, whereas if X contracts only with A, C will be liable. This rather startling conclusion is based on the idea that the words 'does not know or believe him to be a partner' must include the plural 'does not know or believe them to be partners' and that this plural form must be read with the addition 'of another'. Thus if X contracts with A and B jointly, he does not know or believe them to be partners of another, C, and so C cannot be made liable under the section. If X only contracts with A, however, he does know or believe that a is a partner and so both B and C are liable. A contrary argument has been put by J.C. Thomas in an article entitled 'Playing word games with Professor Montrose' (1977) 6 VUWLRI.

I suspect that for those who appreciate word games this is a potentially endless area of fun. But what should the position be? Surely it should depend solely upon whether X believes or knows that he is dealing with a firm or whether he thinks he is dealing solely with an individual. Such a solution would be simple to apply and it would be consistent with the concept of partnership liability. Once again the real culprit in all this is the fact that a partnership is not a separate legal entity. Thus to say that it depends upon whether X believes or knows that he is dealing with a firm is in some ways misleading. More accurately it should depend upon whether X knows or believes he is dealing with a person who has partners in that business. Put that way it should then be irrelevant whether he knows how many or who they are, since a partnership is by its very nature a fluid form and X could quite easily imagine that there are dormant partners involved. (In practice, of course, since X will not be a lawyer he will in any event assume that a firm in this context is some form of 'being' and that he is dealing with all its members.)

Liability for other wrongs

Partners may be liable for wrongs committed by their fellow partners quite independently of any contract. Thus they may be liable for torts or crimes or the misapplication of property entrusted to one partner and for breaches of trust. In practice the principles applicable to all these heads are quite similar but in practice it is easier to consider them under two heads: liability for misapplication of property and breaches of trust, and liability for crimes and other torts. In some cases liability can arise under both heads, so this distinction is for our convenience rather than being indicative of any sharp distinction between them. We will start with the general liability for torts and crimes, i.e., those which do not involve a misapplication of property or a breach of trust.

General liability for torts and crimes

Section 10 of the Act explains the general rule for liability for torts and crimes:

> Where, by any wrongful act or omission of any partner acting in the ordinary course of the business of the firm, or with the authority of his copartners, loss or injury is caused to any person not being a partner in the firm, or any penalty is incurred, the firm is liable therefor to the same extent as the partner so acting or omitting to act.

Thus each partner is liable for the wrongful acts or omissions of his fellow partners provided either that they are acting in the ordinary course of the firm's business or with the authority of their copartners. This provision has been applied to the law of torts so as to create a liability along the same lines as the vicarious liability of an employer for the torts of his employees where liability arises if the tort is committed in the ordinary course of employment. This extends to liability for an unauthorised form of doing what an employee is authorised to do.

So it is with a partnership. Whilst it is possible to argue that it is never in the ordinary course of the business of a firm to commit a tort, the partners will be liable if the erring partner in committing the tort is simply carrying out the ordinary business of the partnership in such a way as to commit a tort. The relevant authority for this is the case of *Hamlyn* v *Houston & Co* (1903). A partner was engaged by the firm to obtain information by legitimate means about the business contracts etc. of its competitors. He bribed the clerk of a rival firm to divulge confidential information about that firm to him and thus committed the tort of inducing a breach of contract. The bribe came out of the firm's money and the resulting profits went into its assets. The rival firm who had lost money as a result sued the other partners in tort. The Court of Appeal allowed the action to succeed. It was within the ordinary scope of the partner's business to obtain the information, so that his object was lawful, and the fact that it was obtained by unlawful means did not take it outside either the ordinary course of the firm's business or his authority.

In fact the partners will be liable for torts committed by a partner if they are committed in attaining some object which is within that partner's actual, implied or apparent authority. In *Hamlyn's* case the partner had actual authority to obtain the information and in doing so he committed the tort. The position would be the same if the partner had apparent authority to obtain the information (i.e., by virtue of a representation by words or conduct to that effect) or even implied authority (i.e., by virtue of his position and status). A more modern example of this idea is the Scottish case of *Kirkintilloch Equitable Co-operative Society Ltd* v *Livingstone* (1972) where a partner in a firm of accountants negligently carried out an audit ostensibly in his private capacity. In fact, however, he used the firm's staff and premises and the fee was paid to the firm. He was judged to have been acting in the ordinary course of the firm's business for the purposes of s. 10 — in effect, he either had implied authority from his position as a partner in an accountancy firm or apparent authority from his permitted use of the partnership facilities. A similar result was obtained in Canada in the case of *Public Trustee* v *Mortimer* (1985) where a solicitor was held to be acting within his apparent authority as a solicitor in the practice when he acted as an executor for a client and as such used all the partnership facilities.

However, if the partner has no authority at all to achieve the end sought, then his partners will not be liable for any tort he may commit in seeking to achieve that end. To go back 170 years from the last case, an illustration of this point is the case of *Arbuckle* v *Taylor* (1815) (which shows that there was more to that year than Napoleon, Wellington etc.). One partner of a firm instituted a criminal prosecution on his own account against the plaintiff for an alleged theft of partnership property. The prosecution failed and the plaintiff now sued the firm for the torts of false imprisonment and malicious prosecution. The claim against the other partners failed. It was not within the general scope of the firm's activities to institute criminal proceedings and the other partners were not liable simply because the property allegedly stolen had belonged to the firm. In the absence of any actual or apparent authority, therefore, the partners could not be liable.

Of course nothing in s. 10 relates to a partner's primary liability as a tortfeasor in his own right. Thus if two partners commit a tort which is not within their authority, each can still be liable for the tort, not vicariously but primarily as joint tortfeasors. So in *Meekins* v *Henson* (1964) where one partner wrote a letter defamatory of the plaintiff but could rely on the defence of qualified privilege since he had not acted maliciously, the other partner was held liable since he had acted maliciously, on the basis that he was a joint publisher of the letter and so a joint tortfeasor. The plaintiff did not have to rely on s. 10 — the liability was *primary*, i.e., being responsible for one's own wrongful act, rather than *vicarious*, i.e., being responsible for the wrong of another. Since the partner writing the letter had committed no tort there would of course have been no liability on the other under s. 10 since there had been no wrongful act by him.

Section 10 also applies to crimes ('any penalty') although, of course, only the partners (and not the mythical firm) can actually be convicted of an offence. Again, therefore, a partner can be liable vicariously for the crimes of his partners if they fall within the authority of the criminal partner in the sense explained above. Similarly a partner can be liable primarily for the crimes committed by his partners if the offence applies to more than the immediate offenders. For example in *Clode* v *Barnes* (1974) a dormant partner was convicted of an offence under the Trade Descriptions Act 1968 since he was deemed to be a joint supplier of the car with the active partner who had actually sold the car.

Liability for misapplication of property and breaches of trust

As we have seen it is quite possible for the general liability under s. 10 of the Act to cover the liability of partners where another partner **misappropriates** money or other property in the course of acting in his actual, implied or apparent authority. The words of s. 10, 'any wrongful act or omission', would seem wide enough to include not only such misapplications but also breaches of trust by one partner. The Act, however, provides special rules for such misapplications in s. 11 and for one particular aspect of a breach of trust in s. 13.

Section 11 provides:

In the following cases; namely —

(a) Where one partner acting within the scope of his apparent authority receives the money or property of a third person and misapplies it; and
(b) Where a firm in the course of its business receives money or property of a third person, and the money or property so received is misapplied by one or more of the partners while it is in the custody of the firm;

the firm is liable to make good the loss.

Paragraph (a) therefore applies where the receipt is by a partner acting 'within the scope of his apparent authority'. Paragraph (b) requires the receipt to be by the firm in the ordinary course of the business and to be still in the firm's custody at the time it is misapplied.

The first important point to grasp is that 'apparent authority' in this section does not just mean authority created by a representation by words or conduct (i.e., in the sense in which I have used that term in this book) although it does include that. It also means authority derived from the nature of the business and the status of the partner (i.e. what I have termed implied authority). As we saw at the beginning of this chapter there is no one meaning of any of the terms applied to authority. Thus s. 11(a) applies where the partner receives the property in the course of his implied or apparent authority — the misapplication need not, of course, be part of that authority.

If the dishonest partner has no such authority there is, therefore, no liability. The best example of this is where the third party is consciously dealing with that partner as an individual and not in his capacity as a partner. Thus in *British Homes Assurance Corporation Ltd* v *Patterson* (1902), the plaintiffs engaged Atkinson to act as its solicitor *vis-à-vis* a mortgage and Atkinson later informed them that he had taken Patterson into partnership. The plaintiffs nevertheless sent a cheque ignoring the new firm name, which was then misappropriated by Atkinson, and sought to recover the amount from Patterson under s. 11(a). The judge, Farwell J, held that Patterson could not be liable because at all times the plaintiffs had dealt with Atkinson as an individual and had elected to continue the contract as one with an individual even after notification of the existence of the firm.

Whether a receipt by a partner is in the course of his apparent or implied authority for the purpose of s. 11(a) depends upon establishing one or other of the concepts. If he receives it in the course of his implied authority it will almost certainly be a receipt in the ordinary course of business by the firm and so also fall within s. 11(b). Thus the two heads are not mutually exclusive. In *Rhodes* v *Moules* (1895), the plaintiff sought to raise money by way of a mortgage on his property. He used a solicitor in a firm who told him that the lenders wanted additional security and so he handed the solicitor some share warrants to bearer (ie., transferable by simple delivery and a fraud's delight). The solicitor misappropriated them and the plaintiff now sued the firm under s. 11. The Court of Appeal held that the firm was liable under both heads. On the evidence the certificates were received in the ordinary course of the firm's business and also within the apparent authority of the partner.

On the other hand there will be occasions where, because liability under paragraph (a) is based on authority arising from a representation by the other partners rather than from the business of the company, paragraph (b) will not be available. Thus in the Canadian case of *Public Trustee* v *Mortimer* (1985) where a solicitor acting as an executor and trustee of a will misapplied the funds under his control his partners were held liable under paragraph (a) of this section (numbered 12 in the Ontario statute just to confuse you). The judge was unsure whether the solicitor *qua* trustee and executor was acting in the ordinary course of business of the firm but:

> There can be no doubt, in my view, that the firm, by permitting Mortimer to use the stationery, accounts, staff and other facilities of the firm in connection with his activities as executor and trustee, had vested Mortimer with apparent authority to receive the money or property of the estate which he subsequently misapplied.

The judge also found the other partners liable under the Ontario equivalent of s. 10 since it was a wrongful act of a partner acting with the authority of his fellow partners. They could not, however, in view of the judge's doubts, have been liable under the Ontario equivalent of s. 11(b) since the receipt (as distinct from this misapplication for the purposes of s. 10) was not clearly within the ordinary course of business of the firm.

If s. 11(b) is relied upon, the receipt must be by the firm in the course of its ordinary business and the misapplication must have been whilst the money or property was still in the firm's custody. Thus the receipt must in effect be by a partner acting within his implied authority and if the misapplication takes place after the property ceases to be in the custody of the firm, e.g., where the money is loaned out again by the firm to a company and a partner fraudulently persuades the company to repay the money to him, there can be no liability under s. 11(b): *Sims* v *Brutton* (1850). Whether the property is in the custody of the firm at the relevant time is a question of fact — the answer would appear to be no if it is in the custody of an individual partner in his own private capacity. In *Tendring Hundred Waterworks Co* v *Jones* (1903), the company employed a firm of solicitors, Garrard and Jones, to negotiate a purchase of land. Garrard was the company secretary and his fees as such were regarded as partnership income. The company stupidly arranged for the land to be conveyed into Garrard's name and the vendors gave him the title deeds. Garrard used the deeds to raise money by way of a mortgage. The company now sought to make Jones liable for Garrard's misapplication.

Farwell J held that this did not fall within s. 11(b) since the deeds were given to Garrard not in his capacity as company secretary or partner but as a private individual who was named in the conveyance as the legal owner. Thus the deeds were not in the custody of the firm — they were in Garrard's custody as a private individual. It is, of course, equally true that the receipt by Garrard was not in the ordinary course of the firm's business — it is no part of the ordinary duty of a solicitor to accept conveyances of land belonging to his clients into his own name. It would be different if a client leaves his deeds with his solicitors in the ordinary course of business and a member of the firm fraudulently deposits them with another in order to raise money on them. In such a case the misapplication would take place whilst they were in the custody of the firm.

The basis of liability for a misapplication by one partner under either part of s. 11 depends primarily, therefore, upon whether the receipt of the property is within the implied or apparent authority of the partner receiving it. The subsequent misapplication need not be within his authority; liability arises out of a misapplication following a relevant receipt. If all this sounds obvious, I am labouring the point because of some confusion caused by a recent decision of Vinelott J where the judge, in applying the law of constructive trusts to partnerships, seems to have treated liability under s. 11 of the Act as at best subsidiary to liability under that head. In order to understand this confusion it is necessary to recall a little of the doctrine of constructive trusts which gives rise to a liability to account as if the person concerned were a trustee.

A constructive trust arises where there is a breach of trust (or fiduciary duty) by X and Y either *knowingly* receives the trust property or he *knowingly* assists in the breach of trust. In both cases Y will be liable as a constructive trustee, which in practice means he will have to account to the injured party for any loss suffered as a result of X's breach of trust. Although the position is not yet exactly clear, it appears that for the 'knowing receipt' category of liability it will be sufficient if Y knew or ought to have known of the breach of trust whereas if only knowing assistance can be proved, Y must either have known of the breach or have turned a blind eye to it (so-called 'Nelsonian notice'). In both cases liability is based on the concept of equitable fraud — it would be unfair to allow Y to escape liability. What is needed, therfore, is a breach of trust and either knowing receipt or knowing assistance on the part of another. However, there has always been an exception to this doctrine where Y receives the trust property merely in his capacity as an agent of the fraudulent trustee. In such cases, provided he acts in a purely ministerial capacity (i.e., does only what he would be expected as agent to do), he will not become a constructive trustee unless, of course, he has actual knowledge of the breach. Thus if Y is X's solicitor he will not, in so far as he acts purely as a solicitor, be liable as a constructive trustee unless he actually knows of X's breach of trust.

How then does the concept of a constructive trust overlap with the liabilities under s. 11 of the Act? Suppose that one partner is a trustee and he receives trust property in his capacity as a partner in the firm (usually of solicitors). If that partner then misapplies the trust property, are the other partners liable either as constructive trustees (knowing receipt or knowing assistance) or under s. 11 (receipt by the partner in the course of his implied or apparent authority)? Ideally the two types of liability should be kept strictly separate since the two questions are quite different: is there a breach of trust followed by knowing receipt or assistance (except as an agent); alternatively is there a receipt in the course of the partner's implied or apparent authority? Unfortuntely as a result of the decision of Vinelott J in *Re Bell's Indenture Trusts* (1980) the two concepts have been mixed up and need to be unravelled.

The facts of the case were basically quite simple. A solicitor was one of three trustees of a trust fund. Money was paid into that solicitor's firm's client account to the credit of the trustees and was then misappropriated by the trustees including the solicitor. His partner had no knowledge of the fraud — he had at all times acted 'honestly and reasonably' — nevertheless, was he liable for the sums misappropriated by his partner either under 'the general principle' of ss. 10 and 11 of the Act or as a constructive trustee? An earlier case, *Blyth* v *Fladgate* (1891), suggested that in such cases all the partners were liable as constructive trustees — they had the knowledge of the guilty partner — but this had been rejected in *Mara* v *Browne* (1896). In his judgment Vinelott J concentrated almost exclusively on liability as a constructive trustee. He quite correctly followed *Mara* v *Browne* and decided that there was no liability under that head.

As we have seen there is no liability for someone who receives trust property in his capacity purely as an agent of the fraudulent trustee without actual knowledge of the breach, and in effect this is what the 'firm' (i.e., the other partner) had been. The guilty partner's conduct did not make the innocent partner a constructive trustee: 'A solicitor has the implied authority of his partners to receive trust moneys as *agent* of the trustees but does not have any implied authority to constitute himself a constructive trustee'. Receipt by the firm was, therefore, as agents of the trustee and not as constructive trustees in their own right and the well recognised exception to constructive trusts could apply. *Blyth* v *Fladgate* was distinguished as applying only to its own facts — the firm in that case could not have received the money as agents of the trustees because there were no trustees at the time of the receipt; therefore they must have received the money as trustees (or constructive trustees) themselves and so were fixed with constructive notice and so liable for knowing receipt.

Thus the innocent partner was quite correctly absolved from liability as a constructive trustee. It is less obvious why he also escaped liability under s. 11 of the Act. Vinelott J seems to have assumed that since the guilty partner had no implied authority to make the innocent partner a constructive trustee that was the end of the matter. But turning to s. 11(a), as we have seen, all that needs to be proved is that the partner *received* the money in the course of his apparent (or implied) authority — it is not necessary to show that the misapplication was also in the course of that authority. That is only relevant for the application of s. 10. In this case, therefore, the real question, which was never asked, was whether the receipt by the firm of the trust money was in the course of the fraudulent partner's apparent or implied authority? It was irrelevant that the act which might have given rise to liability as a constructive trustee (the misapplication) was outside that authority. Again, applying s. 11(b), was the receipt of the trust money into the firm's client account a receipt in the ordinary course of the business of the firm and did the misapplication occur whilst it was still in the custody of the firm? Again no such questions were asked. In short, Vinelott J, by default it seems, applied the authority test to the misapplication and not to the receipt. By referring to ss. 10 and 11 as only creating 'principles' of liability the specific provisions of s. 11 were overlooked in favour of s. 10.

Both parts of s. 11 contemplate receipt by the firm (or partner) as an agent for another and that is exactly how Vinelott J categorised the receipt in order to negative liability as a constructive trustee. Whilst it is not necessarily part of a solicitor's ordinary business as such to act as a trustee (Vinelott J relied on a case dated 1857 to establish that proposition — times and practices would seem to have changed since then — professional trustees abound and many are solicitors), is it not part of a solicitor's ordinary business when acting for a trust to receive trust money on behalf of the trust (especially, as in this case, into its client account) and so create a liability for a misapplication under either part of s. 11? If such a receipt is now usual, and contemporary practice would suggest that it is, it is surely part of the implied authority of a partner and liability on the other partners should follow automatically under s. 11 for any subsequent misapplications. Vinelott J regarded this as a 'somewhat surprising proposition' but this should not seem so for anyone who understands the basic nature of partnership liability.

Some authority for my argument can be found in the Canadian case of *Public Trustee* v *Mortimer* (1985), where one solicitor in his capacity as executor and trustee of a will misappropriated trust property. Without any reference to constructive trusts (an English obsession) the firm was held liable under the Ontario equivalent of s. 11(a) since, by allowing him to use the firm's facilities and staff in his work as an executor, he had received the trust property in the course of his apparent authority — the judge was less sure whether on those facts the partner was acting within his implied authority, although there are strong hints that he was. In *Re Bell's Indenture Trusts* the money was actually paid into the firm's client account and clearly all the business facilities of the firm were used by the partner in acting for the trust. There should be no doubt, therefore, that both halves of s. 11 should have applied in that case. Confusion was caused by the unnecessary application of constructive trusts, which is a separate doctrine. If the result would have been unjust to the honest partner than it must be said that the whole basis of partnership liability must be seen to be unjust.

Before leaving this troubled area of misapplications and breaches of trust we should note s. 13 of the Act which applies in quite limited circumstances:

> If a partner, being a trustee, improperly employs trust-property in the business or on the account of the partnership, no other partner is liable for the trust-property to the persons beneficially interested therein.

Provided as follows —

(1) This section shall not affect any liability incurred by any partner by reason of his having notice of a breach of trust; and
(2) Nothing in this section shall prevent trust money from being followed and recovered from the firm if still in its possession or under its control.

This provision only applies where the trust property is brought into the firm by a partner rather than misapplied by a partner in the course of a business. The other partners are not to be liable to the beneficiaries for this breach of trust unless they have notice of it, i.e., are liable as constructive trustees under the knowing receipt category. Further, in any case, the beneficiaries are not prevented from tracing the trust property (i.e., recoverying the property itself (if identifiable) or the proceeds of that property) under the principles laid down in *Ministry of Health* v *Simpson* (1951).

Nature of the liability

The Partnership Act itself makes a clear distinction between the nature of the liability of partners for debts and obligations on the one hand and for torts, crimes and other wrongs on the other. Section 9 provides that every partner in a firm is liable *jointly* with the other partners for all debts and obligations of the firm incurred while he is a partner — this in effect creates the unlimited liability of a partner. Section 12, on the other hand, provides that for liability under ss. 10 and 11 of the Act every partner is liable *jointly* with his copartners and also *severally* for everything for which the firm becomes liable whilst he is a partner. The distinction in the Act, therefore, is between joint liability for contracts and joint and several liability for torts etc. This distinction has never applied to Scotland where it has always been joint and several liability for all debts and fines etc., nor does it apply against the estate of a deceased partner — again joint and several liability is imposed.

What then is the distinction between joint liability and joint and several liability? The difference is that if liability is only joint the plaintiff has only one cause of action against all the partners in respect of each debt or contract. In *Kendall* v *Hamilton* (1879) the practical consequence of this was spelt out. A creditor sued all the obvious members of a firm and was awarded judgment against them. He failed to recover the debt in full, however, and when he subsequently discovered a wealthy dormant partner he sought to sue him for the balance of the debt. The House of Lords decided that since the debt was a joint one only, by suing the apparent partners the creditor had elected to sue only them and could not now commence fresh proceedings against the other partner. He had exhausted the cause of action. No such fatuous restriction applies to liability under s. 12 for there the liability is several as well as joint so that each partner can be sued in turn or all together until the full amount is recovered — the plaintiff is never put to his election.

The palpable injustice caused by the decision in *Kendall* v *Hamilton* was relieved partly by the disclosure of partners' names on notepaper and partly by the rules of practice which allowed creditors to obtain lists of who were the partners at the relevant time. But it was finally laid to rest by s. 3 of the Civil Liability (Contribution) Act 1978. This provides that:

> Judgment recovered against any person liable in respect of any debt or damage shall not be a bar to an action, or to the continuance of an action, against any other person who is (apart from any such bar) jointly liable with him in respect of the same debt or damage.

In very clear terms, therefore, the old rule in *Kendall* v *Hamilton* has been abolished and the fact that s. 9 of the Partnership Act still provides only for joint liability is of no consequence. The difference between joint and several liability has gone. The amazing thing was that it took a hundred years to achieve.

Duration of the liability

We have seen, therefore, that partners are liable without limit for all debts, obligations, torts, crimes, misapplications etc. committed by the firm *whilst they are partners*. But partnerships are not static — partners come and go and therefore it is necessary to find out when a retiring partner ceases to be liable for the debts etc. of the firm and when a new partner assumes such liability. The answers are to be found in ss. 17 and 36 of the Act, but it should always be remembered that irrespective of these rules, a person can always be liable as if he were a partner under s. 14 of the Act if he either allows himself to be represented as such by the other partners or indeed represents himself as such. This may be particularly relevant where a former partner is involved. Bearing that in mind we should turn our attention to s. 17 which provides the basic rules on a change of partners.

Section 17(1) states that: 'A person who is admitted as a partner into an existing firm does not thereby become liable to the creditors of the firm for anything done before he became a partner', and s. 17(2) accordingly rules that: 'A partner who retires from a firm does not thereby cease to be liable for partnership debts or obligations incurred before his retirement'. Applying these rules therefore presents a neat picture. Suppose A, B and C are partners. C retires and D joins the firm. C is liable for the debts etc. incurred up to the change by virtue of s. 17(2) and D becomes liable only for those debts incurred after the change under s. 17(1). In theory this is perfectly correct — D had no control over debts incurred before he became a partner and C should not be allowed to escape liability for existing debts simply by retiring from the firm. But practice is as usual far less tidy than theory. Contracts made with the firm before the date of change may produce liabilities after the date of change — is the new partner liable for such debts or the old partner absolved?

The answer seems to depend upon whether the contract is a single continuing contract, in which case the former partner remains liable and the new partner is exempt, or whether it is a series of individual contracts in which case the new partner replaces the old for liabilities incurred after the change. An example of a single continuing contract giving rise to a single liability already incurred at the date of change is *Court* v *Berlin* (1897). Court was a solicitor retained by a partnership to recover a debt due to it. The firm consisted of Berlin, the sole active partner, and two dormant partners. During the solicitor's work for the firm the two dormant partners retired. After the proceedings for recovery of the debt were completed the solicitor sued Berlin and the former partners for his costs. The dormant partners claimed that they were only liable for costs incurred up to the date of their retirement. The Court of Appeal held that they were fully liable. The contract entered into whilst they were partners was 'one entire contract to conduct the action to the end'; the solicitor did not need to come for fresh instructions at each step of the action. The dormant partners' liability for costs was for all the costs in the action — it did not arise on a day-to-day basis. Presumably it would have been different if Berlin had then decided to take the matter to an appeal court — that would not have been a single continuing liability since fresh instructions would have been needed.

It was suggested in *Court* v *Berlin* that the retiring partners could avoid liability under a single continuing contract by giving the solicitor in that case express notice of their retirement — in which case presumably the solicitor would have to choose to continue on a new basis or end the contract. If, however, the liabilities accrue on a day-by-day basis, albeit under a single general contract, the retiring partner will cease to be liable on retirement and the new partner will take over from the date of joining. An example of this type of contract is in *Bagel* v *Miller* (1903) where a firm contracted to purchase various shipments of goods. One of the partners died and it was held that his estate was only liable for the goods delivered before his death and not for deliveries afterwards. Those were liabilities accruing after his death. In such standing supply contracts it is the new partner who assumes responsibility: see *Dyke* v *Brewer* (1849).

All this can be inconvenient and so the Act and the common law allow an alternative to ss. 17(1) and (2). Section 17(3) accordingly provides that:

> A retiring partner may be discharged from any existing liabilities, by an agreement to that effect between himself and the members of the firm as newly constituted and the creditors, and this agreement may be either express or inferred as a fact from the course of dealing between the creditors and the firm as newly constituted.

There is no doubt that, since this is simply declaratory of the position at common law, similar principles would apply equally to an incoming partner accepting a liability. What is required is a contract of novation between the creditor, the new or retiring partner and the other partners. This is a tripartite agreement by which the creditor accepts the new firm as taking over liability for the debt from the old firm — it must be a three-way agreement, an internal agreement between the partners cannot affect the rights of the creditor on basic principles of privity of contract.

If such an agreement is express then few problems occur but it is far more likely to be implied from the acts of all concerned. What amounts to a novation in such circumstances is, of course, a question of fact in each case. It is less likely where there is no incoming partner to take over responsibility for the debt but more likely if the debts are difficult to quantify as between before and after the change. The creditor must, however, be aware of the change and that he is looking to the new firm for payment. There are several examples of novation in such circumstances. In *Rolfe* v *Flower Salting & Co.* (1866) three partners took two of their clerks into partnership. The newly constituted firm continued to trade under the old name and no change was made to the business, even the accounts were continued in the same way. The company was owed £80,000 by the old firm (without the clerks). That debt and the interest payable on it had been kept in the accounts and was regularly entered up. The new partners had access to the books. The company continued to trade with the new firm. The Privy Council, agreeing with the Supreme Court of Victoria, found the new partners liable for the old debt on the basis of implied novation. The company, by dealing with the new firm with full knowledge of the change of membership, had impliedly agreed to accept the new firm as debtors in place of the old firm, and the partners, by not objecting to the accounts, had impliedly agreed to accept liability for the debt.

From the point of view of an outsider a change in the firm will often terminate his contract, e.g., to supply goods, and a new contract (usually implied) will be needed. In the case of a guarantee of a firm debt s. 18 of the Act makes it quite clear that such a guarantee comes to an end on a change in the firm — it will only cover debts incurred before the change. This is because if X guarantees a debt owed by A, B and C to Y and is called upon to pay he takes over Y's rights against A, B and C. If C retires X will lose his rights for the future against C and so the guarantee lapses. Like many things, however, this is subject to contrary intention — any contract may provide that it shall continue to apply despite any change in the firm's membership.

So far we have been discussing the liability of a partner for the debts etc. incurred before he retires. He may, however, also be liable for debts incurred *after* he retires, not only under the doctrine of holding out under s. 14, but more specifically under the provisions of s. 36. In effect this provides a retirement procedure whereby the former partner can escape liability for future debts. It provides for three specific situations although all three subsections have to be read together in order to make this clear. The section is as follows:

(1)   Where a person deals with a firm after a change in its constitution he is entitled to treat all apparent members of the old firm as still being members of the firm until he has notice of the change.

(2)   An advertisement in the *London* [or *Edinburgh*] *Gazette*. . . shall be notice as to persons who had not dealings with the firm before the date of dissolution or change so advertised.

(3)   The estate of a partner who dies, or who becomes bankrupt, or of a partner who, not having been known to the person dealing with the firm to be a partner, retires from the firm, is not liable for partnership debts contracted after the date of the death, bankruptcy, or retirement respectively.

Subsection (1) thus extends the liability of a former member of the firm to debts contracted after his departure if he is still an 'apparent member' of the firm and the creditor has no notice of his retirement. This is based on estoppel. But such liability can be defeated either by actual notice to the creditor concerned or by using the provisions of subsections (2) and (3). If the creditor has never dealt with the firm before the change it will be sufficient if the retiring partner has placed an appropriate announcement in the *London Gazette* (for England and Wales), or the *Edinburgh Gazette* (for Scotland). Actual notice, therefore, need only be given to existing customers: prospective customers must read the small print. A complete exemption applies, however, under subsection (3), if the former partner has died or become bankrupt, or if the person dealing with the firm did not know him to be a partner.

The relationship between subsections (1) and (3) was explained in *Tower Cabinet Co Ltd* v *Ingram* (1949) a case we have already discussed in chapter 2 in relation to s. 14. To recap the facts, Christmas and Ingram were partners in a firm which was dissolved in 1947, Christmas carrying on the business under the same name as a sole trader. In 1948 the company agreed to supply some furniture to the business. The order was later confirmed by Christmas on old notepaper which included Ingram's name on its heading. Ingram had no idea that this was being done. The price was never paid and the company now sought to recover the money from Ingram as an apparent partner under s. 36(1). (If you remember they also tried s. 14 but it was held that Ingram had not 'knowingly' allowed himself to be represented as a partner.) The judge rejected the claim under s. 36 holding that s. 36(3) applied and provided a complete defence to the claim.

In coming to this conclusion the judge interpreted the words 'apparent partner' in s. 36(1) as meaning apparent to the particular creditor and not to the public at large. This could arise either because he had dealt with the firm before or he had some other indication of his existence, including the notepaper as in this case. Section 36(1), however, has to be interpreted in the light of s. 36(3). The company had no knowledge that Ingram was a partner at the date of his retirement and in such cases there can be no liability under s. 36(1) because s. 36(3) gave him complete protection. Lynskey J was quite clear:

> If the person dealing with the firm did not know that the particular partner was a partner, and that partner retired, then as from the date of his retirement, he ceases to be liable for further debts contracted by the firm to such person. The fact that later the person dealing with the firm may discover that the former partner was a partner seems to me to be irrelevant, because the date from which the subsection operates is from the date of the dissolution. If at the date of the dissolution the person who subsequently deals with the firm had no knowledge at or before that time that the retiring partner was a partner, then subsection (3) comes into operation, and relieves the person retiring from liability.

A former partner cannot therefore be an apparent partner within s. 36(1) if the creditor never knew him to be a partner before his retirement. It has to be said that the wording of s. 36(1) would seem to be wider than this but the decision in *Ingram's* case is surely correct. Liability for being an apparent partner should stand or fall with s. 14(1) and not s. 36(1) which is specifically related to retirement formalities. The essence of the company's case was that they had been misled by the notepaper but it was equally clear that at no time had that actually been the case.

Section 36 is confusing enough to require a summary to make things clear. A partner who retires will be liable for debts incurred after he retires unless either (a) he gives actual notice of his retirement to existing creditors, (b) he puts a notice in the relevant *Gazette* for prospective creditors or (c) the creditor did not know that he was a partner at the time when he retired. Of course, if he knowingly allows himself to be subsequently represented as a partner none of these will apply; instead liability will fall quite clearly under s. 14(1). If a partner is liable under s. 36 it is an interesting question whether the creditor must choose to sue the new firm, without the retired partner, or the old, and having chosen one cannot then sue the other. This was the position at common law and it is far from clear whether s. 3 of the Civil Liability (Contribution) Act 1978, which allows a creditor to sue joint debtors in sequence, will apply as between two groups who do not, *vis-à-vis* each other, have joint liability.

5

Partners and Each Other

Contract and equity

Partnership is a relationship based on mutual trust which can have far-reaching consequences as respects the partners' liabilities to outsiders. For precisely that reason it has long been established that partners owe each other a duty of good faith, i.e., to act honestly and for the benefit of the partners as a whole. Thus in 1824 in *Const* v *Harris* Lord Eldon could say: 'In all partnerships, whether it be expressed in the deed or not, the partners are bound to be true and faithful to each other'. The foundation of partnership is mutual faith and trust in each other and ever since the development of equity in the 19th century partners have always been regarded as being subject to the equitable duties implied by this 'good faith' principle.

In modern terms partners are said to be in a fiduciary position towards each other, which is to say that they owe each other duties as if each were a trustee and the other partners were beneficiaries under a trust. They are not actual trustees of course but they have similar obligations. Sometimes such fiduciaries are described as being constructive trustees but this may be inaccurate since it suggests that the trustee/partner is the legal owner of something of which the other partners are the beneficial owners (as under a trust), whereas in reality a fiduciary liability probably only gives rise to a duty to account for profits etc. made in breach of those duties. The distinction is important—if the partner concerned becomes insolvent and he is a constructive trustee for another his creditors will be unable to claim the relevant asset. This is not so if he merely has a duty to account which is an equitable remedy and not a proprietary right.

But partnership is more than a fiduciary relationship, it is above all a contractual agreement and therefore subject to the terms of that agreement, which as in contracts generally may be express or implied. The Partnership Act itself contains several implied terms but these can always be excluded or amended either by the express terms of the agreement or by the conduct of the partners. Once again we can say that the Act imposes a largely voluntary framework as between the partners themselves. On similar principles even the express terms of the agreement may be varied by a course of conduct. Section 19 of the Act makes all this quite clear:

> The mutual rights and duties of partners, whether ascertained by agreement or defined by this Act, may be varied by the consent of all the partners, and such consent may be either express or inferred from a course of dealing.

This wording cannot apply to all the fiduciary duties implied by equity since they do not necessarily arise either from the agreement or the Act (although three specific areas are included) but, since it is always a defence to a breach of fiduciary duty that the other party consented to the breach, no difference arises in practice.

Whether an express or implied term of the agreement has been varied by a course of conduct is a question to be decided on the facts of each case. An example is the case of *Cruikshank* v *Sutherland* (1922). By the terms of the agreement full and general accounts had to be drawn up to 30 April each year and the share of a deceased partner was to be ascertained by reference to the accounts drawn up for the year in which the death occurred. The partnership was formed in 1914, renewing an existing partnership. In 1914 the assets of the previous firm were taken over at their book value (the value as shown in the accounts rather than their actual (higher) value) and the accounts for April 1915 and 1916 both showed assets at book value. In October 1915 Cruikshank, one of the partners, died. The other partners argued that because of the previous use of book values in the accounts the deceased partner's share should also be taken at book value and not its actual value. The House of Lords found no such uniform practice. Lord Wrenbury put it this way:

> How could there be a practice and usage uniform and without variation to pay a deceased partner's share on the footing of book values and not of fair values, where no partner had died before and no partner had retired before?

The only practice which existed—and that only on two occasions, namely, in April 1915 and April 1916—was to prepare the accounts, where the interests of all the partners were the same, on the footing of book values. When a partner died or retired, the interests of all the partners were not the same. In the light of that the partnership agreement requiring a 'full' account had to be complied with.

Partners and Each Other

These two aspects of internal partnership relations, fiduciary duties and contractual agreements, are the subject of this chapter.

Fiduciary duties

Partners owe a wide variety of fiduciary duties to each other—in fact since the boundaries of equity in this respect are never closed it is impossible to provide a definitive list. Whilst there have been a few recent cases involving partners many of the current developments have involved their nearest equivalent, the company director, and it is interesting to compare these recent cases with some of the existing ones on partnership. The law of fiduciaries and/or constructive trusts is at present in mid-development and many questions remain unresolved. The Act itself provides for three fiduciary duties which reflect the three main aspects of such liability and it is clear that these duties are applicable to modern situations. In *Floydd* v *Cheney* (1970) Floydd, an architect, engaged an assistant, Cheney, with a view to partnership. There was some dispute as to whether a partnership was ever formed, and when Floydd returned from a trip abroad, Cheney told him he was leaving. Floydd then discovered that certain papers were missing and that others had been photographed. He now sued for the return of all the documents and negatives and for an order restraining Cheney from making use of confidential information. Megarry J decided that even if there was a partnership rather than an employer–employee relationship, the duty of good faith would prevent Cheney acting as he had.

> Such acts seem to me to be a plain breach of the duty of good faith owed by one partner to another. I cannot think it right that even if a partnership is marching to its doom each of the partners should be entitled to a surreptitious free-for-all with the partnership working papers, with the right to make and remove secretly copies of all documents that each partner thinks himself especially concerned with, so that he may continue to work upon them elsewhere.

These fiduciary duties can apply before a formal partnership agreement has been concluded. The High Court of Australia in *United Dominions Corporation Ltd* v *Brian Pty Ltd* (1985), agreed that such duties can apply even if the parties have never reached full agreement on the terms of the partnership. In particular this will be the case where the prospective partners have embarked upon the conduct of the partnership business before the precise terms of any partnership agreement have been settled.

The three main aspects of fiduciary duties incorporated into the Act in ss. 28 to 30 relate to honesty and full disclosure, unauthorised personal profits and conflict of duty and interest. Modern case law may cast a few doubts on the strictness or otherwise of these duties but in essence they remain as they were when the Act was passed.

Honesty and full disclosure

A partnership agreement is one of *uberrimae fidei* (utmost trust) and it is quite clear that each partner must deal with his fellow partners honestly and disclose any relevant fact when dealing with them. A failure to disclose will suffice for a breach of the duty—there need be no proof of common law fraud or negligence. Section 28 is a statutory version of this duty:

> Partners are bound to render true accounts and full information of all things affecting the partnership to any partner or his legal representatives.

This duty is strict and appears to have no exceptions. It applies to 'all things affecting the partnership'. Two examples will suffice to show its scope. In *Law* v *Law* (1905), the two Laws, William and James, were partners in a woollen manufacturer's business in Halifax, Yorkshire. William lived in London and took little part in the running of the business. James bought William's share for £21,000. Later William discovered that the business was worth considerably more and that various assets unknown to him had not been disclosed. The Court of Appeal held that in principle this would allow William to set the contract aside. Cozens-Hardy LJ explained this decision:

> Now it is clear law that, in a transaction between copartners for the sale by one to the other of a share in the partnership business, there is a duty resting upon the purchaser who knows, and is aware that he knows, more about the partnership accounts than the vendor, to put the vendor in possession of all material facts with reference to the partnership assets, and not to conceal what he alone knows.

Thus the ordinary principle of a contract of sale, *caveat emptor* (let the buyer beware), was varied by the fiduciary duty owed by one partner to another. There was no misrepresentation in the common law sense of the word, no actual lies were told but nevertheless the contract was voidable. A more modern example can be found in the Canadian case of *Hogar Estates Ltd* v *Shebron Holdings Ltd* (1980). Hogar and Shebron were partners in a joint land development scheme. Shebron offered to purchase Hogar's interest, stating that the land was not capable of development since planning permission had been refused by the authorities. When that statement was made it was true but Shebron then found out that an important obstacle to the granting of planning permission was likely to be overcome. Shebron did not pass this information on to Hogar and the purchase went ahead. Hogar was granted its request to have the agreement set aside. Shebron's duty to disclose all material facts extended to correcting an earlier true statement when it discovered that it was no longer accurate. Again there was no misrepresentation and no proof of dishonesty but the fiduciary obligation requires neither of these.

Whilst not strictly a fiduciary duty, it is also true that in addition to honesty and full disclosure in partnership affairs, partners must also act without 'culpable negligence'. Thus in *Winsor* v *Schroeder* (1979) where Mrs Schroeder and Mr Winsor bought a house in partnership as a development scheme, the original estimate of £7,000 for the work proved to be optimistic and extra money was needed. Winsor advanced £4,200 and the property was then put on the market at £50,000, the estate agent's valuation being £39,000. A slump in the property market occurred. Whilst Mrs Schroeder was in the Bahamas the estate agents found a purchaser who would offer £36,000 but Winsor turned this down and the property was withdrawn from the market. Eventually the property was sold for £30,000 and £7,000 was paid to Winsor. He claimed a full share from Mrs Schroeder, whose defence was that the loss on the transaction was due in part to Winsor's failure to accept the offer of £36,000. The judge agreed: Winsor had acted honestly and in good faith but his rejection of the offer was below the standard expected of a reasonable businessman in the situation in which he found himself. He should have at least sought additional advice at the time or made further enquiries. We should note that if negligence rather than lack of good faith is alleged there must be a loss as a result of that negligence—an action for breach of contract based on negligence requires proof of loss.

Unauthorised personal profit

It has long been established that a trustee must not profit from his trust and this principle has been broadly applied to fiduciaries such as partners. Thus any private gain, however innocent, which a partner makes as a result of being a partner must be accounted for to the other partners. Difficulties can arise as to what exactly amounts to a profit which results from being a partner, i.e. the fiduciary obligation, and one which results from some other source. Cases involving other types of fiduciary have imposed a strict duty in this respect, applying the full rigours of the rules evolved for trustees, but there are indications that the full consequences might not be extended to the commercial world. The ban on personal profit in the partnership context can be found in s.29 of the Act:

> Every partner must account to the firm for any benefit derived by him without the consent of the other partners from any transaction concerning the partnership, or from any use by him of the partnership property name or business connection.

This is very wide—'any use of the business connection', for example, can extend beyond use of the partnership assets or exploitation of a partnership transaction.

The clearest example of liability under this section is a secret profit;, i.e., where one partner makes a personal profit out of acting on behalf of the partnership, e.g., in negotiating a contract. Thus in *Bentley* v *Craven* (1853), Bentley, Craven and two others were partners in a sugar refinery at Southampton. Craven was the firm's buyer and as such he was able to buy sugar at a discount on the market price. Having bought the sugar at the discounted price he then sold it to the firm at market price. The other partners only later discovered that he had been buying and selling the sugar to them on his own behalf. The firm now successfully claimed his profits from these dealings. It would have made no difference if the other partners could not have obtained a discount so that they in fact suffered no loss since they would have had to pay the market price anyway—the point is that Craven made a profit out of a partnership transaction and he had to account for it. This can be deduced from a similar situation involving a company director in *Boston Deep Sea Fishing & Ice Co.* v *Ansell* (1888), where even though the company could not have obtained the discount the director had to account for it as a secret profit.

It is equally clear that if a partner uses a partnership asset for his own benefit he must account to the other partners for that benefit. Thus in *Pathirana* v *Pathirana* (1967), R.W. Pathirana and A. Pathirana were partners in a service station in Sri Lanka. The station belonged to Caltex (Ceylon) Ltd which had appointed them as agents. R.W. gave three months' notice determining the partnership and during that period he obtained a new agreement with Caltex transferring the agency into his name alone. R.W. then continued to trade in the same way at the same premises under his name. A. successfully applied through the Supreme Court of Ceylon to the Privy Council for a share of the profits from that business under s.29. The agency agreement was a partnership asset and R.W.'s unauthorised use of it was a clear breach of fiduciary duty. Similar use of any asset of the firm will lead to the same result, whether it is a physical or an intangible asset as here.

But what is the position *vis-à-vis* the business 'connection' of the firm? A partner may acquire information, contacts etc. from the firm's business. Is he then forbidden to use such information etc. in any other enterprise not directly connected with the firm's business? Is there liability, in modern terminology, for misuse of a partnership opportunity? The answer depends upon whether it is the source of the information which counts or the use to which it is made. In *Aas* v *Benham* (1891), the defendant was a member of a firm of shipbrokers dealing with the chartering of vessels. He gave considerable assistance in the formation of a company whose objects were the building of ships. He used information and experience gained as a shipbroker in the promotion of the company, even using the firm's notepaper from time to time. He was paid a fee for this work and became a director of the company at a salary. The other partners sought to claim an account of the fee and salary. The Court of Appeal rejected this claim. Information gained in the course of a partnership business could not be used for a partner's own benefit in that type of business, but using it for purposes outside the scope of that business was allowed. In their view it was the use of the information which counted and not the source.

The question is whether that view is still valid in the light of subsequent decisions in fields other than partnership. It is probably true that if the other partners have suffered a loss then the partner will be liable on the basic principle of unjust enrichment. But in other cases, such as in *Aas* v *Benham* where they suffered no loss and the partner acted honestly, it is difficult to justify a duty to account. Yet in the leading case of *Boardman* v *Phipps* (1967), the House of Lords, by a narrow majority, held that a solicitor acting for trustees, who in the course of that work learnt a great deal about a company in which the trust invested, and then dealt personally in the company at a profit, had to account for that profit to the beneficiaries of the trust. This was so even though the enquiries into the company proved to be extremely beneficial to the trust itself and the solicitor's personal investment had in no way deprived the trust of any benefit or opportunity. He had not taken any shares destined for the trust which had invested as heavily as it wanted to. *Aas* v *Benham* was not disapproved of by the House of Lords but the two decisions are not easy to reconcile.

It cannot really be argued that the difference is between the fiduciary duties of a partner, operating in a business environment *vis-à-vis* his partners and those of a solicitor acting for a client in a confidential environment, for much the same result occurred in *Regal (Hastings) Ltd* v *Gulliver* (1942). There, the directors of a company who invested their own money in the purchase of another company as a subsidiary (their original company could only afford to buy 40% of the shares in the second company) and who made a profit when the two companies were later sold, had to account for their profits to the shareholders. Again there was no loss to anyone and no deprivation of an opportunity—further, the only real winners in this case were the new shareholders, i.e. the purchasers, who in effect received a rebate on their purchase price. The House of Lords in deciding this, however, may have doubted the propriety of those who decided that the company could not afford a greater investment since they were the very people who later made the profit.

Another case which suggests that the source rather than the use of the business connection may be more relevant is *Industrial Development Consultants Ltd* v *Cooley* (1972). Cooley was appointed as managing director of the company expressly to attract work from the public sector. He failed to interest the West Midlands Gas Board since the Board did not employ development companies but because of Cooley's record as a public works architect they offered the contract to him personally. Cooley then resigned from the company on the spurious grounds of ill health and took the contract personally. The company now sued for an account of his profits from the contract and won, although it was clear that the company would under no circumstances have been awarded the contract. It has to be said that Cooley's behaviour could not really be described as totally honest and he was specifically employed to obtain for the company that which he so successfully obtained for himself. He had used information given to him in his capacity as a director for his own advantage.

If *Industrial Development Consultants Ltd* v *Cooley* had involved a partnership rather than a company it must be assumed that the decision would have been the same, and in the light of *Boardman* v *Phipps* the liability for use of partnership information or connections would seem to be stricter than in the older case. There are really only two possible defences to an action in such circumstances. The first, and more obvious, is that the profit was made with the knowledge and consent of the other partners. (In *Boardman* v *Phipps* the solicitor had tried to ensure this knowledge and consent but was not considered to have done so.) The second, and more difficult, is that the use of the information took place outside the scope of his fiduciary duties. In that way *Aas* v *Benham* could be interpreted as meaning that an advantage accruing to a partner by use of such information in a totally unconnected environment is outside the scope of the fiduciary relationship called partnership. Suppose the partner receives information as to, say, a business opportunity but he honestly believes that it is too risky to invest partnership money and so he invests personally and makes a profit. Should he have to account for it to the other partners—is that a profit made within the scope of his fiduciary position?

In Canada it was held in *Peso Silver Mines Ltd* v *Cropper* (1966) that if a board of directors rejected such an opportunity for their company, bona fide and honestly, then a director who made a personal investment was immune from liability, and a similar line was taken by the Privy Council in the Australian case of *Queensland Mines Ltd* v *Hudson* (1978). Problems can again arise from the suspicion that the persons rejecting the opportunity for the company are the very persons making the profit and it is clear that the information must not have been given to the directors solely in that capacity, as in *Cooley's* case. The position is far from clear and the ramifications of *Boardman* v *Phipps* have still to be fully worked out. It would be dangerous now to rely on *Aas* v *Benham* as fully authoritative in this area and it would be wise for any partner using the partnership business connection, in however innocent a manner, to obtain a clearance from his fellow partners in order to avoid trouble later on.

The application of the trustee analogy to partnership can be carried even further than the examples used so far. There are technical rules which apply to trustees, such as the rule in *Keech* v *Sandford* (1726) whereby a trustee of a trust which includes a lease as trust property and who acquires a renewal of the lease for his own benefit must hold that lease as a constructive trustee for the beneficiaries. It is possible that such rules apply equally to other fiduciaries such as partners. (In *Re Biss* (1903) the rule was not applied because the person renewing the lease did not clearly occupy a fiduciary position.) The position is less clear when the trustee acquires the reversion on a lease held as trust property and acts honestly and bona fide in so doing. In *Protheroe* v *Protheroe* (1968), the Court of Appeal applied the rule in *Keech* v *Sandford* without question in making the trustee hold the reversion for the benefit of the trust but in earlier cases such as *Bevan* v *Webb* (1905) the rule had only been applied where the lease was renewable by law or custom.

The problem of the purchase of a reversion by one partner when the lease is a partnership asset has arisen in two recent English cases. In *Brenner* v *Rose* (1973), the two partners owned an underlease as a partnership asset. In 1971 the partnership was dissolved and a receiver appointed. At about the same time Rose acquired the leasehold reversion on the underlease and he offered to accept a surrender of the lease in return for disclaiming arrears of rent which the partnership owed. This offer was worth about £750 to the receiver and the top value of the underlease was £1,000. The receiver asked the court whether he could do this. Brightman J held that Rose as a landlord had all the rights of a landlord and the fact that he was a member of the firm which owned the underlease did not affect the position:

> I do not see that the defendant's fiduciary capacity as a member of a partnership which includes the benefit and burden of the underlease raises any sort of equity which should be allowed to prevent him from exercising the rights as landlord which he would have had if he were a stranger to the partnership. I need only refer to *Bevan* v *Webb*.

There are two possible explanations of this decision. Either that *Protheroe* v *Protheroe* is wrong and *Bevan* v *Webb* correct, so that this case merely reflects the general doubts as to the liability of all trustees and fiduciaries in this area, or that, because the partnership was at the time of the acquisition of the reversion at an end, the acquisition did not arise out of his fiduciary position as a partner. If the second explanation is correct it is possible that the main rule in *Keech* v *Sandford* would not have applied either in such circumstances. *Protheroe* v *Protheroe* was neither cited to the judge nor referred to by him so it is difficult to establish definitely which explanation is the correct one. In the following year, however, another judge, Pennycuick V-C, not only approved of *Protheroe* v *Protheroe* but applied it four-square to a partnership situation, this time without any reference either to *Bevan* v *Webb* or *Brenner* v *Rose*.

This second case is *Thompson's trustee* v *Heaton* (1974). Thompson and Heaton were partners and as such acquired a leasehold interest in a farm in 1948. In 1952 the firm was dissolved by mutual consent when it was occupied by Heaton and later by William T. Heaton Ltd, a company controlled by Heaton and his wife. Thompson consented to this occupation. Following the dissolution, the ex-partners made no effective new arrangements with respect to the lease which thus remained an undistributed asset of the partnership. In 1967 Heaton died and Thompson claimed a half share in the lease. In 1967 Heaton's executors purchased the freehold reversion and in 1971 sold the farm with vacant possession for £93,000. Thompson's trustee in bankruptcy sought a declaration that the executors held the reversion as trustees for themselves and Thompson. Pennycuick V-C granted the declaration, applying *Protheroe* v *Protheroe*, and stating the rule that where someone holding a leasehold interest in a fiduciary capacity acquires the freehold reversion he must hold that reversion as part of the trust as being a 'well-known' principle. He regarded the rule as settled and a modern application of the broad principle that a trustee should not make a profit out of his trust.

He thus applied the rule from the law of trusts to partnerships—the fiduciary relationship was established and this could be applied to an undistributed asset of a dissolved partnership—each of the former partners was under the same obligation as he would have been had the partnership still been in existence. The judge limited this rule to those in a fiduciary position but he clearly regarded this as being such. It is difficult, therefore, to reconcile his decision with either of the explanations of *Brenner* v *Rose*. *Protheroe* v *Protheroe* was applied without question, and the purchase of the reversion took place not during the dissolution as in *Brenner* v *Rose*, but after it had finished which must surely be further away from the fiduciary relationship than in the earlier case. The difficulties in the cases can be seen, therefore, either as part of the general uncertainty in this area as applied to all trustees/fiduciaries or as a disagreement as to when the fiduciary relationship between the partners ceases to apply. Either way the future is uncertain.

Conflict of duty and interest

A trustee must not put himself in a position where his duty and his interest may conflict. This applies equally to fiduciaries and so to partners. One example of this duty is that partners must exercise any power of management or finance bona fide for the benefit of the firm and not for their own personal advantage. A clear example of a conflict is where a partner operates a business in competition with the firm. Section 30 of the Act codifies this:

> If a partner, without the consent of the other partners, carries on any business of the same nature as and competing with that of the firm, he must account for and pay over to the firm all profits made by him in that business.

The sole question in this area is whether the business is in competition with that of the firm. If it is, then the liability to account is established and there is no need to show any use of partnership assets etc. in that business as with the previous section.

Whether there is a competitive business is a question of fact. By analogy with the law of trusts it may depend upon how specialised the business is—a yacht chandlery, for example, may require greater protection in terms of area than a firm of newsagents. Thus whilst two yacht chandleries in separate roads may well be in competition it is hard to say the same about newsagents. In the case of *Aas* v *Benham*, which we have just encountered with respect to misuse of the partnership business connection, the Court of Appeal also held that there was no liability under this head. A shipbuilding business was neither the same as nor in competition with the firm's business of shipbroking. The relationship between ss. 29 and 30 should be made clear. Section 29 requires misuse of a partnership asset etc. giving rise to a personal profit but it does not require competition with the firm whereas s. 30 requires competition but no use of partnership assets.

In practice most cases will involve both concepts—misuse of a 'partnership opportunity' and competition with the partnership business. One final example is the case of *Trimble* v *Goldberg* (1906), a decision of the Privy Council on appeal from the Court of Appeal of the Transvaal. In 1902 Trimble, Goldberg and Bennet formed a partnership to try to acquire some properties belonging to a Mr Holland. These properties consisted of 5,500 shares in a company, Sigma Syndicate, and various plots of land, known as 'stands', mainly in Johannesburg. Trimble was given a power of attorney by the other to negotiate the sale and this went very smoothly, the purchase price being satisfied by a down payment and mortgage over the properties. Subsequently Trimble made an offer, through Holland, for other 'stands' belonging to the Syndicate, and was granted an option to buy them for £110,000. He then asked Bennett to join him in this speculation which was accepted. Goldberg knew nothing of these other purchases until nearly a year later. He now applied for a share of the profits of the separate speculation on the basis of a breach of their fiduciary duties by Trimble and Bennett.

The Privy Council rejected this claim, reversing the court below. Lord Macnaghten giving the judgment rejected claims based on both s. 29 and s. 30 of the Act.

> The purchase was not within the scope of the partnership. The subject of the purchase was not part of the business of the partnership, or an undertaking in rivalry with the partnership, or indeed connected with it in any proper sense. Nor was the information on which it seems Trimble acted acquired by reason of his position as partner, or even by reason of his connection with the Sigma Syndicate.

It was neither a misuse of the partnership 'business connection' (after *Boardman* v *Phipps* this is not necessarily certain) nor in competition with the firm. On the latter point, since the syndicate gained £10,000 on the sale which benefited the firm as a shareholder of that syndicate, it could hardly be regarded as being in competition with the firm.

Contract: implied terms

The contractual framework within which a partnership operates and the fiduciary duties of partners apply depends upon the terms of the agreement between the partners. As we have seen, both the written terms and those imposed by the Act may be varied by express or implied agreement under s. 19, and the opening part of s. 24 confirms this. In effect this section, in addition to s. 25 which relates to expulsion clauses, provides nine rules which apply to a partnership unless there is evidence of contrary intention, express or implied:

> The interests of partners in the partnership property and their rights and duties in relation to the partnership shall be determined, subject to any agreement express or implied between the partners, by the following rules.

Leaving aside expulsion clauses for the moment, we can divide these implied terms into three general categories: management and control, finance and change of partners. Since these are all areas where the actual agreement is of supreme importance we can only ascertain guidelines as to the effect and practicality of the rules in s. 24.

Management and control

We have seen enough about partnerships by now to know that they depend upon a joint venture based on mutual trust. It will not surprise anyone therefore that s. 24(5) provides that: 'Every partner may take part in the management of the partnership business'. A right to management participation is a necessary consequence of unlimited liability for the debts of the firm (remember that a limited partner has no rights of management and if he interferes in the business he will lose his limited liability). So basic is this right that even in company law the courts have applied it by analogy to the so-called partnership company cases (i.e., a company which is in economic terms a partnership but in legal terms remains a company) so that withdrawal of the right to participate in the management of such a company can lead to a winding up even though no canon of company law has been infringed (see *Ebrahimi* v *Westbourne Galleries Ltd* (1973)). In fact such companies are defined by reference to an implied right of management participation. It is obvious, therefore, that breach of such a fundamental right can also lead to a dissolution of a partnership and it has also in the past been enforced by injunction.

The nature of partnership as a joint venture is also reflected in s. 24(6), which follows naturally from s. 24(5): 'No partner shall be entitled to remuneration for acting in the partnership business'. The idea is that each partner will receive his reward by a straightforward share of the profits and, possibly, interest on his original capital investment. The basic rule therefore is no additional 'salaries'. (There is an exception, as we shall see in chapter 7, where one partner continues the business for the purpose of a winding up following a dissolution.) On the other hand, it is not unknown for some partners to be more active in the business than others and for those partners to take in addition to a share of the profits a 'salary' to be deducted before the net profits are shared out. Many permutations are possible involving 'senior' partners, 'middle' partners and 'junior' partners who only receive a 'salary'—we have already encountered the problem of 'salaried partners' in chapter 2. The important point to grasp in all this is, of course, that such 'salaries' are not salaries in the ordinary sense of the word but merely a way of apportioning the profits by agreement. For tax purposes, for example, all the profits of a partnership received by a partner are taxable as the receipts of a trade or profession and not as a salary under a contract of employment. The partnership does not 'exist', remember, and a partner cannot employ himself.

Section 24(6) is therefore frequently altered by the partnership agreement, although there must be evidence of such alteration—the fact that one partner is required to do all the work will not in itself, apparently, be sufficient to provide contrary intention. There is Australian authority in *Re Noonan* (1949) for the proposition that if all the partners are required to devote all their time etc. to the partnership business and one fails to do so then the others will automatically be entitled to additional remuneration for covering for him, but this has been widely criticised in its own country and it seems preferable to sue for breach of contract in such circumstances. The combined effect of s. 24(5) and (6) is therefore that in the absence of contrary agreement the law implies that each partner shall participate equally in the work and rewards of the joint venture, guided and controlled by their fiduciary duties to each other (if only Adam had never eaten that apple!).

Equal rights of management presuppose give and take between the partners in the actual decision-making process. The history of the EEC shows how dangerous it is to give each party a veto over virtually everything. Section 24(8) accordingly provides:

> Any difference arising as to ordinary matters connected with the partnership business may be decided by a majority of the partners, but

no change may be made in the nature of the partnership business without the consent of all existing partners.

The distinction is therefore between day-to-day business decisions and the fundamental nature of the business itself (unlike a company, therefore, a partnership cannot alter its objects except by unanimous consent, subject, as ever, to contrary intention). If the matter goes to the fundamental nature of the firm it is equally clear that the implied rule is unanimity—e.g., the admission of a new partner (see below), changes in the deed, sale of a substantial part of the undertaking. It will be a question of fact in each case whether the dispute relates to the running or the structure of the firm.

In *Highley* v *Walker* (1910) three partners ran a large and profitable business. Two of the partners agreed to allow the son of one of them to be taken on as an apprentice to learn the business. The other partner objected and applied for an injunction. Warrington J decided that since the majority had acted properly, discussing the matter with the other partner, listening to his arguments and generally acting bona fide, their decision should stand. It was an ordinary matter connected with the partnership business within s. 24(8) and thus a question for majority decision. This case is a good example of the interaction between the contractual framework and the fiduciary duties. The powers of the majority given by s. 24(8) must be exercised bona fide and not so as to deprive the minority of their rights, or to gain an unfair advantage over them.

What happens if a minority partner suspects that he is being unfairly treated by the majority? He can sue for breach of contract if there has been a specific breach of a particular agreement; he can apply for the appointment of a receiver (see chapter 7) or, in the last analysis, he can apply for a dissolution on the just and equitable ground. There is, however, no equivalent to section 459 of the Companies Act 1985 which allows the court to make any order it wishes to protect a minority shareholder in a company who has been the victim of unfairly prejudicial conduct. All the possible remedies are, however, very public and since most partnerships today are professional partnerships, of doctors, lawyers, accountants etc., it is very common to include in the partnership agreement a clause whereby disputes between the partners are to be referred to arbitration. Whether a particular clause is wide enough to cover the dispute is a question of fact but assuming it is, in the majority of cases the courts will enforce the arbitration agreement and under recent legislation appeals to the court from a decision of an arbitrator are difficult to sustain—it is no longer enough, for example, to allege that the arbitrator might have made a mistake as to the law involved.

On the other hand, under s. 4 of the Arbitration Act 1950 the court can prevent the matter being referred to arbitration at all if it allows a court action to proceed. It seems that this will only be done when third parties are involved or where the allegation involves fraud or charges which would be damaging to the career of a professional man. It is less clear whether the courts will allow an arbitrator to settle dissolution disputes and we will come back to that matter in chapter 7. There is no doubt, however, that the vast majority of partnership disputes are settled quickly and without fuss by arbitration and that this accounts for the relative scarcity of modern cases on the subject. It is this very privacy which attracts modern partnerships to arbitration and one of the reasons why, for the most part, the court will enforce the agreement to do so—the complaining partner contracted on precisely that basis and with precisely that intention.

One problem for a minority partner is to prove unfair treatment. To assist him in this, s. 24(9) provides:

> The partnership books are to be kept at the place of business of the partnership (or the principal place, if there is more than one), and every partner may, when he thinks fit, have access to and inspect and copy any of them.

This unfettered right to inspect the books is a valuable one and again flows from the nature of a partnership. The courts have in fact strengthened this right by allowing a partner to appoint an agent to inspect the books on his behalf. In *Bevan* v *Webb* (1901) the dormant partners in a business were about to sell out to the active partners. They employed a valuer to inspect the books but the active partners refused him access, arguing that s. 24(9) only referred to partners and not to their agents. The Court of Appeal ordered that he be allowed to inspect the books. The purpose of s. 24(9) is to allow partners to inform themselves as to the position of the firm so that if a partner needs an agent to assist him in understanding the position the agent may inspect the books.

The main objection to the use of agents is that they will then have access to confidential information about the other partners. The Court of Appeal in *Bevan* v *Webb* had an answer for this. Henn Collins LJ said:

> There is, of course, a natural common-sense limitation of such a right of inspection. The inspection is to be of books and documents in which all the partners are interested, and the inspection cannot be made in such a way as to curtail the rights or prejudice the position of the other partners. They are all interested in the matter, and one partner cannot assert his

right in derogation of the rights of the others. But the interests of the others can be amply safeguarded by placing a limitation upon the particular agency which the inspecting partner desires to employ. The agent employed must be a person to whom no reasonable objection can be taken, and the purpose for which he seeks to use the right of inspection must be one consistent with the main purposes and the well-being of the whole partnership.

An agent who is employed by a rival firm can thus be excluded. Partners and their agents cannot, of course, misuse any information gained in breach of their fiduciary duties. It is interesting to speculate on the court's attitude to the right of inspection in the light of modern technology. Partnership records etc. may now be stored in a computer or on a floppy disc on a word-processor, and photocopying is an everyday occurrence. We can assume that the word 'books' in s. 24(9) would not be applied literally (although the Companies Act was amended to provide for computer records) and in general the limitation placed on inspection in *Bevan* v *Webb* could be equally well applied in a modern context. A partner has always had the right to take copies and photocopying is at once easier and more susceptible of misuse.

Financial affairs

The essential criterion for a partnership is mutual sharing of profits and losses. It is of little surprise therefore that s. 24(1) provides that, subject to contrary agreement:

> All the partners are entitled to share equally in the capital and profits of the business, and must contribute equally towards the losses whether of capital or otherwise sustained by the firm.

Whilst this may be the ideal position it is in fact rare in practice and often negatived by contrary agreement. Usually capital investment in particular is unequal and in some cases the skill and management of one partner are regarded as his 'capital' investment whilst the dormant partner provides the whole of the actual financial capital. Entitlement to capital is therefore almost always a matter for the particular agreement, express or implied, between the partners, and in such cases the facts themselves will destroy a presumption that capital shares are equal. The rule in the Act is merely one of convenience based on the old stand-by 'equality is equity'.

In practice most problems arise when there have been losses. If there have been losses of capital are these to be borne equally by all the partners under s. 24(1) even though their original contributions were unequal? The point usually arises, of course, on a dissolution when each partner seeks the return of his investment. A loss in capital occurs when a partnership debt cannot be paid without reducing the assets of the firm. An example may help to explain the position. Suppose A, B and C are partners sharing profits equally. A invested £9,000, B £6,000 and C £3,000 into the business. After paying off all the creditors only £12,000 remains. Does each partner bear one-third of the £6,000 loss or do they share the losses in a ratio of 3 : 2 : 1 in accordance with their capital contributions? In other words does A receive £7,000 or £6,000 out of the £12,000 remaining? The problem is even more acute if A invests £9,000, B £6,000 and C nothing and there is a loss of capital. Does C have to reimburse A and B for his share of their loss? The answer is that in the absence of a contrary agreement, yes, and A in the first example above will only receive £6,000. Section 24(1) makes this quite clear—losses even of capital are to be borne in the same proportion as profits are shared even though the capital contributions are unequal. If one partner becomes insolvent so that his share of the capital disappears the other partners, again in the absence of contrary intention, must bear that loss equally.

Although losses are shared equally in this way it is highly unlikely that s. 24(1) will lead to an automatic equal distribution of capital on a dissolution where there have been no losses. Whether this is because s. 24(1), being declaratory, has not altered the existing law on the point or because the fact of unequal contribution will always provide evidence of a contrary intention is probably academic. The Australian court in *Kelly* v *Tucker* (1907) found it difficult to decide which but had no difficulty in coming to the conclusion that on such a dissolution partners are entitled to receive all their capital contributions in full before surplus assets are distributed (in profit-sharing ratio). In this case the dormant partner supplied £800 as the only capital, the other partner to do all the work. On a dissolution the court held that whatever the effect of s. 24(1) there was an implied agreement that the dormant partner should be entitled to repayment of his £800. Higgins J thought that s. 24(1) should also be so construed: 'Prima facie, where one partner has skill, and the other has money, when one departs with his skill, the other—one would think— should be able to depart with his money'.

Thus in our example of A, B and C, each should be entitled to a return of his capital before surplus assets are distributed, so that £18,000 capital does not go as to £6,000 to each of them but as to £9,000, £6,000 and £3,000 respectively. If there are £18,000 additional surplus assets (e.g., undrawn profits) then those will be shared equally. Capital in this context refers to fixed capital, i.e., that which underlies the business as opposed to circulating capital, which is turned over in the course of the business. The distinction is not always easy to make as tax lawyers are continually discovering. Nor is the concept of a profit much easier to define (tax law again has abundant examples) but in the context of internal partnership affairs it probably means whatever the partners have decided it means. Thus a growth in the value of a fixed asset may be regarded as a profit for this purpose unless the partners have agreed to regard it as an increase in capital rather than a profit.

The distinction between capital and profits is important—for one thing we have just seen that profit-sharing ratios rarely apply to capital distributions. For another, s. 24(4) provides that: 'A partner is not entitled, before the ascertainment of the profits, to interest on the capital subscribed by him'. Again this is subject to contrary intention and it is not unusual to find a clause authorising the payment of interest on capital to be paid before the net profits are ascertained. In a sense this is the counterbalance to the payment of a 'salary' to an active partner and it is no more 'interest' in the true sense of that word than the latter is a salary. It is another way of slicing up the profits prior to applying the profit-sharing ratio and, just as a partner cannot employ himself, he cannot truly pay himself interest, and tax is charged accordingly with the interest simply being regarded as an allocation of business profits. (The tax position is more complex when the partner receiving the interest has retired from the firm but has left his capital in the business in return for interest.)

The Act does, however, distinguish between a contribution of capital by a partner and a further advance so as to create a form of partner/creditor in such cases. This is yet another example of the problems caused by lack of legal personality. Section 24(3) provides:

> A partner making, for the purpose of the partnership, any actual payment or advance beyond the amount of capital which he has agreed to subscribe, is entitled to interest at the rate of five per cent per annum from the date of the payment or advance.

Of course any partner making a formal advance by way of a quasi-loan would be unduly benevolent to accept 5% in today's financial climate where 12% would not be regarded as generous. But this section is more likely to apply, in the sense of not being ousted, to cases where the partner settles a partnership debt out of his own money—that is just as much an advance as a formal 'loan' and interest is then payable.

The exact status of this 'loan' is difficult to define. If it is not capital it must be a loan, but a partner cannot *lend* money to himself (the firm doesn't exist, remember). In Australia such advances have been held not to be loans for the purpose of the general law restricting loans, but in *Craig* v *Finance Consultants Pty Ltd* (1964) where a company guaranteed advances by partners to their firm, the Full Court of the New South Wales Supreme Court held that the company was liable on the guarantee even though no final account between the partners had been drawn up (the only way to recover capital). The guarantee could apply on non-payment when the debt was due and payable. This was done apparently on the basis that this is what the business and commercial world would expect to happen being 'unfamiliar with the law and not much interested in its principle'. With respect this seems to create an anomalous situation and there is nothing in s. 25(3) to suggest that an advance is any more recoverable than capital—just that a share of the profits, to be called 'interest', must first be debited from profits before they are distributed. The only need to distinguish an advance from capital, apart from on a dissolution, is that, in respect of an advance, 'interest' is payable subject to contrary intention rather than the other way round. But since 'interest' is frequently payable on capital there is little distinction in practice.

If one partner does settle a partnership debt, either willingly or unwillingly because he is the one who has been sued (remember all are liable for such debts but any one can be sued for the whole amount), he has a right to claim an indemnity from his fellow partners. Thus, s. 24(2) provides that:

The firm must indemnify every partner in respect of payments made and personal liabilities incurred by him—

(a) In the ordinary and proper conduct of the business of the firm; or,

(b) In or about anything necessarily done for the preservation of the business or property of the firm.

Part (a) is reasonably straightforward and is declaratory of any agent's right to reimbursement for expenses etc. incurred whilst acting within his authority as well as providing a machinery for equal sharing of losses under s. 24(1). It probably does not extend to physical as opposed to financial loss, and it must be a 'proper' way of conducting the business, which may imply some financial limit.

An example of the operation of s. 24(2)(a) is the case of *Matthews* v

Ruggles-Brise (1911). Coupe and Matthews took a lease for 42 years from 1879 as trustees for themselves and eight other partners. In 1886 the firm was incorporated and the company took over all the assets and liabilities of the firm. Coupe died in 1886 and in 1887 Matthews assigned the lease to the company. He died in 1891. In 1909 the landlords sued Matthews's executors for arrears of rent and breach of convenant in the lease. The company was insolvent and the action was settled by a surrender of the lease and a payment by Matthews's executors to the landlord of £5,750. They now claimed a contribution from Coupe's executors and the judge agreed. The lease remained the liability of Coupe and Matthews—the company's liability was in addition to it. Thus the payment was a partnership debt and Coupe had to indemnify Matthews for the loss in proportion to their shares in the firm. The assignment to the company did not affect the original nature of the liability.

Part (b) of s. 24(2) is in effect an extension of the agency of necessity whereby an agent can be indemnified even if he acts outside his authority, provided he was unable to communicate with his principal and acted in good faith in doing what was necessary in the principal's interest. Whilst the section does not require proof of lack of communication, it does require good faith (fiduciary duty) and necessity. In fact, however, if there was time to check with the other partners it may well be that failure to do so would amount to lack of good faith and so prevent any recovery. This statutory right of indemnity is also backed up by the common law and the Civil Liability (Contribution) Act 1978 where a partner has, e.g., committed a tort in the authorised conduct of the business. He may not be so entitled, however, if he has acted carelessly in incurring the liability.

Change of partners

Partnership being based on mutual trust, the introduction of a new partner is usually a sensitive issue since the new partner will have the power to impose severe financial burdens on the other partners. It is not surprising, therefore, that the Act does not regard such a matter as one for the majority to decide under s. 24(8); instead it provides in s. 24(7) that: 'No person may be introduced as a partner without the consent of all existing partners'. This has always been the case, even in Roman law, and goes to the root of partnership. However, it is, like all the other provisions of s. 24, subject to contrary intention and a contrary clause in the partnership agreement will be given effect to. Sometimes such clauses are very wide and allow the introduction of a new partner with virtually no restrictions at all, in other cases they are limited to the introduction of a specific person or class of person (e.g., children of existing partners) or limited by some form of veto in the other partners.

In *Byrne* v *Reid* (1902) the clause gave each partner the right to nominate and introduce any other person into the firm. Byrne nominated his son who was employed in the firm, but the other partners refused to admit him. They then consented to his admission but failed to execute any of the documents necessary for this. The Court of Appeal decided that since the clause was so wide and contained no restrictions the other partners had consented in advance to the son's nomination. There was no reason why they should not so agree or give their consent in advance. Thus even without the consent order he would still have had the right to become a partner. The court applied the doctrine in *Page* v *Cox* (1852), that if there is a person validly nominated as a partner under a clause in a partnership agreement, the result is that a trust is created with reference to the partnership assets for the purpose of enabling the nominated person to take that to which he is entitled under the deed—he is a partner in equity.

Since the son could be regarded as a beneficiary under a trust in such a case he was entitled to the equitable remedy of specific performance to ensure that the trust was carried out. He was thus entitled to the execution of two deeds by the other partners—one whereby he was bound to observe the terms of the existing agreement (that appears to have been the real source of the dispute) and one vesting his share of the partnership assets in him—in fact he was to take over his father's share of the business. Provided, therefore, a person has been validly nominated as a partner and there are no conditions to be fulfilled he will be able to obtain specific performance of the trust created by such nomination under the agreement. But this depends, of course, on the nomination's being valid and unconditional—unless both can be established there can be no trust and in the absence of a contract to which he is a party there can be no specific performance—equity will not assist a volunteer.

The Scottish case of *Martin* v *Thompson* (1962) illustrates the difficulties of proving a valid nomination. The agreement between two partners provided that on the death of one of them control of the business was to pass to the survivor but that either partner could by will 'nominate' his widow to his share of the partnership. On the death of one of the partners his whole estate passed under his will to his widow. The House of Lords held that this did not make her a partner, it simply operated as an assignment of her husband's share in the assets. A general bequest of all the estate to his widow could hardly be regarded as a nomination for the purpose of the clause. It might have been different if he had specifically bequeathed her the partnership share—there was no evidence that the widow was being given the right to become a partner. The problems associated with an assignment of a partner's share of the assets (voluntary and involuntary) are dealt with at the end of this chapter. For the moment it is sufficient to note the distinction between a person introducing a replacement for himself into a partnership as a partner (*Byrne* v *Reid*) and an assignment of his share of the assets as in this case—an assignee as such does not become a partner.

Sometimes there are conditions attached to the right to nominate a new partner. Thus in *Re Franklin and Swaythling's arbitration* (1929), the clause allowed a partner to introduce any qualified person as a new partner provided that the other partners should consent to his admission—such consent not to be unreasonably withheld. Franklin nominated his son as a new partner but the other partners refused to admit him. The judge decided that the fact that consent was necessary and had not been given (whether reasonably or unreasonably had not been established) prevented the doctrine of *Page* v *Cox* from applying. Maugham J put the point this way:

> The applicant admittedly is not at present a partner. The applicant admittedly has no contractual rights. The applicant may be able to establish hereafter that he is a cestui que trust under the doctrine of *Page* v *Cox*, but at the present he cannot do anything of the sort; because, for aught I know, the general partners have properly exercised their rights, and in that case he has no more interest in the partnership assets than a stranger.

In fact the son in *Franklin's* case was in even deeper trouble, for the nomination clause went on to say that any dispute as to whether the consent had been unreasonably withheld should be referred to arbitration and his actual application in that case was for the matter to be referred to arbitration. Since he could not take the benefit of a trust without proving that the consent had been unreasonably withheld and that was the issue for arbitration, and since he was not a party to the original arbitration agreement, he had no rights under it to force the matter to arbitration under the Arbitration Act 1950. The position would have been different, however, if the clause had been similar to that in *Byrne* v *Reid* so that by simply being nominated he became a partner in equity. In enforcing that trust the court might well allow the nominee to invoke an arbitration clause to perfect his entry into the firm.

Expulsion clauses

The law has always been keen to protect a partner from being victimised by his fellow partners and s. 25 of the Act is quite clear: 'No majority of the partners can expel any partner unless a power to do so has been conferred by express agreement between the partners'. Thus there can be no expulsion without an express clause to that effect. An expulsion may or may not involve a dissolution; thus if A and B expel C the partnership continues, but if A 'expels' his sole partner B there is in effect a dissolution—this overlap may explain one of the problems associated with such clauses. There are three questions involved in considering expulsion clauses: (a) is the expulsion within the terms of the clause itself; (b) do the rules of natural justice apply to the expulsion procedure and if so have they been complied with; and (c) did the expelling partners act in good faith and in accordance with their fiduciary duties?

If the answer to all these questions is yes then the courts will support an expulsion. Thus in *Carmichael* v *Evans* (1904) where a junior partner in a draper's firm was convicted of travelling on a train without paying his fare and so defrauding the railway company (on more than one occasion) he was held to have been validly expelled under a clause which allowed expulsion for any 'flagrant breach of the duties of a partner'. This was so, even though the offence was not committed whilst on partnership business, because it was inconsistent with his practice as a partner and would adversely affect the firm's business (an account had appeared in the press). Honesty generally was regarded as a duty of a partner, inside or outside the firm. It would clearly depend upon the offence as to whether a criminal conviction would amount to a flagrant breach of the duties of a partner—crimes of strict liability might not always be so regarded.

The first question is therefore whether the expulsion falls within the terms of the clause. Adultery, for example, may be many things but it does not amount to financial misconduct likely to damage a banking business. In *Re a Solicitor's arbitration* (1962) a clause stated that: 'If any partner shall commit or be guilty of any act of professional misconduct the other partners may by notice in writing expel him from the partnership'. One partner, Egerton, served a notice of expulsion on *both* his fellow partners on the grounds of alleged misconduct, claiming that the word 'partner' in the clause could include the plural. This argument was based on s. 61 of the Law of Property Act 1925 which implies the plural for the singular in all deeds unless the context otherwise provides. The judge found that the context did provide otherwise—this clause was designed to allow two partners to expel the third: it did not cover the situation here for that would allow the minority to expel the majority which would be strange when read against the background of s. 25.

On the other hand the courts will not strictly apply the letter of an expulsion clause if that would produce a nonsensical situation. Thus in *Hitchman* v *Crouch Butler Savage Associates* (1983), an expulsion clause required the signature of the senior partner in order for it to be valid. This was held not to apply where the partner to be expelled was the senior partner himself. Although such clauses are strictly construed they must give effect to the intention of the parties in view of the document as a whole. It was not possible for a partner to expel himself since expulsion was dismissal against the will of the person being expelled and so the clause had to be construed so as to dispense with the requirement of the signature.

The second question is whether the rules of natural justice apply to such expulsion procedures and if so whether they have been complied with. Specifically this would require that the partner concerned should be given the precise cause of the complaint against him and be afforded an opportunity to defend himself.

In *Barnes* v *Youngs* (1898), the clause allowed the majority to expel a partner for breach of certain duties and also provided that in the case of a dispute the matter should go to arbitration. The majority purported to expel Barnes but gave no details of the particular act complained of (he was in fact living with his common law wife). Romer J declared the expulsion to be unlawful—the majority had failed to inform him as to the cause of complaint and to allow him to answer the allegation. Good faith required this. However, this approach was totally rejected by the Court of Appeal in *Green* v *Howell* (1910). In this case one partner expelled his fellow partner for what were admittedly flagrant breaches of the agreement—the clause allowed this and provided for reference to an arbitrator in the case of a dispute. The partner protested that he had been given no opportunity of explanation. The Court of Appeal decided that in such circumstances there was no need to observe the rules of natural justice since the expelling partner had otherwise acted in good faith. The expelling partner was acting in an administrative character—he was not acting in a judicial capacity since he was simply serving a notice which could lead to an arbitration where the matter would be considered judicially.

There is some doubt, therefore, as to whether these procedural requirements apply to expulsion clauses. In an article, 'The good faith principle and the expulsion clause in partnership law' (1969) 33 Conv (NS) 32, Bernard Davies argued that *Green* v *Howell* was really a case of dissolution masquerading as an expulsion (only one partner was left) and that it only applied to a notice setting such a dispute on its way to arbitration. *Barnes* v *Youngs* should continue to apply to a genuine expulsion to be decided on by a majority of the partners who must discuss the matter and act in a quasi-judicial manner. Since that article, Plowman J was faced with a similar problem in the case of *Peyton* v *Mindham* (1972). The two doctors had been partners for eight years. The deed provided that if either partner was incapacitated from performing his fair share of the work of the practice for more than nine consecutive months the other partners could determine the partnership by notice. Peyton suffered a cerebral haemorrhage on 2 January 1970 and although he returned on 1 October 1970 he was in fact incapable of performing his share of the practice. On 9 October Mindham served the notice and Peyton argued that this notice was invalid because it was issued before either Mindham could ascertain or Peyton could demonstrate that he could perform his fair share. The judge rejected this defence and allowed the notice to stand since Mindham had otherwise acted bona fide. The reasoning was on a par with *Green* v *Howell*; Mindham had not been acting judicially when serving the notice.

It now seems unlikely that *Barnes* v *Youngs* is good law even though both *Green* v *Howell* and *Peyton* v *Mindham* can be distinguished on the grounds of being dissolution cases in reality and that in both cases the actual complaint had actually been substantiated by the time of the decision on natural justice. The only requirement that probably applies is the general duty of good faith—i.e., in exercising the power of expulsion the partners must have been acting bona fide for the benefit of the firm as a whole and not for their own ends: a specific application of the rule that a partner must not put himself in a position where his duty and interest conflict. Partners, like majority shareholders and directors of companies must exercise their powers in such a way. It is, for example, well established that a majority of shareholders cannot alter the articles of a company to give themselves power to buy out the minority unless it will be for the benefit of the company as a whole (e.g., to remove a competitor from a private company's membership).

The classic example in partnership law is *Blisset* v *Daniel* (1853). The expulsion clause was being exercised by the majority in order to obtain the other partner's share at a discount. The court had little difficulty in holding that the power had been improperly exercised. The judge, Page Wood V-C, said that it was quite clear that the power was being used solely for the majority partners' exclusive benefit and that such use of the power was an abuse and would not be allowed. The power must be used for the purpose it was intended.

Assignment of the partnership share

There is a clear distinction between the introduction of A as a replacement partner for B and the assignment of B's share in the partnership to A. As we have seen, the introduction of a new partner requires the consent of all the other partners unless the agreement provides to the contrary and the intended partner is able to enforce that agreement. In such cases A replaces B totally in the firm and acquires all his rights and liabilities *vis-à-vis* the other partners. An assignment, on the other hand, does not, unless the contrary is agreed, make A a partner in B's place, it simply assigns B's rights in the partnership assets and/or profits to A: A does not become a partner. Such assignments may be commercial, e.g., a mortgage, or personal, e.g., a divorce agreement. An assignment may also occur involuntarily, i.e., by a judgment creditor who, having been awarded judgment against a partner for a private debt, then wishes to levy execution of that debt over the partner's share of the firm's assets. Let us look at the position of these two types of assignee, voluntary and involuntary, in turn.

Voluntary assignments

The rights of a voluntary assignee of a share in a partnership are set out in s. 31 of the Act first as to his rights whilst the partnership is a going concern:

(1) An assignment by any partner of his share in the partnership, either absolute or by way of mortgage or redeemable charge, does not, as against the other partners, entitle the assignee, during the continuance of the partnership, to interfere in the management or administration of the partnership business or affairs, or to require any accounts of the partnership transactions, or to inspect the partnership books, but entitles the assignee only to receive the share of profits to which the assigning partner would otherwise be entitled, and the assignee must accept the account of profits agreed to by the partners.

Such an assignee is therefore considerably restricted in his control of the assigned assets. He cannot interfere in any way in the running of the firm; he cannot inspect the books or demand an account—all he has is the right to the assignor's share of the profits but even then he must accept the other partner's accounts as to the amount of those profits.

This obligation to accept the other partners' accounts was taken to extreme lengths in *Re Garwood's trusts* (1903). Garwood was one of three partners in a colliery business who received an equal share of the profits but took no 'salary' since all the work was done by employees. In 1889 Garwood charged his share of the partnership with payment of £10,000 to two trustees of a settlement for the benefit of his wife on his separation from her. He later agreed to pay all his share of the profits into the settlement. In 1893 the partners, including Garwood, decided to take part personally in the running of the business and that accordingly they should each be paid a salary before net profits were ascertained. Garwood received nothing by way of salary after 1895. Mrs Garwood, whose income under the settlement was thus reduced by the salaries payable to the other two partners, sought to have these payments stopped. Buckley J, applying s. 31(1), held that the decision to pay the salaries was a matter within the administration or management of the firm and so a matter entirely for the decision of the partners and one which could not be challenged by Mrs Garwood as an assignee. She had to accept the account of profits as agreed between the partners.

On the other hand it is clear that in coming to this decision the judge was impressed by the fact that the actions of the partners were bona fide, in the sense that they were not done with the intention of defeating Mrs Garwood's rights nor were they improper or fraudulent. The reason for the partners' increased activity was to superintend sales at the pit-head so as to stop thefts which were occurring. Stopping such thefts would, of course, actually increase the net profits. It follows that if the partners' actions had not been bona fide the result might well have been different. The rule as to s. 31(1) is therefore as laid down by Buckley J in that case:

> The intention of the Acts was to substitute the assignee for the assignor as the person entitled to such profits as the assignor would have received if there had not been an assignment, but to give the assignee no right to interfere at all with anything bona fide done in management or administration.

It is an open point whether a decision to alter the actual profit-sharing ratios would fall within this exception. Presumably if it was done bona fide for management reasons there could be no objection—in any event the practical effect of a 'salary' payment such as in *Re Garwood* is the same as an adjustment of the profit-sharing ratio. As we have seen they are all simply different methods of allocating the profits.

The position of an assignee changes when the partnership goes into dissolution. In such cases s. 31(2) applies:

> In case of a dissolution of the partnership, whether as respects all the partners or as respects the assigning partner, the assignee is entitled to receive the share of the partnership assets to which the assigning partner

is entitled as between himself and the other partners, and, for the purpose of ascertaining that share, to an account as from the date of dissolution.

Thus where the assigning partner is leaving the firm and taking out his share or when the whole firm is being dissolved the assignee has two rights: (a) to the assigning partner's share and (b) to an account as from the date of dissolution to ascertain that share. He is no longer interested in profits as they arise, he needs to quantify the actual share of the assets and so, unlike s. 31(1), he is entitled to an account. If there is no such account the assignee is not bound by the actions of the other partners.

In *Watts* v *Driscoll* (1901), a father lent £1,900 to his son to set him up in partnership, and he secured that sum by taking an assignment of his son's share in the firm. The son fell out with the other partner and sold his share to him for £500. The father claimed an account to enable him to ascertain the value of the son's share irrespective of the agreement. The Court of Appeal agreed. Section 31(2) was intended to give the assignee a right to an account whenever a dissolution takes place irrespective of whether there is a private agreement between the other partners. On the facts no accounts had been taken. The son made up his mind to leave the partnership and made a bargain without the father's knowledge or consent to sell his share for £500. There was no evidence that this was the correct valuation since the agreement took no account of the goodwill—it could not therefore be construed as an unofficial account. The father was entitled to an account properly drawn up to ascertain the true value of the son's share.

Two points need to be made here. First, that the Court of Appeal came to this decision even though there was no evidence of fraud in the conduct of the partners in fixing the share at £500. The decision was that an account had to be taken by virtue of the Act and the existing partners simply could not agree otherwise as between themselves. Second, that the right to have an account is simply the right to an account 'bona fide taken in the course of the partnership on the footing of its being a going concern' according to the Court of Appeal in *Watts's* case. Thus if a bona fide account had shown the share to be worth only £500 that would have been the end of the matter. This was in fact the position prior to the Act and the court was anxious to make it clear that this section had not altered the law by giving a right to a different type of account.

But an assignor is entitled to an account on that basis. Thus in *Bonnin* v *Neame* (1910), assignees were held not to be bound by an arbitration agreement in the deed under which the partners wished to resolve their dispute as to the valuation of their shares on a dissolution. Since the assignees were not parties to the agreement they could not be bound by the arbitration clause—they were entitled to rely on their statutory right to ask the court to order an account. The court refused to stay the action pending the arbitration. Swinfen Eady J summed up the position:

> Then how can an account taken behind their backs, and to which they are not parties, bind them? If I were to determine that they were bound by an account taken as between the partners, it would be not to allow them the right which the statute confers upon them. They are entitled to an account, and to hold that they are to be bound by an account taken in their absence and that unless they can show some fraud or some manifest error they are not to be entitled to come to the court for an account would be to ignore the language of the statute altogether.

There is some doubt as to whether an assignee as such acquires any liability for partnership losses. Of course he will be liable to third parties, by virtue of s. 14, if he represents that he is a partner, but it would seem that otherwise the effect of s. 31(1) is to exempt him—he is by definition not a partner. This is the view taken in Australia but there is some doubt cast on that sensible proposition by the English case of *Dodson* v *Downey* (1901), where Farwell J found that an assignee was liable to indemnify his assignor against partnership losses. This decision has been much criticised and seems to have been based on a misunderstanding of the law of vendor and purchaser which was used by way of analogy. Clearly since an assignee is not a partner he should not be liable as such either—he has no right of management and the law would be inconsistent if the Australian cases were held not to apply here.

Involuntary assignments

Prior to the Partnership Act, if a creditor was awarded judgment against an individual partner in respect of a private (non-partnership) debt he was able to enforce this judgment against the partnership property. This could have dramatic effects on the firm—it could, for example, paralyse its business and injure the other partners who were not concerned in the dispute. For once, the Act changed the law and s. 23 now provides in subsection (1) that 'a writ of execution shall not issue against any partnership property except on a judgment against the firm'. Only firm debts can be enforced against the firm's assets. Instead a private creditor has to rely on subsection (2):

> The High Court, or a judge thereof, or a county court, may, on the

application by summons of any judgment creditor of a partner, make an order charging that partner's interest in the partnership property and profits with payment of the amount of the judgment debt and interest thereon, and may by the same or a subsequent order appoint a receiver of that partner's share of profits (whether already declared or accruing), and of any other money which may be coming to him in respect of the partnership, and direct all accounts and inquiries, and give all other orders and directions which might have been directed or given if the charge had been made in favour of the judgment creditor by the partner, or which the circumstances of the case may require.

Thus a judgment creditor can ask the court to make him in effect an assignee of the debtor's share in the partnership. He is entitled to ask for any order to effect this, including the appointment of a receiver—but such a receiver will only be able to collect the sums due to the debtor, he cannot interfere in the running of the firm. Section 23 does not apply to Scotland (s. 23(5)).

The courts have interpreted this section strictly against the judgment creditor. In *Peake* v *Carter* (1916), the Court of Appeal held that if there was a dispute as to whether particular assets were partnership assets or belonged solely to the debtor there could be no execution against the assets without the other partners' being given a chance to interplead in the proceedings making the order. Further if the dispute, as in that case, related to whether the assets were partnership assets or the sole property of an innocent partner, no execution at all could be levied against the property because of s. 23(1). The matter would have to be resolved by an inquiry under s. 23(2) to ascertain the particulars of the partnership assets and of the debtor's share and interest in them. Further in *Brown, Janson & Co.* v *Hutchinson (No. 2)* (1895), where an order had been made under s. 23(2) charging a partner's interest in the firm for payment of a private debt, the Court of Appeal refused to make an additional order for an account. Such an order, although provided for in s. 23(2), will only be made in exceptional circumstances.

The reasoning behind this is that the court regards an involuntary assignment under s. 23(2) as being similar to an assignment under s. 31 where there is, as we have just seen, no right to demand an account. This analogy should be adhered to in ordinary cases. As the Court of Appeal said: 'As a general rule, a judgment creditor of a partner must be treated in the same way as the assignee of the share of a partner'. If this is so, it is conceivable that the judgment creditor's rights may be frustrated by a device such as used in *Re Garwood* to reduce the debtor's share of the profits, provided of course it is a bona fide management decision. One snag to that is, of course, that the creditor would simply hang around for longer than he would otherwise do with the additional possibility that he would go back to the court for an order for account, which he could not do as an assignee under s. 31.

If the other partners object to the imposition of a charge under s. 23(2) they have two alternative courses of action. First, under s. 23(3) they are 'at liberty at any time to redeem the interest charged, or in case of a sale being directed, to purchase the same'. Alternatively, under s. 33(2), they may dissolve the partnership and in that case all will be worked out in the winding-up process which will follow. If they redeem the charge by paying the amount owed into court then, of course, the debt will be transferred to them and they can recover it from the debtor at their own convenience. Dissolution is a rather drastic step and would have the same practical effect as if s. 23 had never been passed, i.e., bringing a possibly prosperous business to an end because of the private folly or ill luck of one of the partners.

If the other partners decide to purchase the debtor's share, and s. 23(3) seems to give them a pre-emptive right to do so (although the language of the section is not that strong, such an interpretation would be in accord with the other parts of the section), they must be careful not to fall foul of s. 28 and their fiduciary duty of avoiding a conflict of interest. A trustee may not purchase trust property and although this may not apply strictly to fiduciaries it would be very wise to employ an independent valuer to advise the debtor. The fact that it was sold to a partner at an auction will not in itself suffice to negative the obligation of full disclosure etc. It seems that, at least prior to the Act, where such a sale was set aside on the grounds of breach of a fiduciary duty, the other partners lost their right to dissolve the firm. Nor can partnership money be used to purchase the share since it will then simply become partnership property itself.

6

Partnership Property

Problems and possibilities

In the previous chapters we have seen something of the importance of distinguishing between property which belongs to all the partners as partners (i.e., to the firm) and property which remains that of an individual partner, or partners, as individuals. Sometimes the distinction is quite clear but it can become blurred in relation to assets used by the firm. It is then possible for such an asset to be owned by one partner and used by the firm under some form of agreement or even for it to be owned by all the partners as individuals and used by them as partners under a similar arrangement. On the other hand such assets can be owned and used by the firm as partnership property. Circulating capital, e.g., stock in trade, work in progress etc., is highly likely to be partnership property, but much more difficulty arises with fixed capital, e.g., the freehold or leasehold business premises, plant and machinery etc.

Before we attempt to solve some of these problems, however, we should clarify why this distinction between partnership and other property needs to be made. There are four potential problem areas, although one is now of historical importance only. First, as we shall see in the next chapter, the basic rule for insolvency at present is that the creditors of the firm must proceed first against the assets of the firm whereas an individual partner's creditors must proceed first against his individual assets, or estate as it is called in such circumstances. If all the partners are insolvent this means that each set of creditors has first go at the relevant estate in priority to the others, and so it is of great importance to sort out which asset belongs to which estate and so is available first to pay off which set of creditors. Second, if an asset increases in value, that increase will be attributed to the firm if it is partnership property and obviously to the individual owner(s) otherwise.

The third reason is the technical one that partnership property is held by the partners beneficially as tenants in common whereas it is possible for other property to be held by the individual owners as joint tenants. The difference, for those who prefer to forget their encounter with land law, or even managed to avoid it altogether, is that a tenant in common owns an 'undivided share' in the property (i.e., an unseparated but otherwise quantifiable share in the whole) which he can sell, mortgage, bequeath etc. A joint tenant, on the other hand, has no such share: each one owns everything and so he has no 'share' to sell etc. In particular a joint tenant cannot leave his share in a will so that with a joint tenancy the right of survivorship applies. Thus if A and B own an office block and A dies leaving all his property to X, X can only inherit A's 'half' if A and B were tenants in common. Otherwise B becomes the sole owner.

Equity has always regarded partners as tenants in common even if the formal transfer of property to them suggests that they are joint tenants. Normally this depends upon whether 'words of severance' such as 'equally' or 'in equal shares' are used—at common law only if there are such words of severance will there be a tenancy in common. Equity, however, regards a joint tenancy, with its right of survivorship, as being incompatible with a commercial enterprise such as a partnership and so always implies a tenancy in common behind a trust. Particularly in the older cases, therefore, this has been the cause of the dispute as to the nature of an asset's ownership—i.e., are the partners co-owners as individuals, and so possibly as joint tenants, or as partners and so as tenants in common?

Finally it has always been the rule that the doctrine of conversion applies to partnership property. This means that even land is regarded as personal property if it is a partnership asset—i.e., it is regarded as being held on a trust for sale and since equity 'looks upon that as done which ought to be done' the partners' interests are regarded as being in the proceeds of sale. Prior to 1925 this distinction between real and personal property was important in connection with intestacy (one went to the 'heir' and the other to the 'next of kin'). There are still some differences, e.g., for tax purposes on death, but since 1925 all land, whether partnership land or otherwise, held in any form of co-ownership is held on a statutory trust for sale and so is all regarded as personalty under the same doctrine. This distinction between partnership and other land held in co-ownership is therefore of no importance now but again it explains some of the earlier disputes in the cases.

What is partnership property?

The Act provides only a basic definition of what amounts to partnership property, although as we shall see later, it does provide additional guidelines for subsequent acquisitions out of profits. Section 20(1) provides:

All property and rights and interests in property originally brought into the partnership stock or acquired, whether by purchase or otherwise, on account of the firm or for the purposes and in the course of the partnership business, are called in this Act partnership property, and must be held and applied by the partners exclusively for the purposes of the partnership and in accordance with the partnership agreement.

This section covers two distinct features. One the existence of partnership property and the other the nature of a partner's interest in that property. Identifying the property is one thing, describing the partner's interest in it another. Let us cover these two aspects in reverse order (it is actually easier that way round).

Nature of a partner's interest

Section 20(1) requires partnership property to be held for partnership purposes and in accordance with the partnership agreement. It seems clear that this gives each partner an interest in the property which at the end of the day can only be realised by a dissolution and the lien which each partner then has by virtue of s. 39 on the partnership assets to have them first applied in payment of partnership debts (see chapter 7). Thus it is a chose in action, a piece of property which can only be enforced by an action. However, it is more than that, for, as we have seen, all partnership property is held by the partners as co-owners under a trust for sale—it is therefore also a form of equitable interest under a trust. Section 22 of the Act codifies the doctrine of conversion, mentioned above, which provides the consequences of this—all partnership property is to be regarded as personal and not real property.

The Australian cases have struggled with the attempt to define a partner's interest in partnership property. In *Canny Gabriel Castle Jackson Advertising Pty Ltd* v *Volume Sales (Finance) Pty Ltd* (1974), partners were held to have an equitable interest capable of taking priority over a later equitable interest such as an equitable charge ('where the equities are equal the first in time prevails'). In *Federal Commissioner of Taxation* v *Everett* (1980) the court preferred to class the interest as an equitable interest in the nature of a chose in action. As we have seen this interest can be assigned under s. 31 of the Act and in Canada it has been held to be capable of being insured. Finally it is, of course, subject to the fiduciary duties imposed on partners and must not be used for private benefit or gain by the partners, and to the ordinary conveyancing rules imposed on the legal title of a trust for sale—s. 20(2) makes the latter quite clear. Under the Law of Property

Act 1925 the first four partners named on a conveyance will be the trustees of the property (as joint tenants), holding for all the partners beneficially as tenants in common, and the fact that it is partnership property makes no difference to the rules relating to the legal estate held by the trustees for sale.

Identifying partnership property

Returning to the words of s. 20(1), partnership property can either be brought into the firm or acquired on account of the firm. Thus property brought in as capital is partnership property and subsequent acquisitions of capital are also included. If the property is itemised in the accounts as partnership property there is little difficulty. In other cases the court will have to infer an implied agreement that the property was to be brought in or acquired as partnership property from the surrounding circumstances, which can include the subsequent treatment of the asset. In general it can be said that the courts are very reluctant to imply that an asset has become partnership property—presumably because by doing so they are depriving the original owner of his title simply by implication from surrounding facts. Two cases illustrate the problems which can arise in such cases.

In *Miles* v *Clarke* (1953) the two men were partners at will in a photography business. Miles was a well-known photographer who brought with him his reputation, whereas Clarke owned the lease of the studio and the equipment used in it. Miles also brought with him his existing negatives. Both partners, however, contributed to the stock in trade used in the business. The partners never agreed as to the formal listing of the assets, all that they agreed was to share the profits equally. On a dissolution the question arose as to who owned what. Harman J refused to imply any terms as to change of ownership so that Clarke retained the lease and equipment whilst Miles retained his previous goodwill and negatives. The only terms implied as to partnership property were those necessary to give business efficacy to the relationship. e.g., concerning the stock in trade, negatives taken during the partnership etc.: 'Therefore, in my judgment, nothing changed hands except those things which were actually used and used up in the course of the carrying on of the business.'

In *Harvey* v *Harvey* (1970), the Australian High Court similarly declined to hold that a farm owned by one Harvey had become an asset of a partnership which he concluded with an existing firm consisting of his brother and his brother's sons. They agreed that Harvey should bring in the farming stock and implements and that the original firm should supply only labour and skill in farming the land. Profits and expenses were to be borne equally. It was intended to improve the farm but nothing was said about either its ownership or how it was to be improved. The partnership was dissolved and the farm, having been improved out of the profits of the business, was now substantially more valuable. Harvey's nephews claimed that it had become a partnership asset. The evidence was, however, contradictory—at one stage, for example, it had been said that the farm was to be available for Harvey's son (aged nine at the time)—and the fact that the improvements had come out of the profits was simply in accordance with the agreement and not sufficient to outweigh the other evidence.

Even if there is an agreement, the courts will also construe it strictly before including a doubtful asset as being partnership property. In two recent cases, *Singh* v *Nahar* (1965) and *Eardley* v *Broad* (1970), general words such as 'assets' have been held not to be specific enough to include a valuable lease. Evidence may, of course, point the other way, e.g., payment of insurance premiums relating to the asset, payment of rates or other taxes—but once again we are forced to the conclusion that there are no absolutes—each case has to be taken on its own facts. Mere use of the asset is clearly not enough as *Miles* v *Clarke* and *Harvey* v *Harvey* both show. The fact that the property, e.g., land, is registered in the name of one of the partners is not conclusive either way. It is possible, for example, as in *Singh* v *Nahar*, for the court to imply that some assets owned by an existing business owner were brought into the partnership when he took a partner whereas others were not. (Horatio's philosophy would indeed be stretched.)

If the dispute relates to property subsequently bought with partnership profits two other sections of the Act may apply. Section 21 provides:

> Unless the contrary intention appears, property bought with money belonging to the firm is deemed to have been bought on account of the firm.

Thus property so acquired is not automatically partnership property. It is also true that an asset acquired at the expense of an individual partner may still be a partnership asset. The fact that an asset was acquired out of the partnership account, therefore, puts the burden of proving that it is not a partnership asset onto the individual so claiming. It is important to note that s. 21 only applies to property bought out of 'money belonging to the firm', i.e., money which is itself partnership property. As such, therefore, it does raise a presumption which needs to be rebutted.

One example may show how this section works. In *Jones* v *Jones* (1870),

Partnership Property

two brothers, T and A, were general dealers and out of the profits of the partnership they bought a shop to use in the business. The land was conveyed to them as tenants in common. T died intestate. If the land was partnership property it was personalty under the doctrine of conversion and so passed to his next of kin; if it was not then it remained realty and descended to the heir (remember this distinction is now obsolete). Since the property had been acquired out of partnership profits and used for the partnership business the evidence was that it was partnership property and not owned by them as individuals.

The other section which applies to subsequent acquisitions is s. 20(3). This deals only with one specific situation, however:

> Where co-owners of an estate or interest in any land, . . . not being itself partnership property, are partners as to profits made by the use of that land or estate, and purchase other land or estate out of the profits to be used in like manner, the land or estate so purchased belongs to them, in the absence of an agreement to the contrary, not as partners but as co-owners for the same respective estates and interests as are held by them in the land or estate first mentioned at the date of the purchase.

It is useful to remember that s. 2(1) provides that co-ownership of land does not of itself make that land a partnership asset even though the profits from it are shared by the co-owners as partners. Just as that section applies to land already owned, s. 20(3) applies to property bought out of those profits and used 'in like manner' to the original land.

In such cases it is clear that something more than mere use of the property in the business is needed to make it a partnership asset. Although the section only applies to subsequent purchases, it has also been applied by analogy to improvements to the original property out of profits. Thus in *Davis v Davis* (1894), a father left his freehold business premises to his two sons as tenants in common. They carried on the business under an informal agreement and subsequently borrowed money by raising a mortgage on the premises. They used the money to expand the workshops. One brother died and it became important to decide (for intestacy purposes again) whether the improvements were partnership assets or not. North J applied s. 20(3) even though it did not strictly cover the situation:

> In the present case, the money which was borrowed was not employed in paying for the additional piece of land which was brought into the business; if it had been the case it would have been exactly within that subsection; but the case seems to me so like that, that, although it is not

literally covered by the subsection, the same law applies to it.

The improvements remained outside the partnership.

Section 20(3) is different from s. 21 in that it presupposes that the profits used to buy the land are the partners' own which they may spend at their will rather than profits which remain partnership money. Contrary intention can be shown, however, so that subsequent property may indeed become a partnership asset, even though the original land remains outside. There are many examples of this, cited by North J in a useful summary in *Davis* v *Davis*, including *Waterer* v *Waterer* (1873). There a nurseryman carried on a business with his sons, although not in partnership. He died and left his estate, including the goodwill of the business and the land, to his sons as tenants in common. They carried on the business in partnership and bought more land for the purpose of the business, paying for it out of the father's estate. One son died and the others bought his share of the business, using money raised by a mortgage of the additional land. On that evidence and the fact that the new land had been included in the sale of the deceased brother's share, the judge was able to decide that the new land had been 'substantially involved' in the business and so had become a partnership asset.

Even if property is transferred or acquired in one partner's name so that there is no apparent co-ownership, the property may still be partnership property under the concept of a presumed resulting trust. In essence this applies where A and B jointly purchase an asset, which is then conveyed into A's name only. A is then presumed to hold the property on trust for A and B. If A and B are partners it may well be that such an asset then becomes partnership property. The rule is only a presumption and can be rebutted by evidence that B intended to make a gift of his share to A, but in the case of partnership with its fiduciary duties that may be very difficult to show. (There is a complication if A and B are married, for a husband in such cases is presumed to have made a gift to his wife, which presumption then has to be rebutted. Partnership would be good evidence for that purpose, however, and in any event modern judges are rather doubtful as to the force of this presumption of advancement.) A modern example of a resulting trust is the Australian case of *Carter Bros* v *Renouf* (1962). A partner took out a life assurance policy in his own name. When the firm was in difficulties the benefit of the policy was assigned to a creditor subject to a proviso for redemption. The policy was for a larger amount than the debt. When the partner died there was a dispute as to which set of creditors was entitled to the balance of the policy money after paying off the secured creditor. Since the premiums had been paid by the firm it was held that the benefit of the policy belonged to the partners; there was no evidence to rebut the presumption of a resulting trust. Thus the balance was available first to the partnership creditors.

A resulting or even a constructive trust can also arise if one person spends money on improving or extending the property of another. Thus if the firm uses its money to extend the business premises owned by one partner, it would be possible to argue that a limited interest arises in favour of the firm. The position is far from clear, however, and the better view is probably that such a trust, if it arises at all, is better classified as a constructive trust, i.e., one imposed by law on the grounds of equity rather than from a joint contribution to the purchase price. In any event it may well be that the investment can be classified as a loan and the judges in more recent cases have been careful to point out that a loan is a loan and does not give the lender rights in the asset as a constructive trustee. He has his rights as a creditor, and it is quite possible for the other partners to be creditors against the separate assets of one partner.

Business premises: leases and licences

Most modern problems relating to partnership property revolve round the business premises of the firm. The simplest situation is where the freehold or leasehold premises are themselves partnership property and so held by the partners as co-owners under the rules set out above. If the premises are held on a lease from a third party, however, problems can arise on a change of partners. In such circumstances, can the old firm transfer the lease to the new firm, or surviving partners, even though there is a prohibition against an assignment in the lease? (Landlords take such covenants to protect themselves against finding themselves with unsuitable tenants by assignment.) In *Varley* v *Coppard* (1872) it was held that the landlord's consent had to be obtained to any such assignment. One reason for this was that in that case the former partners would have ceased to be liable on the covenant in the lease if the assignment had gone through, since they were not parties to the original lease but were all tenants by assignment in the first place. Thus having themselves assigned the lease they could not be liable either under privity of contract (no contract with the landlord) or under privity of estate (being no longer tenants by assignment). In Australia in *Cook* v *Rowe* (1954) the court held that the position would therefore be different if the retiring partners were in fact the original tenants and so would remain liable on the covenants even after the assignment on the basis of privity of contract. Whether a breach of a covenant against assignment should depend upon such technical considerations is a matter for doubt, however, and there are no English cases in support.

Since such a lease will usually be a lease of business premises the partners will be able to take advantage of Part II of the Landlord and Tenant Act 1954, which enables a business tenant to claim renewal of a business tenancy at the end of the lease unless the landlord has a valid objection under the Act. This valuable right is available where the membership of the firm is different at the time of claiming a renewal from that at the grant of the lease, following s. 9 of the Law of Property Act 1969, which reversed an unfortunate decision to the contrary. Similar rules apply to farming partnerships under the Agricultural Holdings Act 1948. In practice considerable care is needed in drafting business leases, not only as to renewals but also as to rent review procedures, which have become part of life since inflation appeared on the scene. Failure to follow set procedures can be expensive for any business whether carried on in partnership or not.

It is equally possible for the freehold or leasehold business premises to be owned by all the partners as co-owners and not as a partnership asset. No difference will arise in practice in the case of a leasehold interest from the position set out above, and the freehold, being held separately from the partnership property, will be governed by the ordinary rules of land law. One point to note, however, is that in such a case the partners, as co-owners, cannot grant a lease to themselves as partners. The House of Lords so held in *Rye* v *Rye* (1962)—partners cannot contract with themselves (yet another problem caused by the lack of legal personality). In such cases where a lease is attempted, the premises might well be construed as being partnership property in any event. Otherwise, one idea may be to form a company to hold the freehold which can then lease it to the firm, the firm paying rent and the partners receiving it back as dividends from the company. The point is that the rent comes equally off each partner's share of the profits, but is then distributed as dividends according to their respective shares in the property which need not necessarily be the same as the profit-sharing ratio.

The most complex cases arise where the premises are owned by one partner and then used by the firm. The firm will almost certainly be using the premises either under a lease or a licence from the owner/partner. It is clear that the law allows him to grant a lease either to his co-partners or even, following s. 72 of the Law of Property Act 1925, to all the partners including himself. Strangely, however, it was held in *Harrison-Broadley* v *Smith* (1964) that he cannot confer a licence on the whole firm, i.e., including himself. Whilst there are technical distinctions between leases and licences this does seem to be a peculiar one although it can be argued that in the absence of a statutory provision a partner cannot confer a licence upon himself.

The position of a partner/landlord is also unclear. As a partner he owes fiduciary duties to fellow partners but as a landlord he has certain rights both at common law and under various statutes. The exact relationship has never been clarified. One possible conflict could arise where the firm applies for a renewal of the tenancy under the Landlord and Tenant Act 1954, mentioned above, and the landlord/partner opposes it. Must he act for the benefit of the partnership as a whole or can he exercise his statutory rights as a landlord irrespective of such considerations? The answer will depend upon whether the court regards his activities in this respect as being within the scope of his fiduciary position. The problem is similar to that encountered in the previous chapter in relation to the purchase by one partner of the reversion to a partnership lease, where the position is also far from clear and so it is difficult to draw any analogy.

A licence, being implied in most cases, will normally be for the duration of the partnership and so will end on a dissolution, and after that any other partner will become a trespasser unless he can show that he needed to enter in order to protect his interests—see *Harrison-Broadley* v *Smith*. On the other hand, although a lease granted for the duration of the partnership was upheld in *Pocock* v *Carter* (1912), later cases have suggested that tenancies for an uncertain period are not allowed. Clearly a fixed-term lease is preferable and in the light of the lease-renewal protection in the statutes, not unduly hard on the other partners.

Goodwill: a note

All businesses generate goodwill, i.e., the difference between the value of the business as a going concern and the value of its assets. Partnerships are no exception to this and clearly the goodwill of the business will usually be a partnership asset (but remember *Miles* v *Clarke* (1953) where the 'goodwill' attaching to the active partner when he entered the partnership remained his at the dissolution). In most cases questions as to valuing the goodwill will only arise on a partial dissolution of a partnership where one or more of the partners wish to carry on the business and so have to buy the retiring or deceased partner's share of the goodwill, or on the introduction of a new partner who must buy himself into the firm, i.e., purchase a share of the goodwill. Although it is illegal to sell the goodwill of an NHS general practice, under s. 54 of the National Health Service Act 1977, all other professional partnerships would appear to have a potential goodwill attached to them which needs to be valued in this way, despite the odd decision to the contrary.

Partnership Property

There are two problems associated with goodwill: first as to identifying and valuing it and second the consequences for the vendor and purchaser of such a sale. In the absence of agreement in the partnership deed the position is governed entirely by case law and is unaffected by the Partnership Act. It is not, therefore, specifically a partnership problem and the following is simply a note of some of the points which can arise. First, what exactly is goodwill? Two classic statements are those of Lord Eldon in *Cruttwell* v *Lye* (1810): 'The goodwill which has been the subject of sale is nothing more than the probability that the old customers will resort to the old place'; and of Lord Macnaughten in *Trego* v *Hunt* (1896):

> It is the whole advantage, whatever it may be, of the reputation and connection of the firm, which may have been built up by years of honest work or gained by lavish expenditure of money.

More graphically the Court of Appeal in *Whiteman Smith Motor Co.* v *Chaplin* (1934) divided up the goodwill into four animal groups. Some customers are 'cats' since they remain with the business whoever runs it; some are 'dogs', they will follow the proprietors wherever they go; others are 'rats' since they will drift away from both business and proprietors; and yet others are 'rabbits'—they come only because the premises are close by.

Valuation of the goodwill is a skilled affair and a matter for specialists. Lawyers are naturally more concerned with the consequences of a sale. Again I must stress that we are only dealing with the tip of the iceberg here but the following are three points which seem to have emerged from the cases, assuming that there is no contrary agreement.

(a) A person who acquires the goodwill alone may represent himself as continuing or succeeding to the business of the vendor (*Churton* v *Douglas* (1859)).

(b) The vendor may, however, carry on a similar business in competition with the purchaser though not under a name which would amount to a representation that he was carrying on the old business (*Trego* v *Hunt* (1896)).

(c) The vendor may publicly advertise his new business, but may not personally or by circular solicit the customers of the old business (*Curl Bros Ltd* v *Webster* (1904)).

It is clear, therefore, that the purchaser of the goodwill should take additional steps to protect himself against competition from the vendors.

The partnership agreement can, of course, provide what it will in relation to goodwill. It may give it a nominal or nil value. In chapter 3 we saw in the case of *Deacons* v *Bridge* (1984) an example of the former so that a new partner paid very little for the goodwill but equally received little for it on his departure. Such solutions are, of course, the easiest course and place the emphasis instead on restricting the departing partner's activities. Alternatively the agreement may provide for some amateur solution as to quantifying the goodwill, e.g., by reference to throughput of work. This again is now an easier option since precise records are kept in any event for the VATman to inspect (VAT being a tax on turnover). Such solutions may appeal to the less numerate professions, and it is usually better to have some form of agreement than to rely on the old and somewhat complex cases.

7

Dissolution and Winding Up

Dissolution

'In my beginning is my end' wrote T.S. Eliot, and whilst it may seem unduly pessimistic it has to be said that many of the problems associated with partnerships are concerned less with their inception or active life than with their demise. We have seen how easily and informally a partnership can be created and run but, like most things in life, partnerships are easier to start then to finish. The analogy with marriage, with which I started the book, is again quite appropriate—a dissolution is often the result of ill feeling and mistrust on all sides where every detail is a potential source of dispute. But of course not all dissolutions are like that—many arise on the death or retirement of one partner where the business is carried on by the surviving partner(s) often quite amicably.

There are, therefore, really two entirely different types of dissolution— one where the firm and the business simply split up and the other where the surviving or continuing partners take over the whole business. In the first case a dissolution is followed by a full winding-up of the business, in the second it is a question of valuing the outgoing partner's share of the continuing business. Insolvency may, of course, be involved in either case and this presents particular problems which are dealt with later in this chapter. Let us start, however, with the grounds upon which a partnership may be dissolved. These divide into three categories: contractual, automatic and those made under court orders.

Contractual grounds for dissolution

Partnership has a contractual basis and so it is perfectly possible for the agreement itself to provide express terms as to when that agreement can be terminated. True to form, however, the Act also provides five implied terms to that effect, four of them subject to the usual contrary agreement. We have in fact already encountered the first three, contained in s. 32 of the Act, when we discussed the duration of a partnership in chapter 2. Section

Dissolution and Winding Up

32 provides for a dissolution: (a) if a partnership is entered into for a fixed term by the expiration of that term; (b) if for a single adventure or undertaking by its termination; and (c) if for an undefined time, by a notice at any time given by one partner to his fellow partners. In chapter 2 we also encountered the relationship between this section and s. 26 (partnerships at will)—remember that the key is that a partnership for a fixed term in s. 32(a) includes any partnership with a time-limit, however vague or uncertain, and that a partnership for an 'undefined time' in s. 32(c) must be read in the light of that as including only totally open-ended agreements. The agreement itself may, of course, contain its own arrangements as to time and dissolution.

Section 33 implies two further terms relating to dissolution:

(1) Subject to any agreement between the partners, every partnership is dissolved as regards all the partners by the death or bankruptcy of any partner.

(2) A partnership may, at the option of the other partners, be dissolved if any partner suffers his share of the partnership property to be charged under this Act for his separate debt.

Subsection (2) needs no contrary intention in the deed to oust it—it is only an option given to the partners where one partner's share in the partnership assets has been charged with payment of his individual debt under the procedure set out in s. 23 of the Act—i.e., the involuntary assignment procedure which we have already discussed in chapter 5. The Act does not provide for an automatic dissolution on such a charge being created since that was the very thing that s. 23 was passed to prevent.

It may be highly inconvenient for a large modern partnership to subject itself to the whole dissolution process under subsection (1) every time one partner dies or becomes insolvent. In either case it will be much easier to value the relevant partner's share and provide some method of sorting things out whilst preserving the partnership business. It is usual to provide in respect of death at least the necessary contrary intention to negative s. 33(1). A modern example can be seen in the Scottish case of *William S. Gordon & Co. Ltd* v *Mrs Mary Thompson Partnership* (1985) (remember in Scotland a partnership does have a separate legal personality). The company was the landlord of two fields let to the defendant firm. The firm had three partners, one of whom, Mrs Mary Thompson, died in 1981. The landlords argued that by virtue of s. 33(1) her death had dissolved the firm and so terminated the lease and they now sued the remaining partners for possession of the fields. The remaining partners relied on a clause in the

Dissolution and Winding Up

partnership agreement that on such a death: 'the remaining Parties shall decide within two months of the death . . . either to wind up the partnership business or to take over the estate and assets of the partnership business and to carry on the business to the exclusion of the representatives of the deceased . . . with exclusive rights to the goodwill and use of the firm name'. They had in fact so continued the business and the Court of Session agreed that this clause amounted to a contrary agreement sufficient to act as an antidote to s. 33(1). The chosen alternative allowed by the deed was not to wind up the firm but on the contrary to carry on the partnership business, and was thus another way of saying that the surviving partners could choose to carry on the partnership. Of course, each clause has to be construed on its own wording and a contrary decision was reached in *IRC* v *Graham's Trustees* (1971).

There are also many examples of express dissolution clauses in partnership agreements which expand the available grounds for dissolution rather than ousting the implied terms in the Act. These are particularly important for professional partnerships where reputation and professional integrity are paramount. Thus in *Clifford* v *Timms* (1908), one dentist in a firm was held to be entitled to a dissolution, under a clause in the deed allowing him to do so if his partner was 'guilty of professional misconduct', where the other partner became involved in a company which produced scurrilous pamphlets etc. as to the activities, both dental and sexual, of other dentists. Lord Loreburn LC was sufficiently outraged: 'for my part, if this be not disgraceful conduct, if it be not professional misconduct, I know not what the terms mean'. Sometimes in such cases 'conduct unbecoming' will suffice even though it is not directly related to the firm's business—remember the draper convicted of travelling on a train without a ticket in *Carmichael* v *Evans* (1904) (see chapter 5). Other express clauses relate to incapacity such as the one in *Peyton* v *Mindham* (1972), which we also discussed in chapter 5 with reference to expulsion clauses. Remember also that when exercising the power of dissolution under all such clauses the partners remain subject to their fiduciary duty of good faith not to act solely for their own personal advantage.

Automatic dissolution

There can, however, be no contracting out of s. 34 of the Act. This is obligatory, although it only reflects the common law position:

> A partnership is in every case dissolved by the happening of any event which makes it unlawful for the business of the firm to be carried on or

Dissolution and Winding Up

for the members of the firm to carry it on in partnership.

Again we are going over old ground—illegality was one of the subjects in chapter 3. Most of the cases involve enemy aliens in times of war. Thus in *R* v *Knupfer* (1915) the court was able to say: 'The declaration of war had the effect of dissolving the partnership by operation of law'. A more modern example is *Hudgell Yeates & Co.* v *Watson* (1978) where one of three solicitors in a firm forgot to renew his practising certificate without which he was forbidden to practise under the Solicitors Act 1974. The Court of Appeal was quite clear that this automatically ended the partnership under s. 34 even though the partners were all unaware of the circumstances and in fact had continued as before. Waller LJ, reviewing the earlier cases, held that s. 34 operates by force of law and not by any intention of the partners:

> If the partnership was dissolved by force of law and since it is illegal for someone who is not qualified to be in partnership with a solicitor, it is inevitable in my view that if there is a partnership of solicitors it cannot include the unqualified man.

(For more details of this case turn back to chapter 2 and the discussion of s. 14 of the Act.)

Dissolution by the court

Even if there is nothing in the agreement, express or implied, one partner may apply to the court for a dissolution order under one of six heads, and it is clear that the courts will not always allow an arbitration agreement to prevent access to the courts under these heads. We can take the six heads in order before returning to the arbitration question. They are set out in s. 35 of the Act: 'On application by a partner the court *may* decree a dissolution of the partnership in any of the following cases':

(a) *Insanity*. The actual wording of s.35(a) was repealed by the Mental Health Act 1959. The procedure now is that if a partner becomes a patient under the Mental Health Act 1983 his receiver or the other partners may apply to the Court of Protection for a dissolution which can be given if the person is incapable of managing his property and affairs.

(b) *Permanent incapacity*. Section 35(b) refers to a partner becoming 'in any other way permanently incapable of performing his part of the partnership contract'. Thus the analogy is with insanity, formerly in paragraph (a). It is of course, a question of fact, in each case as to whether this situation has arisen. It will depend upon the partner's duties and it could hardly apply to a dormant or limited partner. The incapacity must be permanent, however, and in *Whitwell* v *Arthur* (1865) evidence of an improvement in the affected partner's condition (he had been subject to a stroke) prevented an order being made. As a result, express clauses, such as that in *Peyton* v *Mindham* (1972), usually specify a period of incapacity.

(c) *Prejudicial conduct.* Section 35(c) requires proof of conduct by one partner which the court, having regard to the nature of the business, regards as 'calculated to prejudicially affect the carrying on of the business'. This heading includes conduct not directly connected with the business and there is no need to prove actual loss or public knowledge—the test is objective: would a client knowing of this conduct have moved away from the business?

(d) *Persistent breaches of the agreement.* Section 35(d) requires evidence that the offending partner 'wilfully or persistently commits a breach of the partnership agreement, or otherwise so conducts himself in matters relating to the partnership business that it is not reasonably practicable for the other partner or partners to carry on the business in partnership with him'. The problem for the courts in such cases is to avoid the Draconian solution for petty internal squabbles and yet to end matters if the other partners really cannot continue with him. In *Cheeseman* v *Price* (1865) the offending partner had failed to enter small sums of money received from customers into the accounts as he was required to do under the agreement. This had happened 17 times and that was sufficient to tip the scales in favour of a dissolution.

(e) *Carrying on the business at a loss.* Section 35(e) is straightforward: 'When the business of the partnership can only be carried on at a loss'. Current solvency will not prevent such an order being made if that situation cannot continue. On the other hand there must be proof that making a profit is impossible in practice. In *Handyside* v *Campbell* (1901) a partnership had been running at a loss but this was shown to be the result of the absence of the petitioning partner due to illness and that given proper attention the business could run at a profit. The judge, Farwell J, refused to make the order. The loss was attributable to special circumstances and not to any inherent defect in the business.

(f) *Just and equitable ground.* Section 35(f) has been the subject of many recent cases because it has a direct counterpart in company law and has been applied by analogy to justify the winding up of a small 'partnership company'. It allows an order to be made: 'Whenever in any case circumstances have arisen which, in the opinion of the court, render it just and equitable that the partnership be dissolved'. In *Re Yenidje Tobacco Co. Ltd* (1916), the following were suggested as examples of such circumstances: refusal to meet on matters of business, continued quarrelling and a state of animosity that precludes all reasonable hope of a reconciliation and friendly cooperation. In general the courts require evidence of acts which show that there has been such a breakdown of the mutual confidence and trust that are required in a partnership as to make it impossible for it to continue. In *Ebrahimi* v *Westbourne Galleries Ltd* (1973), the House of Lords, in the company context, applied this section where one 'partner' was excluded from management participation in breach of a clear understanding that he would be so entitled. Unlike company law, however, there is no 'alternative remedy' for such cases as can be found in s. 459 of the Companies Act 1985.

The question now arises—can the partners effectively oust the jurisdiction of the courts by providing that all such disputes shall go to arbitration? The best answer was provided by Roxburgh J in *Olver* v *Hillier* (1959), where he considered that the court has a discretion in each case whether to allow the court action to proceed or to stay the case and allow the arbitration to go ahead. It is never an easy decision. After all, in a professional deed the partners have agreed to arbitration and so why not let them take the consequences? (Assuming that the arbitration clause is wide enough to cover dissolution—if it does not then the problem cannot arise.) On the other hand if the dispute relates to s. 35(f), the just and equitable ground, it would seem to involve the exercise of judicial discretion and so the courts are more likely to take matters into their own hands. That was certainly the basis of the actual decision in *Olver* v *Hillier* against staying the action. On the other hand if the dispute is more limited, e.g., as to the return of an alleged premium, perhaps an arbitration will be allowed: *Belfield* v *Bourne* (1894). Modern arbitration statutes preclude judicial review of an arbitrator's decision in most cases so that the distinction has since been sharpened and the matter is of more concern. One factor mitigating in favour of arbitration, however, is the lack of publicity attached to it, and the courts should be wary of allowing one embittered partner deliberately seeking publicity to harm his fellow partners in this way.

Rescission of the partnership agreement

A partnership agreement, like other contracts, may have been induced by a misrepresentation by one partner to another, be it a fraudulent, negligent or innocent misrepresentation. In this respect the partner so induced can rescind the contract which, of course, has the effect of dissolving the partnership. In addition he may sue for damages if the misrepresentation is either fraudulent (in the tort of deceit) or negligent (under s. 2(1) of the Misrepresentation Act 1967), although it is by no means clear whether under the general law there is such a remedy for an innocent misrepresentation (s. 2(2) of the Misrepresentation Act is subject to dispute on this point). The law on misrepresentation has thus moved significantly since the Partnership Act was passed but s. 41 of the Act provides additional remedies for misrepresentation in the partnership context. Section 41 provides:

> Where a partnership contract is rescinded on the ground of the fraud or misrepresentation of one of the parties thereto, the party entitled to rescind is, without prejudice to any other right, entitled—
>
> (a) to a lien on, or right of retention of, the surplus of the partnership assets, after satisfying the partnership liabilities, for any sum of money paid by him for the purchase of a share in the partnership and for any capital contributed by him, and is
> (b) to stand in the place of the creditors of the firm for any payments made by him in respect of the partnership liabilities, and
> (c) to be indemnified by the person guilty of the fraud or making the representation against all the debts and liabilities of the firm.

The right to rescission applies even though there is no fraud or negligence. In *Senanayake* v *Cheng* (1966) a statement that the business was a 'gold-mine' when in fact it had enormous bad debts enabled the court to rescind the contract.

The additional rights given by s. 41 reflect the fact that entering into a partnership agreement brings about liabilities to third parties and thus the rights of subrogation in paragraph (b) and indemnity in paragraph (c) will apply even if the misrepresentation was innocent. The right to rescind is lost under the general law if there has been undue delay in claiming the remedy, if the affected partner has continued in the partnership after discovering the misrepresentation or if a third party becomes involved. The effect of the Misrepresentation Act 1967 has been to reduce the scope of s. 41 but it remains available as an alternative basis of claim.

Winding up

The effect of a full dissolution is to finish the partnership as a going

Dissolution and Winding Up

concern. The next step is to wind up the business, i.e., to collect in and value the assets, pay off the partnership debts and distribute the surplus, if any, to the former partners. This can be contrasted with a partial dissolution, i.e., any dissolution where the business *per se* is to continue in the hands of one or more of the former partners. That produces different problems which are dealt with later. The problems associated with a final account and the actual distribution of the assets arise mainly with regard to insolvency and will also be considered later. For the moment we should concentrate on the mechanics of a full (and sometimes acrimonious) dissolution. The first question is who is to carry out the winding up? There are two basic choices: the existing partner or partners or a receiver appointed by the court.

Winding up by the existing partners

Partners, as we know by now, are all agents of each other whilst the partnership is a going concern and can bind each other to contracts etc. if they are acting in the course of their actual, implied or apparent authority. If it is decided that the partners are to conduct the winding-up operations personally then they continue to do so as agents for their fellow partners. Thus each will bind his fellow partners in the same manner as when the partnership was a going concern—and again questions of actual and apparent authority will be decided as questions of fact. Did the partner have actual permission to enter the contract on behalf of the firm or is the firm estopped from denying that he had authority because of their representations to that effect by words or conduct? Implied authority is, however, a question of law governed, whilst the partnership is a going concern, by s. 5 of the Act (see chapter 4 again). In this respect the position is altered in the case of a winding up, since s. 5 is qualified by s. 38:

> After the dissolution of a partnership the authority of each partner to bind the firm, and the other rights and obligations of the partners, continue notwithstanding the dissolution so far as may be necessary to wind up the affairs of the partnership, and to complete transactions begun but unfinished at the time of the dissolution, but not otherwise.

This section covers two things—one, the implied authority of a partner (but clearly not his actual or apparent authority), and two, the fiduciary duties which are equally preserved.

Anything 'necessary to wind up the affairs of the partnership' is thus included in this implied authority and it is suggested that that authority

Dissolution and Winding Up

should take precedence over the limitation as to completing transactions in existence at the date of dissolution. Clearly to dispose of stock is necessary for a winding up even though it will involve new transactions. Perhaps the easiest way is to regard the authority relating to completing existing transactions as being in addition to that relating to winding up *per se*. An example of s. 38 is *Re Bourne* (1906). A surviving partner continued to run the business after the death of his partner until it was wound up. He continued the firm's bank account which was overdrawn at the date of the death and remained overdrawn until the final account. He paid money into and drew money out of the account, and to secure the overdraft he deposited the title deeds of certain partnership land with the bank. Did this bind the executors of the deceased partner? The Court of Appeal held that it did. A partner has a duty and the authority to do all such acts as are necessary for a winding up. Vaughan Williams LJ was quite clear: 'And if it is necessary for such winding up either to continue the partnership business, or to borrow money, or to sell assets . . . the right and duty are coextensive'.

In most cases a winding up will be carried out 'in-house' in this way. It is cheaper, quicker and more private than the alternative. It also preserves the confidentiality between the partners (and the Revenue!). Section 38 is construed as imposing a duty to wind up the firm and to complete existing transactions. It will therefore apply unless the court orders otherwise and appoints a receiver because the lack of trust is terminal. One aspect of this duty means that failure to complete an existing transaction may give rise to an action for negligence by the third party so let down, e.g., by a firm of solicitors not pursuing an action so that it becomes statute-barred: see *Welsh* v *Knarston* (1972). Finally there is a proviso to s. 38 whereby the firm is not bound by the acts of a bankrupt partner unless a partner has since held himself out as being a partner of the bankrupt.

Partnership receivers

Receivers may be appointed by the court even if the partnership is a going concern, in which case the person appointed will be a receiver and manager. In such cases some evidence of fraud or unfair conduct needs to be procured. It is much more common, however, for the court to be asked to appoint a receiver on a dissolution to supervise the winding-up process. A receiver in such a case is not like a receiver appointed by a creditor in company law since a partnership receiver is charged with acting in the best interests of all the partners. The court has an absolute discretion as to whether to appoint a receiver. Two recent decisions have, however, laid down a few guidelines for future reference. In *Floydd* v *Cheney* (1970) an architect and his assistant/partner quarrelled and the latter disappeared with many documents relating to the business. When sued for their return he argued that there was a partnership and asked for the appointment of a receiver. The fact that a partnership was disputed did not preclude the appointment of a receiver, although it was a factor which the court could take into account. Another factor was that since the partnership involved a professional practice the court should be wary of appointing a receiver since such an appointment might harm the 'delicate blossom' of a professional man's reputation. On that basis, and the fact that he thought that it was unlikely that a partnership would in fact be established, the judge, Megarry J, refused to appoint a receiver.

In *Sobell* v *Boston* (1975), Goff J refused to appoint a receiver where one partner retired and the remaining partners were continuing the business. In other words, a receiver will not usually be appointed in a partial dissolution, i.e., where there is no winding up but simply the buying out of a retiring partner, even though such an appointment might speed up events. Such a partner's rights lie in s. 42 of the Act (see below) and not in the appointment of a receiver. He also reiterated Megarry J's point *vis-à-vis* professional partnerships—in this case it was a firm of solicitors. The position might be different if there was evidence of fraud or that the assets were somehow in jeopardy. In effect the only complaint in this case was the delay in payment and the unsatisfactory nature of s. 42.

Frequently the court will appoint one of the partners as a receiver, providing, of course, there is no evidence against him. Once appointed, a receiver is an officer of the court and his actions cannot be interfered with. Thus in *Dixon* v *Dixon* (1904), when a receiver and manager was appointed following a dissolution, one of the former partners set up a rival business and attempted to persuade his former employees to give proper notice and to join his new business. He also attempted to obtain the lease of a field used by the partnership business. The court granted an injunction restraining him from interfering in this way with the activities of the receiver. A receiver's management of the business is sacrosanct and even though there were no obvious breaches of contract by anyone, the acts of the former partner amounted to interference with the receiver's management. Swinfen Eady J said: 'I am of opinion that any act calculated to destroy property under the control of a receiver and manager is an interference with the management of the receiver and manager, even though it may not involve a breach of contract'.

A receiver appointed by the court is to be paid both his costs and his remuneration out of the assets of the firm. This is apparently so even though the receiver is a former partner who owes money to the firm which he cannot pay. This was the position in *Davy* v *Scarth* (1906). Davy and Scarth were partners. Davy died and Scarth was appointed as receiver by the court. The accounts showed that he had £1,392 in his hands as partnership assets and that in addition he owed the firm some £14,450. His remuneration as receiver was fixed at £280 and his costs at £48. The judge allowed him to deduct his fees and expenses from the £1,392 before paying it over to Davy's executrix. Farwell J gave this graphic reason: 'I think he is entitled to have the remuneration, irrespective of his debt to the partnership, so as to keep himself alive while he is doing his work as receiver'.

On the other hand he has no rights against the partners personally—he can only look to the assets of the firm. In *Boehm* v *Goodall* (1911) a receiver made such a claim on the basis that he had been appointed with the consent of the partners. Warrington J in declining his request spelt out the true nature and position of a partnership receiver and we will leave the subject with him:

> Such a receiver and manager is not the agent of the parties, he is not a trustee for them, and they cannot control him. He may, as far as they are concerned, incur expenses or liabilities without their having a say in the matter. I think it is of the utmost importance that receivers and managers in this position should know that they must look for their indemnity to the assets which are under the control of the court. The court itself cannot indemnify receivers, but it can, and will, do so out of the assets, so far as they extend, for expenses properly incurred; but it cannot go further.

Return of premiums

If one partner has paid a premium to the others on joining the firm he may be entitled to reclaim part of this on a dissolution. A premium has to be distinguished from a payment of capital. The latter is an investment in the business and forms part of the partnership assets, whereas a premium is a 'joining fee' which goes to the other partner(s). The premium is paid in return for being allowed to join the partnership and to remain a partner for a specified period. If the firm is dissolved prematurely, therefore, the payer has not received full consideration for his payment and can recover an

Dissolution and Winding Up

appropriate amount from the other partner(s). Premiums, as I have said, are not capital and are thus considered separately (and indeed usually first) in a winding up. The Act deals with premiums in s. 40 and they have been the subject of some complex case law. Today, however, they are an endangered species—few professional firms now take a premium from a new partner, whereas even in the early 1970s they were reasonably common. In the light of this modern development the following is a somewhat brief survey of the rules as to the return of premiums.

Section 40 codifies the pre-Act law exactly:

Where one partner has paid a premium to another on entering into a partnership for a fixed term, and the partnership is dissolved before the expiration of that term otherwise than by the death of a partner, the court may order the repayment of the premium, or of such part thereof as it thinks just, having regard to the terms of the partnership contract and to the length of time during which the partnership has continued; unless

    (a)   the dissolution is, in the judgment of the court, wholly or chiefly due to the misconduct of the partner who paid the premium, or
    (b)   the partnership has been dissolved by an agreement containing no provision for a return of any part of the premium.

Little further comment is needed. A partnership will presumably be for a 'fixed term' if it is not entirely open-ended (see the discussion on ss. 26 and 32 in chapter 2)—there can be no recovery of a premium paid on the ending of a partnership at will since the payer was allowed to join a partnership which he knew could be ended at any time and he has thus received full consideration. There is equally no recovery on a dissolution caused by death (insolvency is not mentioned) or, under paragraph (a), if the dissolution is caused by the misconduct of the payer. In *Brewer* v *Yorke* (1882), however, it was held that mere incompetence did not amount to misconduct for this purpose, at least in the absence of proof of damage caused by the incompetence. Paragraph (b) allows the parties, as usual, to contract out of the section.

Since the payer will usually have received partial consideration for his payment he will receive only part of his premium back. This can be done on a simple mathematical basis—i.e., the proportion of the time remaining in the term to the whole term, but other factors may intervene. The payer may have already received valuable benefits, such as training or acquiring business contacts and acumen, which may well reduce the amount returnable. On the other hand the premium may itself have been induced by a misrepresentation in which case a substantial part of it will be recoverable. Each case will ultimately depend upon its facts but it may well be that there will be no more cases of this nature and premiums will be consigned to history and Dickensian England.

Application of assets

On a dissolution the partners have certain rights as to how the firm's assets are to be dealt with. We have already spent some time in chapter 6 defining both these assets and the nature of a partner's interest in them. The latter is usually described as a partner's lien, which arises from s. 39 of the Act but this is misleading in that it has little in common with the possessory liens like those of an unpaid vendor or garage (i.e., a right to retain goods until payment). It is, as we have seen, a form of equitable interest in the nature of a chose in action. Another possible analogy is with a floating charge, except that it does not crystallise on a dissolution, for creditors will always be paid in priority to the partners and at the end of the day it is probably no more than an entitlement to a share of the surplus assets after the creditors have been paid. Whatever these rights are they arise from s. 39:

> On the dissolution of a partnership every partner is entitled, as against the other partners in the firm, and all persons claiming through them in respect of their interests as partners, to have the property of the partnership applied in payment of the debts and liabilities of the firm, and to have the surplus assets after such payment applied in payment of what may be due to the partners respectively after deducting what may be due from them as partners to the firm; and for that purpose any partner or his representatives may on the termination of the partnership apply to the court to wind up the business and affairs of the firm.

The real importance of this section is that it separates partnership assets from an individual partner's assets and allows the former to be kept for partnership creditors rather than those of an individual partner. Thus, in the venerable case of *Skipp* v *Harwood* (1747) the partners' lien was held to defeat a creditor of an individual partner seeking redress against partnership property.

The usual way of operating s. 39 in a winding up is to realise the partnership assets by a sale, and any partner can apply to the court if necessary for such an order. If the sale is undertaken by some of the partners then they will be bound by their fiduciary duties to the others—in effect that will be a partial dissolution. In addition there are cases where a sale is no longer a practicable alternative. The most recent example of this is the decision of the Privy Council on an appeal from the Fijian Court of Appeal in *Latcham* v *Martin* (1984).

In this case Latcham and Martin were partners in a firm called 'Brunswick Motors' in Fiji. The firm was dissolved in 1978 and the business had since been continued by Latcham. A dispute arose as to how Martin was to be bought out. The Fijian judge refused to order a sale of the assets under the Fijian equivalent of s. 39 of the UK Act because such a course had ceased to be practical. The book value of the assets at dissolution was $379,901 and whilst their market value would have been established by a sale at that time, that could no longer be done. Latcham had continued to use the assets and four years had elapsed since the dissolution and the nature and possibly the quality of the assets had changed. Instead the judge regarded Latcham as having purchased the assets in 1978 at their book value and awarded Martin $257,387, representing the payment of the debt due to him from the firm and his share of the capital. The Fijian Court of Appeal dismissed Latcham's appeal. So too did the Privy Council. To permit Latcham to delay matters even further while the accounts of the partnership were reinvestigated at great expense would be a denial of justice. Section 39 does not require a sale. The court's power was not confined to ordering a sale but was a broader one, i.e., to wind up the affairs of the partnership in such a manner as to do justice between the parties.

Thus there are may ways of enforcing s. 39 but it should be remembered that the partners' rights under the section are equitable and so subject both to prior equities and to later purchasers for value of the legal estate without notice of their interest. The section does, however, provide the basic framework for a winding up. However, before we proceed to the final part of the process—the final account and distribution of the assets—we must first turn to the problems associated with a partial dissolution—i.e., where the business is not being wound up but is being continued by some of the former partners.

Partial dissolution

There are three areas which present problems when one partner leaves a partnership and the other partners carry on the business. First, the departing partner should take steps to avoid liability for future debts etc. of the firm. Second, his interest in the capital and undrawn profits of the firm must be valued and then purchased by the continuing partners, and third, whilst that process is going on his rights as to the profits etc. made by the firm between his retirement and the date when his share is finally acquired by the other partners must be determined. The position is basically the same whether the former partner has retired, been expelled or has died, and whether the business is being carried on by one surviving or remaining partner as a sole trader or by two or more such partners in partnership. Many variations are possible, particularly with professional firms. The common theme is that there is no winding up of the business.

We have already encountered the first of our three problems. We saw in chapter 4 that a former partner can be liable for debts etc. incurred after his departure unless he complies with the notice provision of s. 36 and avoids being represented as a partner under s. 14. In brief he must inform existing clients of the firm of his departure, put a notice to that effect in the *London* (or *Edinburgh*) *Gazette* and, if he is wise, check that all the headed notepaper has been altered or destroyed. We need only mention in addition s. 37 of the Act which provides:

> On the dissolution of a partnership or retirement of a partner any partner may publicly notify the same, and may require the other partner or partners to concur for that purpose in all necessary or proper acts, if any, which cannot be done without his or their concurrence.

In theory this section will not apply where a partner dies and the deed provides that there is no dissolution on such an event but it is unlikely that the court will accept such an argument. In effect this section is an example of the fiduciary duties of the partners and they are owed equally to the deceased's estate.

Valuation of a partner's share in the assets

Valuation of assets is a skilled business normally outside the province of a lawyer. However, there are certain guidelines established by the cases as to the criteria to be used when ascertaining the sums due to an outgoing or deceased partner in a partial dissolution. In general such a partner will be entitled both to his share of the capital and assets of the firm and of the profits made prior to his departure and not withdrawn by him during his time as a partner. In practice the disputes seem to fall into two categories: first, is the outgoing partner's share of the capital and assets to be valued according to their book value, i.e., as shown in the accounts, or at their fair or market value? Second, what exactly is meant by phrases such as 'profits', 'net profits' and 'undrawn profits' in such context? Each case will, of course, depend upon the particular terms of the partnership agreement if

Dissolution and Winding Up

any but it is possible to find some principles from the decisions.

The basic rule relating to capital and assets was laid down by the House of Lords in *Cruikshank* v *Sutherland* (1922). In that case the agreement required a full and general account of the partnership dealing and of its property to be made each year and provided that the share of a deceased partner was to be calculated by reference to the annual accounts. The House of Lords held that in the absence of any direction in the agreement as to the principles to be adopted in preparing such accounts, it must be an account in which property was brought in at its market value. This case has been followed many times since and it is clear that, in the absence of contrary agreement, an outgoing partner is entitled to take his share of the firm's capital gains, i.e., the difference between the book values of the assets (usually at cost value) and their current market value.

The most recent example of the application of this principle is the Scottish case of *Clark* v *Watson* (1982). Two dentists practised in partnership until one of them died in August 1977. There was a dispute as to the valuation of his share. The surviving partner claimed that the value should be taken from accounts prepared on the basis used during the continuance of the partnership which showed land and equipment at cost price. The deceased partner's executrix claimed that realistic values should be used. The agreement itself provided that the deceased partner should be paid the 'capital standing at the credit of the deceased partner in the accounts of the partnership'. The judge, Lord Dunpark, agreed with the executrix and applied *Cruikshank* v *Sutherland* (1922) with the modification that the account based on market values should be drawn up at the date of death and not at the date of the last annual accounts prior to the death. He explained his decision as follows:

> Now the general rule, that the share of capital due to the estate of a deceased partner falls to be calculated on the basis of a fair valuation of the assets, applies whether that value has to be inserted in the last balance sheet prepared prior to his death or in the next balance sheet prepared after his death. The fact that partners have agreed to the insertion of book values in balance sheets prepared during the continuance of the partnership does not mean that they have agreed to the insertion of book values in the balance sheet which governs the distribution of the assets on dissolution of the partnership by death or retiral. For that result to follow there must be an agreement to that effect, either expressed or plainly to be implied. I find nothing in the terms of this contract which points to such an agreement.

Contrary agreement is, however, possible even though such a result seems inequitable. A recent example is another Scottish case, that of *Thom's Executors* v *Russel & Aitken* (1983). The agreement in this case provided that on the death of a partner his representatives were not entitled to an account made up to the date of death but to his share of the capital 'standing at his credit' as determined by the firm's auditors. The particular firm was an old and well-established firm of solicitors in Falkirk and Edinburgh, which had been operating from the same building for nearly 200 years. The judge, Lord Jauncey, held that the deed itself entitled the deceased partner only to his share of capital as stated in the accounts (i.e., at book value) and that there was no provision for a revaluation of the assets to increase this share. He also decided that the conduct of the partners showed that they had all impliedly agreed to this. The provision for determination by the auditors did not import a revaluation requirement: that clause could equally well apply to changes in the firm's membership since the last annual accounts. In coming to this conclusion the judge relied on a narrow definition of the word 'capital' as applying only to the sum originally brought in as such and regarded as capital and not including all the assets of the firm which can vary from time to time. In general, however, the decision will usually be to the contrary since the courts regard provisions made for the partnership as a going concern inappropriate for a valuation on a partial dissolution.

Turning from capital to profits, these will normally be calculated annually for tax purposes either on an earnings (or invoice) basis, i.e., sums earned less expenses incurred in earning them, or on a cash basis, i.e., sums received less expenses paid out in any particular year. The latter does not attempt to marry up receipts and expenses for each piece of work. Thus any outgoing partner's share of those profits due to him at his withdrawal can be ascertained by applying the profit-sharing ratio to the profits so ascertained. Complications can, as ever, arise. In the absence of any agreement to the contrary it seems that for partnership, if not for tax, purposes, the cash basis will be used to calculate profits. In *Badham* v *Williams* (1902) one partner was entitled to a fixed amount of profits until 1885 and from then on to a proportion of the profits. He left the firm in 1899 without having received any such share of the profits and the question arose as to whether he was entitled to a proportionate share of the money received after 1885 for work done prior to 1885. The judge applied the cash basis rule so that the outgoing partner was entitled to a share of all sums received since 1885, even though they were attributable to work done prior to that date.

As we have seen, partners may decide on various ways of sharing the profits, paying themselves 'salaries' or 'interest' before sharing out the residue. Such complex arrangements can cause problems when assessing the amount of profits due to an outgoing partner. In *Watson* v *Haggitt* (1928) the partners agreed to pay themselves a salary and to divide the 'net profits' after that equally. On the death of a partner, the survivor was to pay his estate one-third of the 'net annual profits'. Did this latter amount include provision for the salary payable to the continuing partner? No, said the Privy Council. Net profits in relation to a dissolution did not have the same meaning as given to it whilst the partners were alive. No allowance could be made for deduction of a salary.

Careful planning is needed in this area. A recent example is the case of *Smith* v *Gale* (1974). Three partners in a firm of solicitors kept their accounts on a cash basis. The junior partner agreed to be 'bought out' and an agreement was drawn up whereby he was to be paid a lump sum (for capital) and the amount of 'undrawn profits' due to him as certified by the auditors. The accounts showed this amount as £2,237—his share of the cash received less expenses. The other partners now claimed that this was a false amount since new premises had recently been bought on a mortgage and no deductions had been made from each partner's current (profit) account for the cost although the lump sum took the value of the premises into account. Undrawn profits, they argued, impliedly meant the current account less some provision for the cost of the premises. Goulding J rejected this argument (which would have reduced the figure to £13). The words 'undrawn profits' must bear their ordinary meaning—profits contained in the partner's current account. There had been no implied variation as alleged by the other partners and the original figure must stand. An expensive error for the other partners.

Partner's share in profits etc. after dissolution

The process of valuing the outgoing partner's share can be a complex affair and thus take a long time, particularly if there is a reluctance on the remaining partners to settle matters. What right does the outgoing partner have *vis-à-vis* the profits made by the continuing partners from 'his' share of the assets during that period, i.e., from the partial dissolution to the final settlement? Section 42(1) provides the answer:

> Where any member of a firm has died or otherwise ceased to be a partner, and the surviving or continuing partners carry on the business of the firm with its capital or assets without any final settlement of accounts as between the firm and the outgoing partner or his estate, then, in the

absence of any agreement to the contrary, the outgoing partner or his estate is entitled at the option of himself or his representatives to such share of the profits made since the dissolution as the court may find to be attributable to the use of his share of the partnership assets, or to interest at the rate of five per cent per annum on the amount of his share of the partnership assets.

The outgoing partner has a clear choice—a share of the profits or 5% interest on his share of the assets. We have already seen that the partner has to choose one or the other—he cannot have a receiver appointed even where there is undue delay in coming to a final account (*Sobell* v *Boston* (1975))—the partner is merely an unsecured creditor for whichever sum he chooses to accept. Section 43 of the Act makes this clear—such a sum is a debt accruing at the date of dissolution or death.

The right to some return is in effect no more than an example of the fiduciary duties of partners. A recent example is the Privy Council decision in *Pathirana* v *Pathirana* (1967), where one of the partners continued the business (a petrol station) after the departure of his partner and exploited an agency agreement with an oil company for his own benefit even though it belonged to the firm. He had to account for his post-dissolution profits. We have already come across this case in connection with fiduciary duties in chapter 5.

If the outgoing partner opts for a share of the profits he can only receive a share of the profits 'attributable to the use of his share of the partnership assets', and this may not necessarily be his pre-dissolution share. In particular, the surviving or continuing partners can deduct an allowance for the management of the business during this period. The position was explained by Romer J in *Manley* v *Sartori* (1927). Whilst emphasising that s. 42(1) provides that the outgoing partner is prima facie entitled to a share of the profits proportionate to his share in the assets of the partnership, the judge considered it possible for the continuing partners to show that the profits have been earned wholly or partly by means other than by utilising the partnership assets. They are entitled, for example, to an amount for their trouble in carrying on the business. He also outlined some of the factors which might be used by the continuing partners to rebut the presumption in the section:

> [I]t may well be that in a particular case profits have been earned by the surviving partner not by reason of the use of any asset of the partnership, but purely and solely by reason of the exercise of skill and diligence by

Dissolution and Winding Up

the surviving partner; or it may appear that the profits have been wholly or partly earned not by reason of the use of the assets of the partnership, but by reason of the fact that the surviving partner himself provided further assets and further capital by means of which the profit has been earned.

The alternative to a share of profits is interest at 5% on his share of the partnership assets. On the face of it this sounds a poor option since current interest rates are more than double that amount and in *Sobell* v *Boston* (1975) Goff J suggested that an amendment increasing the rate should be considered 'by those charged with considering law reform'. It is certainly a prima facie unrealistic choice unless the profits are very low. On the other hand new light was thrown upon this option by the case of *Barclays Bank Trust Co. Ltd* v *Bluff* (1982). A father and son carried on a farming partnership at will until the father died in 1972. The son carried on the business for several years, whilst negotiating with his father's executor, Barclays, for the purchase of his share of the business. Nothing was ever agreed, however, and in 1977 Barclays issued a summons asking for a declaration from the court that if it opted for the 5% interest payment in lieu of profits, it would still be entitled to share in the increased value of the assets between dissolution and a final account. The farm had increased dramatically in value during that time as all land did in that period, the difference by the date of trial being about £60,000. The son's defence was based on two contentions. First, that an election for interest rather than a share of the profits excluded the right to all post-dissolution profits, including capital profits arising from an increase in the value of the assets. Second, that the bank had in any event already elected for interest and so could not opt for a share of profits, capital or otherwise.

The judge rejected both arguments. On the main issue he decided that the word 'profits' in s. 42(1) only included profits accruing in the ordinary course of carrying on the firm's business pending realisation—in this case the earnings derived from the disposal, in the ordinary course of trade, of livestock and produce. It did not include capital profits. Thus an election to take the 5% interest instead of profits under the section had no effect on the executor's rights to a share in the increased value of the assets. In such cases the outgoing or deceased partner has a right to share in capital profits in addition to interest.

Such increase in value cannot be regarded as having been brought about by the efforts of the [son] and it is difficult to see any rhyme or reason why he should have the whole benefit of it even if the [father's executor] has chosen to take interest of 5% per annum in lieu of a share of profits by way of income for the period between dissolution and sale of the partnership business. After all, the [son] is not the sole beneficial owner of the farm. He is a trustee of it for the deceased's estate and himself. In that situation a fortuitous accretion to the value of the farm ought surely to ensure to the benefit of all the beneficiaries interested in the property.

This decision is apparently contrary to the earlier Irish case of *Meagher* v *Meagher* (1961), but the position there was complicated by the fact that the income profits arose from buying and selling land. The judge in the *Barclays Bank* case regarded the alternative view as being inequitable and on principle he must be right. The key is to distinguish between capital and income profits, only the latter are subject to s. 42(1). The distinction is not unknown to tax lawyers! In cases such as this therefore where a 5% interest return is larger than a pro rata return on the profit basis, the interest option under s. 42(1) is much more attractive than might originally be supposed.

The case also raised two points in relation to the son's second argument that the bank had already made an election. This was based on two letters written by the bank's solicitors but the judge rejected this, first because the letters were ambiguous and subsequent actions by both sides showed that they still regarded the matter as open. An election under s. 42(1) must therefore be clear and unambiguous to be effective. The second reason given by the judge was that in any event the bank was an executor and as such owed a fiduciary duty to the father's estate in making its choice. The bank could only have made an election, therefore if it had considered the advantages and disadvantages of each course of action. For that it would have needed information as to the profits made since dissolution, i.e., to see the farm accounts which had in fact been withheld from it. Thus the bank *as an executor* could not on the facts have made a valid election binding on the estate.

The partners may, of course, contract out of s. 42(1), and s. 42(2) provides an example of this:

> Provided that where by the partnership contract an option is given to surviving or continuing partners to purchase the interest of a deceased or outgoing partner, and that option is duly exercised, the estate of the deceased partner, or the outgoing partner or his estate, as the case may be, is not entitled to any further or other share of profits, but if any partner assuming to act in exercise of the option does not in all material respects comply with the terms thereof, he is liable to account under the foregoing provisions of this section.

It will be a question in each case whether the option has been exercised 'in all material respects' and, of course, the fiduciary duties will apply.

We have now reached the final part of our journey, the last act of the play. Whether there is a partial dissolution or a winding up there must be a final account, a total or partial distribution or purchase of assets. It is at this stage that we must include some consideration of insolvency, either of one partner or all the partners.

Distribution of assets: insolvency

Once the assets have been valued or realised the final stage is either to pay off a departing partner or to distribute the assets amongst all the partners in accordance with the final account, according to whether there is to be a total or a partial dissolution. This process will be carried out against one of three backgrounds: (a) the firm and all the partners are solvent; (b) one partner is insolvent but the other partners, and so the firm, are solvent; (c) all the partners and so, of necessity, the firm are insolvent.

Where all the partners are solvent

The rules for distributing the assets in such a situation are contained in s. 44 of the Act. Since all the partners are by definition solvent the creditors of the firm will be paid in full and the only problems which arise are therefore among the partners themselves. There are in fact two possibilities: (a) where the firm has traded at a profit so that all its capital remains intact; (b) where it has traded at a loss so that after paying off the outside creditors part or the whole of the original capital has been lost. In (a) the question is who receives the surplus assets and in (b) who bears the capital loss. Section 44 provides some of the answers:

> In settling accounts between the partners after a dissolution of partnership, the following rules shall, subject to any agreement, be observed:
>
> (a) Losses, including losses and deficiencies of capital, shall be paid first out of profits, next out of capital, and lastly, if necessary, by the partners individually in the proportion in which they were entitled to share profits:
>
> (b) The assets of the firm, including the sums, if any, contributed by the partners to make up losses or deficiencies of capital, shall be applied in the following manner and order:

Dissolution and Winding Up

    1. In paying the debts and liabilities of the firm to persons who are not partners therein:
    2. In paying to each partner rateably what is due from the firm to him for advances as distinguished from capital:
    3. In paying to each partner rateably what is due from the firm to him in respect of capital:
    4. The ultimate residue, if any, shall be divided among the partners in the proportion in which the profits are divisible.

Assuming that all the outside creditors have been paid, paragraph (b) therefore provides that partner/creditors are to be paid next, followed by repayments of capital, and then the surplus is to be divided in the profit-sharing ratio, irrespective of capital contributions. For a partner/creditor, i.e., a partner claiming repayment of an advance made by him over and above his contribution to capital, this procedure of a final account in accordance with s. 44 is the only remedy available. In *Green* v *Hertzog* (1954), the Court of Appeal refused to allow a partner to bring an ordinary action for the recovery of a debt against his fellow partners. The distribution order in paragraph (b) can be varied by contrary intention, i.e., by dividing the surplus according to the capital rather than the profit-sharing ratio, although on general contractual principles any such agreement cannot affect the outside creditors.

The position is more complex where there has been a loss of capital. There is by definition no surplus, and s. 44(a) will apply so that, prima facie, the partners are bound to make good those losses in profit-sharing ratio (rather than in proportion to their capital entitlement). To take an example: A contributed £10,000, B £5,000 and C £2,000 into a partnership as capital but they shared profits equally. After paying off the creditors, only £11,000 capital remains so there has been a loss of £6,000 from the £17,000 originally invested. According to s. 44(a) this loss must be borne equally, i.e., in profit-sharing ratio, so that each partner will have to contribute an additional £2,000 into the capital. In effect this means that A will receive £8,000 net, B £3,000 net and C nothing. In percentage terms, A will have lost 20% of his investment, B 40% and C 100%. Again, however, this rule can be varied by contrary agreement so that it is open to the partners to agree that losses shall be borne according to capital entitlements—in our example in the ratio 10 : 5 : 2 so that the percentage of loss of each partner will be the same.

Paragraph (a) was further explained by Joyce J in *Garner* v *Murray* (1904). In that case one of the partners was unable to contribute his share of the capital loss. The judge held that the other partners were not liable to make good his share so that his trustee in bankruptcy could not obtain any further assets in this way. Instead the loss will be borne by the solvent partners when the final distribution occurs under paragraph (b) of s. 44. An example should help to explain: A contributed £10,000, B £5,000 and C £2,000 capital into a partnership and they shared profits equally. After paying off the creditors only £8,000 capital remains, giving a loss of £9,000 so that under s.44(a) each partner is liable to contribute £3,000. If all the partners were solvent this would happen as in the example above and C would in fact suffer a further loss of £1,000 (i.e., a 150% loss). But suppose C is insolvent and cannot pay. *Garner* v *Murray* establishes that A and B need only contribute £3,000 and not £4,500 each, so that the capital available for distribution will be the £8,000 remaining plus the £6,000 contributed by A and B i.e., £14,000. This will be distributed under s. 44(b) according to capital entitlement.

Nothing in *Garner* v *Murray* affects outside creditors. A and B, in our example, will have to make good all outside debts under the general principle of unlimited liability for partnership debts. The costs of the winding up etc. rank as a deferred debt so that they will be paid after outside and partner creditors but before repayments of capital and distribution of surplus assets. If one partner owes money to the firm he cannot claim his costs until he has repaid his money. We have already mentioned the payment of a receiver's fees and expenses where the position is slightly different.

Where some but not all the partners are insolvent

In this case, under the general principles of liability for partnership debts, the firm's creditors will be paid in full in any event, if necessary by the solvent partners making additional contributions to the partnership assets. The fact that one partner is insolvent does not, of course, mean that the firm or other partners are insolvent. The insolvent partner's trustee in bankruptcy will, of course, take by way of assignment that partner's share in the partnership which will then become available for his separate creditors. But the solvent partners will almost certainly have suffered a loss as a result of his insolvency—as we have just seen, *Garner* v *Murray*, for example, provides that they will bear his inability to contribute to capital losses in the final distribution. Although the separate creditors of an insolvent partner have no right to recover their debts from the other solvent partners, problems arise where the solvent partners seek to recover their losses from the insolvent partner's separate estate.

These problems are much worse in the case of a partial dissolution—i.e., where the solvent partners are carrying on the business and the firm is in effect continuing. Because the partnership creditors are creditors of both solvent and insolvent partners there is a clear rule, applied in *Re Howes* (1934), that the solvent partners cannot provide (apply for payment) against the insolvent partner's separate estate in competition with the partnership creditors, since that estate will include his share of the partnership assets to which the joint creditors also have a claim. Since, as we shall see, the partnership creditors themselves cannot at present claim against that estate until all the separate creditors have been paid in full, the practical effect of this is that the solvent partner's claim will also be so postponed. This somewhat arbitrary rule of bankruptcy law does, however, have three exceptions.

The first exception is, if the partnership creditors have been paid in full out of the partnership assets or it is clear that there will be no available surplus from the insolvent partner's individual estate after paying off the separate creditors, so that the partnership creditors cannot recover anything out of it. In both these cases the partnership creditors have no interest in the individual partner's estate and the solvent partners cannot be regarded as competing with them. Accordingly they may prove in the separate estate in competition with the separate creditors: see *Re Head* (1894). The second exception is based on fraud. Where a solvent partner has been defrauded by the insolvent partner he can prove against the separate estate for any loss occasioned by the fraud, irrespective of the partnership creditors. Such a claim would not be based on contract but in equity. The third exception is where the debt owed to the solvent partners arises out of a transaction between the insolvent partner and the firm arising out of the ordinary course of a separate business carried on by the insolvent partner.

Where the partnership and its business continue despite the insolvency of one of the partners, i.e., the partners have contracted out of s. 33(1) of the Act, the insolvent partner's trustee in bankruptcy is an assignee of that partner's share in the firm. But true to form he does not thereby become a partner. He is allowed access to the firm's books but he has no right to possession of them. Above all he has no right of management and cannot interfere with anything done bone fide by the solvent partners in the ordinary course of the business. The easiest solution for the solvent partners in this situation is to purchase the insolvent partner's share from his trustee in bankruptcy.

Far fewer problems arise in the case of a full winding up of the firm. The partnership creditors will have been paid off in full by the solvent partners so they can proceed against the insolvent partner's estate for debts due to them without any problems as to competition with the joint creditors. Usually one or more of the solvent partners will undertake the winding up and *Garner* v *Murray* will apply as to losses of capital. Such problems as these will arise from the bankruptcy laws and not from partnership.

Where all the partners are insolvent

In this situation both the partnership creditors and the individual partners' creditors will be competing for payment of their debts. In reality the firm itself will be insolvent, yet since it has no legal personality that simply means that all the partners are insolvent. A bankruptcy notice can be addressed to the firm and if it is not complied with will amount to a joint act of bankruptcy by the partners. It is thus possible for a joint creditor for a partnership debt to bring a single action to bankrupt all the partners—that is the nearest thing under English law to bankrupting the firm. In such a case all the property of the partners, both joint (i.e., partnership assets) and separate, will vest in a single trustee in bankruptcy.

How then are the various creditors to be dealt with? The rules are clear, if arbitrary: the administration of the joint and separate estates must be kept quite separate. This is a strict rule so that, for example, a joint creditor who has security against the separate estate of one partner can prove against the joint estate for his full debt without giving up his security. The rules as to priority are at present contained in s. 33(6) of the Bankruptcy Act 1914. The joint estate is applicable first in the payment of the partners' joint (i.e., partnership) debts and the separate estates of each partner in the payment of their separate debts. If there is a surplus in the separate estate, after paying all the separate creditors, it goes into the joint estate. If there is a surplus in the joint estate, it is to be allocated to the various separate estates of the partners according to their shares in the partnership assets. This rule tends to favour the separate creditors since partners are more likely to have personal assets, whereas the business may have few remaining assets. When the Insolvency Act 1985 comes into force, however, this rule of priority will disappear and all creditors will be able to petition equally against each estate.

Within this framework it should be noted that not all creditors are equal. Some creditors, e.g., the Inland Revenue, are preferred creditors who rank before other creditors. Others will be secured creditors, e.g., mortgagees, who can take the security to pay off their debt before handing any surplus over to the general estate. Yet others will be deferred creditors, e.g., persons who have lent money to the firm under s. 2(3)(d) and (e) of the Partnership Act and whose debts are postponed by s. 3 of the Act.

Dissolution and Winding Up

Insolvency is a complex topic and the above is just a glimpse of the problems which can arise out of partnership involvement. I should like to finish this book where I began, with a plea for legal personality for partnerships—this would make the law so much easier in many situations, of which insolvency and taxation are merely the most obvious examples. It would also enable modern group and linked partnerships to operate in a simpler way. In fact, examiners apart, it would make life easier for everybody.

Index

Agency concepts 71–85
Agent
  actual authority 72, 73
  apparent authority 72, 73
  authority of 71 et seq
  implied authority 72, 73
    belief of third party, and 81–6
    construction of contract, and 82
    'in the usual way' 76–81
    'kind of business' 74–6
    knowledge of third party 81–6
    modern judicial approach 80
    representation of other partners 76
    statutory provisions 80–1
    trading partnerships, and 77–80
    undisclosed principal, doctrine of 81–6
  ratification of contract, and 73
Assignment of partnership share 127–33
  account, entitlement to 130–1
  dissolution of partnership, and 129–30
  involuntary 131–3
  judgment creditor, and 132
  liability for losses, and 131
  voluntary 128–31
Association
  partnership by 32 et seq
  see also Partnership by association

Breach of trust
  knowledge of partners, and 95
  liability for 88–95
Business
  meaning of 6
Business name 66–8
  disclosure requirements 67
  fraud, and 68
  restrictions on choice of 66–8
Business premises 141–3
  lease of 141–2
  licence of 143
  owned by one partner 142–3

Capacity 60–1
Capital
  profits distinguished 120
Change of partners 122–4
Company
  development of concept 17–18
  limits on ability to do things 23
  modern concept 16
  partner, as 22–4
    ultra vires rule, and 23–4
  partnership, and 1
  quasi-partnership 18
Constructive trust 91–4
  arising, when 92
  innocent partner, and 92–3
  ordinary business, and 94
  partnership property, and 141
Contract
  continuing, liability under 97
  liability of partners for 71–86
Contract of service 7
Crime
  liability for 86–8

Death of partner
  dissolution, and 147–8
  partnership by representation, and 46
Dissolution of partnership 146–52
  assets, application of 158–9
  automatic 148–9
  carrying on business at loss 150
  contractual grounds 146–8
  court, by 149–51
  death of partner, and 147–8
  distribution of assets 167–72
    all partners insolvent, where 171–2
    all partners solvent, where 167–9
    some but not all partners insolvent, where 169–71
  insanity, and 149
  just and equitable ground 150–1

Index

Dissolution of partnership—*continued*
  ouster of jurisdiction of court 151
  partial 159–67
  see also Partial dissolution
  partner's share in profits after 163–7
  permanent incapacity, and 149–50
  persistent breaches of agreement 150
  prejudicial conduct 150
  rescission of partnership agreement, and 151–2
  return of premiums on 156–8
Duration of partnership 29–32
  fixed term partnership, and 32
  notice of dissolution
    form of 31–2
  partnership at will 29–31
  right to dissolve 29–30

Edinburgh Gazette
  announcement of retirement in 99–100
Employee
  legal protection of 53
  partner, and 52–7
  third parties, and 53–4
Estoppel 42
Establishing a partnership 25–57
  commencement 28–9
  duration of partnership 29–32
  see also Duration of partnership
  freedom of contract, and 28
  'insider question' 25–6
  'outsider question' 25
  taxation, and 26
European Community
  development of concept of partnership, and 19–20
Expulsion clauses 124–7
  natural justice, and 126
  procedural requirements 126–7
  scope of 125

Fiduciary duties
  application before formal agreement 104
  conflict of duty and interest 112–13
  'culpable negligence', and 106
  full disclosure 105–6
  honesty 105, 106
  owed by partners to each other 104–13
  partnership opportunity, misuse of 113
  unauthorised personal profit 106–12
  see also Unauthorised personal profit
Financial involvement
  partnership by association, and 33–42
Formal partnerships
  establishment of 27–32

Freedom of association
  restrictions on 65–6
Freedom of contract
  restrictions on 60–5

Goodwill 143–5
  identification of 144
  meaning of 143
  valuation of 144–5
Goodwill, sale of
  partnership by association, and 40, 41
Group partnerships 20–1

Illegality 61–2
  bookmaking permit, and 62
  common law 61–2
  third party, and 62
Implied trust
  partnership property, and 141
Income tax 68
Incorporated limited firm
  proposal for 19
Insanity
  dissolution of partnership, and 149
Internal partnership relations 102–33
Investing in a partnership 46–7

Judgment creditor
  assignment of partnership share, and 132

Lease
  reversion of,
    unauthorised personal profit, and 110–12
Legal controls 58–69
  business name, *see* Business name
  capacity, *see* Capacity
  freedom of association, restrictions on 65–6
  illegality, *see* Illegality
  laissez-faire attitude of courts 58
  private 58–60
  public 58–60
  restraint of trade clauses, *see* Restraint of trade clauses
  restrictions on freedom to contract 60–5
Legal procedure 68–9
Limited partnerships 11–12, 47–52
  disadvantage 52
  dissolution 51–2
  insolvency of general partners, and 49
  liability to bear losses out of entitlement to share in profits 49
  limited partner, meaning of 48–9
  management of business, and 50–1

Index

Limited partnership—*continued*
  modification of general law, and 51–2
  protection of 49–50
  registration
    purpose of 49
  similarity to ordinary partnerships 48
  statute 47
Loan agreement
  partnership by association, and 39–40
London Gazette
  announcement of retirement in 99–100
Loss-sharing
  evidence of partnership, as 35–6
Losses
  right to equal shares 118–22

Management
  day-to-day business decisions 116
  right to participation in 114–18
Marriage
  partnership, and 1–3
Maximum number of partners 65
Medical partnerships
  restraint of trade clauses, and 63–4
Members' clubs 8
Minority partner
  unfair treatment by majority 116–17
Minors 60–1

Natural justice
  expulsion clauses, and 126
Negligence
  fiduciary duty of partners to each other, and 106
  partnership by representation, and 44
New partner
  introduction of 122–4

Partial dissolution 159–67
  notification 160
  profits, sharing of 162–3
  share of assets during period from partial dissolution to final settlement
    choice of outgoing partner 164–6
  valuation of partner's share in assets 160–3
Partner
  company as 22–4
  employee, and 52–7
  retirement of, *see* Retirement
Partners and each other 102–33
  indemnity, right to 121–2
Partners and outsiders 70–101
  breach of trust, liability for 88–95
  contract 114–24
    implied terms 114–24

Partners and outsiders—*continued*
  crimes, liability for 86–8
  duration of liability 96–101
  financial affairs 118–22
  joint and several liability 95–6
  joint liability 95–6
  misapplication of property, liability for 88 et seq
  torts, liability for 86–8
Partnership
  carried on in common 9–12
  common law, and 4–5
  company, and 1
  definition 1–3
  development of 16–17
  equity, and 4–5
  essentials of 6–15
  history of 15–18
  legal controls on, *see* Legal controls
  management control 11
  marriage, and 1–3
  public domain, and 68
  with a view of profit 12–15
Partnership Act 1890 3–4
Partnership agreement 27–8
Partnership at will
  dissolution of 29–31
Partnership books
  inspection of 117–18
Partnership by association 32 et seq
  distinction between partner and creditor 38
  financial involvement 33–42
  loan agreement, and 39–40, 41
  loss-sharing 35–6
  profit-sharing 33–5
  remuneration, and 37
  sale of goodwill, and 40, 41
Partnership by holding out 42, 45
Partnership by representation 42–6
  'credit', and 44–5
  deceased partner, and 46
  fact, question of 43
  'knowingly' 43–4
  negligence, and 44
  reliance 45
Partnership deed 27–8
Partnership names
  Business Names Act 1985 5–6
Partnership property 134–5
  acquisition of 137–8
  bought with firm's money 138
  business premises 141–3
  see also Business premises
  constructive trust, and 141
  conversion, doctrine of 135

Index

Partnership property—*continued*
  distinction from other property 134
  equity, and 135
  goodwill, *see* Goodwill
  identifying 137–41
  implied trust, and 141
  meaning of 135–6
  nature of partner's interest 136–7
  property transferred or acquired in one partner's name 140–1
  subsequent acquisitions 139
  use of property in business, and 139
Pension schemes 37–8
Premiums 156–8
  return on dissolution 156–8
Profit-sharing 12–15
  evidence of partnership, as 33–5
Profits
  capital distinguished 120
  right to equal shares 118–22
Promoters 8–9

Quasi-loan
  formal advance by way of 120–1
Quasi-partnership 42

Receiver 154–6
  appointment of partner as 155
  costs of 156
  court, appointment by 154–6
  nature of 156
  position of 156
  remuneration of 156
Registrar of Companies
  administration burden on 19
Rescission
  partnership agreement, of 151–2
Restraint of trade clauses 62–5
  medical partnerships 63–4
  reasonableness 62–3
  solicitors 64–5
Retirement
  Edinburgh Gazette, announcement in 99–100

Retirement—*continued*
  liability in contract, and 97–101
  London Gazette, announcement in 99–100
  notice of 97–8

Salaried partners 54–7
  meaning of 54–5
  rules as to 54–7
Self-employment 6–7
Solicitors
  restraint of trade clauses, and 64–5
Subpartnerships 21–2

Taxation
  establishment of partnership, and 26
  modern partnership usage, and 18–19
Tax planning 13–14
Tort
  liability for 86–8
Trading partnership
  implied authority, and 77–80
Trust
  breach of, *see* Breach of trust
  constructive, *see* Constructive trust

Unauthorised personal profit 106–12
  business 'connection' of firm, and 108
  defences to action 109–10
  reversion of lease, and 110–12
  secret profit 107
  use of partnership asset 107–8
Undisclosed principal
  doctrine of 81–6
Unjust enrichment 108–9
Undue influence 60–1

Winding up 152 et seq
  effect of 153
  existing partners, by 153–4
  'in-house' 154
  realisation of assets by sale 158–9
  receiver, *see* Receiver